Self-Leadership
The Definitive Guide to Personal Excellence

Second Edition

Christopher P. Neck
Arizona State University

Charles C. Manz
University of Massachusetts Amherst

Jeffery D. Houghton
West Virginia University

Los Angeles | London | New Delhi
Singapore | Washington DC | Melbourne

FOR INFORMATION:

SAGE Publications, Inc.
2455 Teller Road
Thousand Oaks, California 91320
E-mail: order@sagepub.com

SAGE Publications Ltd.
1 Oliver's Yard
55 City Road
London, EC1Y 1SP
United Kingdom

SAGE Publications India Pvt. Ltd.
B 1/I 1 Mohan Cooperative Industrial Area
Mathura Road, New Delhi 110 044
India

SAGE Publications Asia-Pacific Pte. Ltd.
18 Cross Street #10-10/11/12
Chine Square Central
Singapore 048423

Acquisitions Editor: Maggie Stanley
Editorial Assistant: Janeane Calderon
Production Editors: David C. Felts and
Veronica Stapleton Hooper
Copy Editor: Liann Lech
Typesetter: Hurix Digital
Proofreader: Jeff Bryant
Indexer: Will Ragsdale
Cover Designer: Gail Buschman
Marketing Manager: Sarah Panella

Printed in the United States of America

Library of Congress Cataloging-in-Publication Data

Names: Neck, Christopher P., author. | Manz, Charles C., author. | Houghton, Jeffery D., author.

Title: Self-leadership : the definitive guide to personal excellence / Christopher P. Neck, Arizona State University, Charles C. Manz, University of Massachusetts Amherst, Jeffery D. Houghton, West Virginia University.

Description: Second Edition. | Thousand Oaks : SAGE Publications, [2019] | Revised edition of the authors' Self-leadership, 2017. | Includes bibliographical references and index.

Identifiers: LCCN 2018054211 | ISBN 9781544324302 (pbk. : alk. paper)

Subjects: LCSH: Leadership—Psychological aspects. | Self-perception. | Self-esteem.

Classification: LCC BF637.L4 N43 2019 | DDC 158/.4—dc23 LC record available at https://lccn.loc.gov/2018054211

This book is printed on acid-free paper.

19 20 21 22 23 10 9 8 7 6 5 4 3 2 1

BRIEF CONTENTS

DETAILED CONTENTS

To bring anything into your life, imagine that it's already there.

—Richard Bach

The quote above truly captures the essence of this book. Self-leadership is a process of leading yourself to overcome obstacles to your goals. We believe that everyone practices self-leadership, but not everyone practices self-leadership effectively. This book is a comprehensive self-help guide that is thoroughly grounded in sound principles and research. It addresses the most interesting subject you will ever encounter—yourself. If you want to be more effective in your work and life, this book is for you. It provides powerful advice and the tools you need to lead yourself to personal excellence, offering a practical perspective that should serve as the foundation for the study of management. The book is based on a simple yet revolutionary principle: *first learn to lead yourself, and then you will be in a solid position to lead others effectively.*

Consider the following:

- **Sandra Day O'Connor**, the first woman on the U.S. Supreme Court, could not get a job as a lawyer on graduating from law school. The only job offered to her was that of a legal secretary.

- **Michael Jordan**, arguably the best basketball player of all time, was cut from his high school basketball team.

- **Ludwig van Beethoven**, one of the world's major composers, was told by a music teacher that he had no talent for music. In fact, this teacher once remarked about Beethoven, "As a composer he is hopeless."

- As a young man, **Walt Disney**, the great cartoonist and movie producer, was advised to pursue another line of work by a newspaper editor in Kansas City, who told Disney, "You don't have any creative, original ideas."

- A Munich schoolmaster told ten-year-old **Albert Einstein**, who later became a brilliant scientist, "You will never amount to much."

- In 1962, Decca Records turned down the opportunity to work with an unknown music group called the **Beatles**. The company's rationale was, "We don't like their sound and guitar music is on the way out." This unknown singing group subsequently became legendary.

- **Dr. Seuss**'s first children's book, *And to Think That I Saw It on Mulberry Street*, was rejected by twenty-seven publishers. The twenty-eighth, Vanguard Press, sold 6 million copies of the book.

- The book *Chicken Soup for the Soul*, written by **Jack Canfield** and **Mark Victor Hansen**, was turned down by thirty-three publishers before Health Communications agreed to publish it. Major New York publishers said, "It is too nicey nice" and "Nobody wants to read a book of short little stories." Since the first book came out in 1993, more than 80 million copies of the *Chicken Soup for the Soul* series have been sold worldwide, with translations in thirty-nine languages.

- In 1935, the *New York Herald Tribune*'s review of composer **George Gershwin**'s now-classic opera *Porgy and Bess* stated that the work was "surefire rubbish."

- **Thomas Edison**, the inventor of the electric light, the phonograph, and more than a hundred other useful items, was told by a teacher that he was too stupid to learn anything.

- During their first year in business, the founders of the **Coca-Cola Company** sold only four hundred bottles of Coke.

- In response to **Fred Smith**'s term paper proposing the creation of a reliable overnight delivery service, a Yale University management professor wrote, "The concept is interesting and well formed, but in order to earn better than a C, the idea must be feasible." Smith went on to establish the Federal Express Corporation based on the ideas in this "average" paper.

- Inventor **Chester Carlson** pounded the streets for years before he found backers for his photocopying process and subsequently helped to establish the Xerox Corporation.

- Before he founded Apple Computer, **Steve Jobs** was rejected by Atari and Hewlett-Packard during his attempts to get companies interested in his idea about a personal computer. Hewlett-Packard personnel remarked, "Hey, we don't need you. You haven't gotten through college yet." Jobs pursued the idea himself, and Apple's first-year sales exceeded $2.5 million.

- In December 1977, with only $20,000 to his name, **Michael Burton** was laughed at by colleagues and bankers when he quit his lucrative small business consulting job and vowed to turn his "snowsurfing" concept into a popular sport. By 1998, Burton was owner of Burton Snowboards, the largest pure snowboarding company in the world, with annual sales of more than $150 million. Because of Burton's promotional efforts, some 8 million people worldwide enjoy snowboarding, and it officially became a medal sport in the 1998 Winter Olympics. Who's laughing now?

These are just a few illustrations of people who persevered—who led themselves by using their strengths, skills, and determination to overcome the "can'ts" in their lives, who knew in their own minds that they could succeed. They did not let initial failures rob them of their dreams. They followed their inner voices and kept forging ahead until their fantasies became realities.

What is your dream? Is it perhaps to become a doctor? A lawyer? A supermodel? A CEO? Is it to start your own business? To raise a healthy and happy family? To become a teacher? A rock star? A television news anchor? Maybe you want to win an Academy Award? Possibly even become president of the United States? Despite what some may try to tell you, whatever you want to become, you can! As William A. Ward once wrote,

If you can imagine it, you can achieve it;

If you can dream it, you can become it.

Do you believe in yourself and your ability to make your dreams come true? We hope this book provides you with the skills to lead yourself toward living your goals and dreams. We hope our words solidify your belief in your potential and abilities, so that you can achieve and become whatever you desire. Most of all, we hope the knowledge within the following pages will help you to travel the paths of Michael Jordan, Walt Disney, Dr. Seuss, Albert Einstein, and others. These individuals believed that the impossible was possible, that the unthinkable was thinkable, that the undoable was doable. These remarkable individuals thought they could; these go-getters knew they could! It is our hope that this book will help you lead yourself to personal excellence, too!

KEY NEW FEATURES FOR THE SECOND EDITION

1. Real-World Self-Leadership Cases: New and updated cases focusing on more contemporary individuals and organizations that include questions for class discussion or personal reflection

2. Profiles in Self-Leadership: New and updated profiles featuring current examples of people who have applied self-leadership concepts in their lives

3. Self-Leadership in the Movies: New movie examples from recent popular movies that illustrate self-leadership concepts discussed in the chapters

4. Self-Leadership Research: New and updated boxed features that highlight the most recent and cutting-edge self-leadership-related studies available and make application to the chapter material

5. Self-Assessments and Experiential Exercises: Assessments and exercises designed to help you assess your level of self-leadership skills and apply self-leadership processes in real-world contexts

Visit https://study.sagepub.com/selfleadership2e for additional resources!

ACKNOWLEDGMENTS

As with most worthwhile projects, a great many people have contributed to this book. In particular, we would like to thank Jim Knight, Hank Sims, Craig Pearce, Frank Shipper, Glenn Sumners, Greg Stewart, Bob Marx, Vikas Anand, Peter Hom, Heidi Neck, Brent Neck, Greg Moorhead, Jeff Godwin, Mike Goldsby, Jordan Jensen, Wanda Smith, Krishna Kumar, Bob Dintino, Judi Neal, Tony Butterfield, Cyle Compton, Eric Compton, George Probst, Trudy DiLiello, Kevin Knotts, Sherry Maykrantz, Sarah Hohmann, Kevin Murphy, Tristan Gaynor, George Heiler, and Stuart Mease for their collegial support of us and our work over the past several years. Chuck Manz also wants to thank those individuals who helped shape his early thoughts on the issue of self-leadership, including Art Bedeian, Kevin Mossholder, Bill Giles, Kerry Davis, and Denny Gioia.

We gratefully acknowledge the special inspiration we have received from the work, ideas, and thoughtful encouragement of Richard Hackman, Ed Lawler, Chris Argyris, Fred Luthans, Ted Levitt, Rosabeth Moss Kanter, Richard Walton, John Kotter, Kenneth Cooper, Brent Neck, Damian Luckett, and Dick Heinrich.

We also would like to recognize our respective universities—Arizona State University (especially the W. P. Carey School of Business and The University College), University of Massachusetts at Amherst (especially the Isenberg School of Management), and West Virginia University (especially the John Chambers College of Business and Economics)—for supporting our research and writing. Our thanks extend to our special colleagues Bruce Skaggs and Mark Fuller. Charles Manz truly thanks the generosity of Charles and Janet Nirenberg, who funded the Nirenberg Chair of Business Leadership, the position he holds at the University of Massachusetts. Chris Neck would especially like to thank the thousands of students at Arizona State University and Virginia Tech who have inspired and encouraged him to test and develop many of the ideas presented in this book.

Chris additionally would like to acknowledge the kindness of Jay Heiler, Tyler Chapman, and Tom Hatten for believing in his teaching philosophy and supporting his teaching approach. He would also like to thank Brian Slingerland, Jim Knight, Hank Sims, and Art Bedeian for providing guidance and support during his career. In addition, we want to express our appreciation to the SAGE team for their assistance in converting our ideas into a book.

We would also like to thank the following reviewers for their helpful input: Catherlyn F. Brim, Warner University; John T. Byrd, Bellarmine University; Tara Clark, University of California, Santa Barbara; Betty Dorr, Fort Lewis College; Jeffrey L. Godwin, Saint Vincent College; Mike Goldsby, Ball State University; John M. Gould, Drexel University; Jordan R. Jensen, Freedom Focused LLC; James R. Johnson, Purdue University Calumet; S. Krishnakumar, North Dakota State University; Patricia K. O'Connell, Lourdes University; Antonio A. Padilla, San Antonio College; Duncan Simpson, Barry University; David M. Tack, Minnesota State University Moorhead;

Joshua H. Truitt, University of Central Florida; Lisa Tyson, Evangel University; Kim Bianca Williams, Housatonic Community College.

We would also like to acknowledge the work of the two ancillary content preparers: Kevin Knotts, Marshall University; and Jordan D. Jensen, founder and CEO of Freedom Focused, LLC.

We want to express our gratitude to our families for their patience during our long hours under lamplight writing away. We especially want to thank our wives, Karen, Jennifer, and Loree, who positively shaped the contents of this book through their listening, guidance, encouragement, and understanding. As with most things in our lives, Karen, Jennifer, and Loree made this book better by their magic touch!

Finally, Chuck Manz would like to thank the late Mike Mahoney, who helped provide the direction and shape to his growing desire to explore the realms of the vast potential locked in each living person—especially those who have the good or bad fortune to have to work for a living. Chris Neck would like to thank Dr. Joseph Patin for the encouragement and support he provided during those "killer" runs together many years ago and for helping him believe in his ability to lead himself.

ABOUT THE AUTHORS

Dr. **Christopher P. Neck** is currently an Associate Professor of Management at Arizona State University, where he held the title "University Master Teacher." From 1994 to 2009, he was part of the Pamplin College of Business faculty at Virginia Tech. He received his PhD in management from Arizona State University and his MBA from Louisiana State University. Dr. Neck is the author and/or coauthor of the books *Self-Leadership: The Definitive Guide to Personal Excellence* (SAGE, 2017); *Get a Kick Out of Life: Expect the Best of Your Body, Mind, and Soul at Any Age* (2017); *Fit to Lead: The Proven 8-Week Solution for Shaping Up Your Body, Your Mind, and Your Career* (2004, 2012); *Mastering Self-Leadership: Empowering Yourself for Personal Excellence*, 6th edition (2013); *The Wisdom of Solomon at Work* (2001); *For Team Members Only: Making Your Workplace Team Productive and Hassle-Free* (1997); and *Medicine for the Mind: Healing Words to Help You Soar*, 4th edition (2012). Dr. Neck is also the coauthor of the principles of management textbook *Management: A Balanced Approach to the 21st Century* (SAGE, Forthcoming, 3rd edition); the introductory entrepreneurship textbook *Entrepreneurship* (SAGE, 2017); and the introductory organizational behavior textbook *Organizational Behavior* (SAGE, 2017).

Dr. Neck's research specialties include employee/executive fitness, self-leadership, leadership, group decision-making processes, and self-managing teams. He has over 100 publications in the form of books, chapters, and articles in various journals. Some of the outlets in which Dr. Neck's work has appeared include *Organizational Behavior and Human Decision Processes, Journal of Organizational Behavior, Academy of Management Executive, Journal of Applied Behavioral Science, Journal of Managerial Psychology, Executive Excellence, Human Relations, Human Resource Development Quarterly, Journal of Leadership Studies, Educational Leadership*, and *Commercial Law Journal*.

Due to Dr. Neck's expertise in management, he has been cited in numerous national publications including the *Washington Post, Wall Street Journal, Los Angeles Times, Houston Chronicle*, and *Chicago Tribune*.

Dr. Neck was the recipient of the 2007 Business Week Favorite Professor Award. He is featured on www.businessweek.com as one of the approximately twenty professors from across the world receiving this award.

Dr. Neck currently teaches a mega section of Management Principles to approximately 800 students at Arizona State University. He received the Order of Omega Outstanding Teaching Award for 2012. This award is given to one professor at Arizona State by the Alpha Lambda Chapter of this leadership fraternity. His class sizes at Virginia Tech filled rooms up to 2500 students. He received numerous teaching awards during his tenure at Virginia Tech, including the 2002 Wine Award for Teaching Excellence. Also, Dr. Neck was the ten-time winner (1996, 1998, 2000, 2002, 2004, 2005, 2006, 2007, 2008, and 2009) of the "Students' Choice Teacher of the Year Award" (voted by the students for the best teacher of the year within the entire university). Also, some of the organizations who have participated in his management development training include GE/Toshiba, Busch Gardens, Clark Construction, the United States Army, Crestar, American Family Insurance, Sales and Marketing Executives International, American Airlines, American Electric Power, W. L. Gore & Associates, Dillard's Department Stores, and Prudential Life Insurance. Dr. Neck is also an avid runner. He has completed 12 marathons, including the Boston Marathon, the New York City Marathon, and the San Diego Marathon. In fact, his personal record for a single long distance run—is a 40-mile run.

Charles C. Manz, PhD, is a speaker, consultant, and best-selling business author. He holds the Charles and Janet Nirenberg Chair of Leadership in the Isenberg School of Management at the University of Massachusetts. His work has been featured on radio and television and in the *Wall Street Journal, Fortune, U.S. News & World Report, Success, Psychology Today, Fast Company*, and several other national publications. He received the prestigious Marvin Bower Fellowship at Harvard Business School that is "awarded for outstanding achievement in research and productivity, influence, and leadership in business scholarship." He earned a PhD in business, with an emphasis in organizational behavior and psychology, from The Pennsylvania State University and MBA and BA degrees from Michigan State University.

He is the author or co-author of over 200 articles and scholarly papers and more than 25 books, including the bestsellers *Business Without Bosses: How Self-Managing Teams Are Building High-Performing Companies*, the Stybel-Peabody prize-winning *SuperLeadership: Leading Others to Lead Themselves, The Leadership Wisdom of Jesus: Practical Lessons for Today* (3 editions), *The Power of Failure: 27 Ways to Turn Life's Setbacks Into Success*, and Foreword Magazine best book-of-the-year Gold Award winner in the self-help category *Emotional Discipline: The Power to Choose How You Feel*. Other books by Dr. Manz include *The New SuperLeadership, The Wisdom of Solomon at Work: Ancient Virtues for Living and Leading Today, Company of Heroes: Unleashing the Power of Self-Leadership, For Team Members Only: Making Your Workplace Team Productive and Hassle-Free*, and *Teamwork and Group Dynamics*. Some of his newer books include *The Virtuous Organization: Lessons From Some of the World's Leading Management Thinkers; Mastering Self-Leadership: Empowering Yourself for Personal Excellence* (6 editions); *Nice Guys Can Get the Corner Office: Eight Strategies for Winning in Business Without Being a Jerk; The Greatest Leader Who Wasn't: A Leadership Fable; Fit to Lead: The Proven Solution for Shaping Up Your Body, Mind, and Career; The Power to Choose How You Feel* (short book format); and *Temporary Sanity: Instant Self-Leadership Strategies for Turbulent Times*. His most recent books include *Self-Leadership: The Definitive Guide to Personal Excellence; Twisted Leadership: How to Engage the Full Talents of Everyone in Your Organization*; and *Share, Don't Take the Lead*. His books have been translated into many languages, as well as featured in book clubs and on audio tape and CD.

Dr. Manz has served as a consultant for many organizations, including 3M, Ford, Motorola, Xerox, the Mayo Clinic, Procter & Gamble, General Motors, American Express, Allied Signal, Unisys, Josten's Learning, Banc One, the American Hospital Association, the American College of Physician Executives, the U.S. and Canadian governments, and many others.

Jeffery D. Houghton completed his PhD in management at Virginia Polytechnic Institute and State University (Virginia Tech) and is currently associate professor of management at West Virginia University (WVU). He has taught college-level business courses at Virginia Tech, Abilene Christian University (Texas), Lipscomb University (Tennessee), the International University (Vienna), and CIMBA Italy (Paderno del Grappa), and for the U.S. Justice Department–Federal Bureau of Prisons. Prior to pursuing a full-time career in academics, he worked in the banking industry as a loan officer and branch manager.

Dr. Houghton's research specialties include human behavior, motivation, personality, leadership, and self-leadership. A member of the Honor Society of Phi Kappa Phi, he has published more than fifty peer-reviewed journal articles and book chapters, and his work has been cited more than 3,500 times in academic journals. He is co-author of *Management: A Balanced Approach to the 21st Century* (SAGE, Forthcoming, 3rd edition) and *Organizational Behavior: A Critical-Thinking Approach* (SAGE, 2017). He currently teaches undergraduate-, master's-, and doctoral-level courses in management, organizational behavior, and leadership. Dr. Houghton was named the 2013 Beta Gamma Sigma Professor of the Year for the WVU John Chambers College of Business and Economics, an honor awarded annually to one faculty member within the college as selected by a vote of the student members of Beta Gamma Sigma. In 2008 he received the Outstanding Teaching Award for the WVU John Chambers College of Business and Economics, which is presented annually to one faculty member for outstanding teaching.

In addition to his research and teaching activities, Dr. Houghton has worked as a consultant and has conducted training seminars for organizations such as the Federal Bureau of Investigation, Pfizer Pharmaceuticals, and the Bruce Hardwood Floors Company. In his spare time, he enjoys traveling, reading classic mystery novels, playing racquetball, and snow skiing. In addition, he has trained for and completed two marathons: the Marine Corps Marathon in Washington, D.C., and the Dallas White Rock Marathon in Dallas, Texas.

To Jumper, Bryton, and GiGe,
Thank you for helping me to realize what is truly important in my life.
Each of you in your own way has made me a better self-leader.
CN

To Karen, Mom, and Dad, the three people who contributed the most
to my acquisition of self-leadership sufficient to write this book.
CM

To Loree, Pierce, and Sloan,
For your love, support, and encouragement in helping me to become
the best person and self-leader that I can be.
JH

1

AN INTRODUCTION TO SELF-LEADERSHIP

The Journey Begins

It is not easy to find happiness in ourselves, and it is not possible to find it elsewhere.

—Agnes Repplier

"I can do it!" he shouted at the figure across the room. "All my life you've been holding me back, beating me down—I've had it! Why? Why can't you just let me be? I could really be somebody," he continued, now in a pleading voice.

For a while he was quiet except for the sound of his own deep breathing. He just stared at what he now realized was his ultimate adversary. The figure was still; it said nothing. He sighed deeply and shifted his gaze away from the figure to the bright lights of the city below. Beginning to see the possibilities for his life, he felt a surge of excitement, of potential purpose, go through his every fiber.

He was lost somewhere in his imagination for what seemed several minutes. Suddenly reality hit him squarely and coldly again. His sense of possible escape was lost. He felt the chains weighing heavy on his soul. And he returned his gaze slowly, steadily, helplessly toward his oppressor. Once more he looked squarely into the eyes of the figure in the mirror before him.

Learning Objectives

After studying this chapter, you should be able to do the following:

1. Provide a basic definition of leadership.

2. Contrast the three primary sources of leadership: external leadership, participative leadership, and self-leadership.

3. Explain how we all lead ourselves.

4. Provide a basic definition of self-leadership.

5. Examine the concept of self-leadership in the context of social cognitive theory and intrinsic motivation theory.

6. Recognize that we choose what we become.

This book will encourage you to "look into the mirror." It emphasizes that we choose what we are and what we become. It recognizes that the world does not always cooperate with our goals, but that we largely create the personal world with which we must cope. It also points out that we influence our own actions in countless ways, some of which we might not even recognize.

The world is experiencing a knowledge explosion. It is frightening to realize that what we learn often becomes obsolete in a short time. What doesn't change, however, is our need to deal effectively with this complex world and to lead ourselves to fulfillment in life. If we can develop the ability to renew ourselves continually and to overcome the obstacles on our way to life's exhilarations, we can become what we choose for ourselves.

LEADERSHIP

This book is not about leadership of others. Instead, it is about something more fundamental and more powerful—*self*-leadership. It is about the leadership that we exercise over ourselves. In fact, if we ever hope to be effective leaders of others, we need first to be able to lead ourselves effectively. To understand the process of self-leadership and how we can improve our capability in this area, it is useful first to explore the meaning of the term *leadership*.

Leadership has been defined and described in a seemingly endless number of ways—largely as a result of the work of the vast numbers of persons who have researched and written about the subject (and the equal vastness of their different viewpoints). One widely recognized name associated with the topic is that of Ralph M. Stogdill, who authored a handbook on leadership, published in 1974, that reviewed theory and research on the subject. Subsequently, that book was revised several times by Bernard M. Bass, most recently in 2008.[1] The book points out that leadership has been conceived of in many ways, including as the art of inducing compliance, a personality concept, a form of persuasion, a set of acts or behaviors, an instrument of goal achievement, an effect of group interaction, a differentiated role, and the exercise of influence. All of these descriptions have some merit. The most useful definition of leadership for our purposes—to focus on the idea of self-leadership—however, is simply that it is a process of influence for directing behavior toward accomplishing goals.[2] This short definition is a broad and meaningful one that recognizes the importance of human influence in determining what we are and what we do and the complexity involved. (Influence takes place not as an isolated event, but as a process involving many parts.)

The existing literature on leadership focuses almost universally on influence exercised by one or more persons over others (in other words, influence exercised by "leaders" on others). The first step in a journey toward an understanding and improvement of our own self-leadership is to recognize that leadership is not just an outward process; that is, we can and do lead ourselves.

SOURCES OF LEADERSHIP

Leadership (the process of influence) can originate from a number of sources. The most commonly recognized source of leadership involves the influence that leaders exercise over their followers. This is also the most externally oriented view of leadership. It does not recognize the influence that we exercise over ourselves. An example of this external view is the giving of orders and the use of other methods of influence (such as rewards and punishments) by a formal organization manager over his or her followers.

Figure 1.1 is a pictorial representation of different sources of leadership. It depicts leadership as ranging from an entirely external influence process at one extreme to a self-imposed process at the other. The latter focus is the primary topic of this book. Between these two extremes, leadership influence consists of different combinations of external influence and self-influence. When a manager and a follower set a goal jointly, a participative leadership process is at work.

At this point, we are ready to take the next step of our journey—that is, the journey toward the realization that we do lead ourselves.

WE ALL LEAD OURSELVES

Even in the most highly controlled situations, we influence our own behavior in various ways. If you have a boss who gives you detailed orders and frequently checks your progress (and is not shy about letting you know what you're doing wrong), you still possess a great deal of discretion. The methods you use and the order in which you complete tasks, for example, are left to you. What you think about while you work is also up to you. If you choose to set a higher or lower personal goal for yourself than what your boss expects, that too is up to you. You can feel good about your progress or be tough on yourself for even the smallest of mistakes if you choose.

The point is that you are your own leader much of the time. Even if you are faced with influential external leaders, they are not likely to be staring over your shoulder every minute. In their absence, who is in charge? You are, of course. Even if they are present, they cannot look into your mind. In fact, we are our own ultimate leaders. We are capable of negating anything we hear externally and substituting our own internal communication. (From boss: "You're loafing, and what little work you *are* doing is poor quality." To self: "Everyone around here knows I'm the best worker in our department—obviously, the boss is being unreasonable today.")

Consider the following story:

On a construction site in the Southwest, when the lunch whistle sounded, all the workers would sit together to eat. Every day Joe would open his lunch pail and start to complain. "Gosh darnit," he'd cry, "not again—a bologna sandwich and corn chips." Day after day, week after week, Joe would moan and groan and say, "Not again—a bologna sandwich and corn chips."

Figure 1.1   Sources of Leadership

Weeks passed, and other workers were getting tired of his complaining. Finally, one of Joe's fellow construction workers said, "C'mon, Joe, what's your problem? Every day you complain about your bologna sandwich and corn chips, so, for Pete's sake, who in the heck makes your lunches?"

Joe replied, "I do."

What this story suggests is that what we do with our lives, including where we work and for whom we work, is largely left to us. In other words, we make our own lunch. If we need more training to obtain the kind of job we really want, it's up to us to lead ourselves to make the kinds of sacrifices necessary to achieve our ends. We are not trying to say that this is an easy process. In fact, leading ourselves to do what we really want is difficult, but we can do it if we know how to go about it.

Belief in your ability to "make your own lunch"—that is, to lead yourself—can be a life-or-death matter. A substantial amount of research evidence suggests that work stress, which may be caused in part by feelings of little or no control at work, explains why rank-and-file employees appear to have a greater risk of coronary heart disease (as much as 50 percent higher) than do those in management and professional jobs.[3] This book can provide you with the tools to lead yourself, to gain a feeling of more control in all aspects of your life, and thus to reduce your risk of experiencing such helpless feelings.

Condoleezza Rice

Condoleezza Rice is an excellent example of someone who has used self-leadership to overcome obstacles on the way to becoming an exceptional leader of others. Rice was the first African American woman (and only the second woman) to become U.S. Secretary of State. She was also the first woman to serve as National Security Advisor and has held the position of Provost at Stanford University. But her rise to such influential leadership roles was far from easy and presented many difficult challenges and failures along the way. Rice grew up in racially segregated Birmingham, Alabama, but from an early age her parents taught her that through hard work and determination she could move beyond the difficult circumstances of her childhood environment. The family motto was "no victims, no excuses" and her parents stressed that she would "have to be twice as good as everyone else to succeed in this world."

Rice's efforts to lead herself began at an early age. When she was only three years old, her parents gave her a toy piano with a limited range of keys that allowed her to play only certain songs. Just before she turned four, she asked her parents for a real piano. Her parents told her that if she could learn to play "What a Friend We Have in Jesus" perfectly, then they would get her a piano. She sat at her tiny piano for an entire day, practicing the song over and over. When her parents returned home from work that evening, she played the song flawlessly and, within a week, she had her piano.

Rice's dream was to become a concert pianist. Through hard work and self-leadership she was accepted as a piano major at the University of Denver. In her

(Continued)

(Continued)

sophomore year, Rice participated in a piano recital in Aspen where the level of talent was so high, she realized that if she continued on her current career track, she would end up "playing the piano in a department store," as she later quipped. Despite her abilities to effectively lead herself, Rice was facing a major roadblock on her path to success. But as we will discuss in detail in Chapter 5, significant success often requires failure. Failure can provide opportunities to learn, grow, and possibly change directions if necessary. Rice returned to Denver looking for a new major. One day she found herself in an International Politics class taught by Soviet expert Josef Korbel. This experience kindled her interest in international affairs and launched her on a journey that would eventually lead to President George H. W. Bush introducing her to Soviet President Mikhail Gorbachev by saying, "This is Condoleezza Rice. She's my Soviet Specialist. She tells me everything I need to know about the Soviet Union." Through a combination of hard work, preparation, and self-leadership, Condoleezza Rice was able to overcome obstacles and failures on her way to becoming one of the most influential leaders of our time.

Sources/Additional Readings

Griffin, Jill. 2018. "Condoleezza Rice: A Lesson in Overcoming Hurdles." *Forbes,* July 17, 2018. https://www.forbes.com/sites/jillgriffin/2018/07/17/condoleezza-rice-a-lesson-in-overcoming-hurdles/#b6f1bd139f37

Rice, Condoleeza. 2010. *Extraordinary, Ordinary People: A Memoir of Family.* New York: Three Rivers Press.

Trice, Laura. 2010. "Condoleezza Rice: A Role Model for Overcoming Adversity." *Huffington Post,* October 21, 2010. https://www.huffingtonpost.com/laura-trice/condoleezza-rice-an-ameri_b_771253.html.

Who provided the leadership for successful businesspeople like Bill Gates in founding Microsoft, Sir Richard Branson in building Virgin Group, Tory Burch in launching her self-titled lifestyle brand, or Arianna Huffington in creating the Pulitzer Prize–winning Huffington Post? Largely, leadership came from within for each of these world-famous visionaries. Tennis star Serena Williams provides an excellent example of leading from within. Over the course of her brilliant career, she has won 23 Grand Slam singles titles, the most by any tennis player in the Open Era. Katrina Adams, president of the United States Tennis Association, has said, "Serena Williams is the ultimate champion. She knows what it takes to get to the top. She started at the bottom from Compton, worked her way up through the ranks of the professional tour to No. 1 in the world."[4] How did Williams rise from her humble origins in the dangerous Los Angeles suburb of Compton to become one of the greatest female athletes of all time? While many observers emphasize her physical presence, including her beauty, physical features, and fashion sense, others argue that her inner leadership—based on her mental strength, and not her body—is her greatest attribute.[5] As Williams herself has noted, "My game is my mental toughness. Just not only to be able to play, to win, but to be able to come back when I'm down. Both on the court and after tough losses, just to continue to come back and continue to fight, it's something that takes a lot of tenacity."[6] Although leadership from

Does Self-Leadership Influence Individual Outcomes?

Approximately thirty years of self-leadership research says yes! Studies have consistently shown a relationship between self-leadership and a variety of individual outcomes, including job satisfaction, self-efficacy, creativity and innovation, and job performance. For example, a recent multi-source diary study with a sample of fifty-seven unique leader-employee dyads found that employees were more engaged at work and were given higher performance ratings by their leaders when the employees used more self-leadership strategies.[1] In fact, a recent meta-analysis of self-leadership research examining thirty-nine effect sizes across thirty-two studies found that self-leadership is positively related to individual outcomes and that this relationship is moderated by a number of contextual factors, including outcome type, country, and national culture.[2] Thus, the evidence suggests that self-leadership has impressive potential for improving performance.

SELF-LEADERSHIP RESEARCH

Notes

1. Kimberley Breevaart, Arnold B. Bakker, Evangelia Demerouti, and Daantje Derks, "Who Takes the Lead? A Multi-Source Diary Study on Leadership, Work Engagement, and Job Performance," *Journal of Organizational Behavior* 37, no. 3 (April 2016): 309–25.
2. Kevin Knotts, Huaizhong Chen, Lu Amy Zuo, and Jeffery D. Houghton, "Self-Leadership and Individual Outcomes: A Meta-Analytic Review" (paper presented at the annual meeting of the Southern Management Association, St. Pete Beach, FL, 2015).

external sources, including her father and her coaches, undoubtedly has had an impact on Williams's career, much of her success has resulted from her ability to lead herself.

As these examples help to show, we all lead ourselves. This is not to say that we are all effective self-leaders. On the contrary, we all have weaknesses in our self-leadership process. In some people the process of self-leadership is dysfunctional. Many lead themselves into the wrong lines of work and into the wrong jobs; even more lead themselves into unhappiness and discontentment with their lives. Perhaps the saddest of all are those who give up much of their self-leadership potential to others and are led into equally negative conditions. The point is that you are your own leader, and just like any leader you can be a good one or a bad one. In the pages that follow, we will attempt to help you understand your self-leadership patterns and how to improve them. The ideas you choose to adopt for yourself, however, are up to you. After all, you are your own leader.

SELF-LEADERSHIP

Building on the definition of leadership presented earlier in this chapter, self-leadership can best be described simply as the process of influencing oneself.[7] This definition is general and does not provide the detail necessary to enable a better understanding or a more effective execution of the process. It does point out, however, the global target on which this book is focused—the process that we experience in influencing ourselves. As we will describe in greater detail throughout the remainder of the book, self-leadership is a comprehensive process of self-influence that involves specific behavioral and cognitive strategies. These strategies are designed to help us address not only *what* we need to do (e.g., determining the standards and objectives) but also *why* (e.g., strategic analysis) and *how* we should do it (e.g., strategic implementation). Therefore, they stress the importance of both intrinsic motivation and effective cognitive processes.[8]

SELF-LEADERSHIP IN THE MOVIES

Rocky (1976)

Three scenes from the Academy Award–winning movie *Rocky* work very well to provide an overview of the entire self-leadership process and why it is important. *Rocky* tells the story of an unknown amateur boxer who is given an opportunity to fight for the World Heavyweight Championship. The first scene begins (at approximately 54 minutes into the movie) with Rocky (Sylvester Stallone) entering Mr. Jergens's office and presenting his card. Mr. Jergens explains that he is offering Rocky the opportunity to fight Apollo Creed for the championship. The second scene begins (at approximately 1 hour, 10 minutes) with Rocky's alarm clock ringing at 4:00 A.M. and Rocky dragging himself out of bed to go for a training run. The scene ends with a discouraged and clearly out-of-shape Rocky panting for breath at the top of the steps of the Philadelphia Museum of Art. The final scene—one of the iconic scenes in the movie—begins (at approximately 1 hour, 30 minutes) with the familiar theme "Gonna Fly Now" and shows Rocky engaging in various forms of training in preparation for the fight. The scene ends with Rocky, now fit and in excellent condition, sprinting triumphantly to the top of the museum steps.

Discussion Questions

1. Does Rocky appear capable of reaching his goal of becoming heavyweight champion after the second scene?

2. Specifically, what does Rocky have to do in order to reach his goal?

3. How does Rocky motivate himself toward accomplishing his goal?

4. Who provides the influence or leadership to move Rocky toward achieving his goal?

5. Does Rocky effectively lead himself?

6. What specific aspects of self-leadership does Rocky use to motivate himself toward achieving his goal of becoming heavyweight champion?

The concept of self-leadership is derived primarily from research and theory in two areas of psychology. The first, *social cognitive theory*, views the adoption and change of human behavior as a complex process with many parts.[9] It recognizes that we influence and are influenced by the world in which we live. We will expand on this idea in Chapter 2. Social cognitive theory places importance on the capacity of a person to manage or control him- or herself—particularly when faced with difficult yet important tasks. This viewpoint serves as the primary basis for Chapter 3. Social cognitive theory also recognizes the human ability to learn and experience tasks and events through vicarious and symbolic mechanisms—that is, by observing others and by using imagination. Chapter 5 addresses these ideas. Finally, social cognitive theory stresses the importance of our perceptions of our own effectiveness or potential to be effective, a topic we examine in Chapter 8.

The second important area of knowledge for this book is that of *intrinsic motivation theory* (or, even more specifically, *self-determination theory*).[10] This viewpoint emphasizes the importance of the "natural" rewards that we enjoy when we take part in activities or tasks that we like. The ideas included in the writings on intrinsic motivation focus on the potential we have to harness the motivational forces available when we do things that we really enjoy. Chapter 4 addresses these ideas.

The knowledge offered by these two insightful theories concerning human behavior represents an important foundation for this book. We also borrow ideas from other bodies of knowledge, including motivation theory and leadership theory. Overall, this book will demonstrate the importance of the forces that we use to influence ourselves (often without being aware of them) and the potential we have to alter our worlds so that they are more motivating to us. At this moment, to help you visualize the concept of self-leadership and its application to your life, we ask you to ponder the following poem:

Leading the Band

He was going to be the President

Of the U.S. of A.

She was going to become an actress

In a Broadway play.

As youngsters—these were their dreams;

The visions they aspired to.

They truly thought these aspirations,

Eventually, would one day come true.

But he did not become President.

The reason is the ultimate sin.

He never ran for office.

He feared he would not win.

She didn't make it to New York City.

In fact, never set a foot on the stage.

She thought she'd forget her lines.

In other words—she was afraid.

The lesson in these stories

Is that you must get up and try.

If you let your fears control you,

Your dreams will quickly die.

Because if you want to hit a home run,

You have to go up to the plate.

If you want to meet that special person,

You have to ask them for a date.

The biggest crime in life

Is to forget what you have dreamt.

It's not the act of losing

But to have never made the attempt.

So as you battle with your fears in life,

Remember this brief command:

"If you're not afraid to face the music,

You may one day lead the band."[11]

In short, the goal of this book is to help you develop a framework that will enable you to motivate yourself to achieve your personal goals—to help you "lead the band" in your personal and professional lives. The journey has begun—lead onward.

J. K. Rowling

Joanne Kathleen Rowling, better known to the literary world and legions of Harry Potter fans as J. K. Rowling, was born in Chipping Sodbury, Gloucestershire, England. She studied French at the University of Exeter in preparation for a career as a bilingual secretary, but she soon found that work as a secretary was not to her liking. Looking back, she has described herself as lacking in organizational skills. She found meetings tedious and often spent her time in them writing down story ideas rather than taking notes.

Shortly after the unexpected death of her mother in 1991, Rowling moved to Portugal to teach English. She took with her a manuscript that she had recently begun about a boy wizard named Harry Potter. Although she had been writing since she was a child, she felt that the adventures of Harry and his friends at Hogwarts School of Witchcraft and Wizardry were her best ideas yet. She loved teaching English in the afternoons and evenings because it left her mornings free for work on her manuscript. She married a Portuguese journalist, and in 1993 her daughter Jessica was born. In 1994, after her marriage had ended in divorce, Rowling moved with Jessica to Edinburgh, Scotland, to be near her younger sister.

Rowling intended to begin teaching full-time again, but she realized that if she ever intended to finish her novel she needed to do it before taking a teaching job. A single mom, depressed and angry about the failure of her marriage and feeling like she had let her daughter down, she was living in a mouse-infested flat, with no job and very little money. Nevertheless, she set to work, staunchly determined to finish her novel and get it published. After Jessica fell asleep in the evenings, Rowling would rush to the nearest café to get in a few hours of writing.

Finally the novel was finished, but no publisher seemed interested. Rowling was told that the book's boarding school setting was too unusual and politically incorrect and that her plot and sentence construction were far too complicated. She refused to become discouraged, however, and finally found a publisher, Bloomsbury. The first book in the Harry Potter series was published in June 1997, and before long, awards and accolades began to pour in. The series went on to become one of the most popular in history, with more than 250 million books sold in more than two hundred countries and in more than thirty different languages. By some estimates, J. K. Rowling will eventually become the first billionaire author in history. Rowling suggests that success is not just a matter of luck. Much like her famous creation, she believes that when you are down on your luck you can't just feel sorry for yourself—you have to work hard to change your fortunes for the better.

Questions for Class Discussion

1. Do you consider J. K. Rowling to be a leader? If so, in what ways?

2. What source of leadership did Rowling use to accomplish her goal of writing a novel and getting it published?

3. What types of external influences and obstacles did Rowling have to overcome?

4. In what ways is Rowling an effective self-leader?

Sources/Additional Readings

"About J. K. Rowling," http://www.jkrowling.com.

Boquet, Tim. 2000. "J. K. Rowling: The Wizard behind Harry Potter." *Reader's Digest*, December 2000.

Kirk, Connie Ann. 2003. *J. K. Rowling: A Biography*. Westport, CT: Greenwood Press.

Smith, Sean. 1999. *J. K. Rowling: A Biography*. London: Michael O'Mara Books.

THE CONTEXT OF SELF-LEADERSHIP

Mapping the Route

The wisest of insights that can be gained by any man or woman is the realization that our world is not so much what it is but what we choose it to be.

—Statement made by a wise individual (or if it wasn't, it should have been)

What do Elon Musk, founder of SpaceX and cofounder of PayPal and Tesla Motors, and Steve Jobs, cofounder of Apple, have in common? In addition to being groundbreaking entrepreneurs, both have been described as possessing the ability to create a "reality distortion field." Reality distortion field? Yes! Inspired by a *Star Trek* episode in which aliens create a new world by mental force, the term was first used in relation to Steve Jobs in the early 1980s by Apple employee Bud Tribble. "In his presence, reality is malleable," Tribble explained to colleague Andy Hertzfield. "He can convince anyone of practically anything."[1] The ability to create a reality distortion field helped Jobs to dramatically shape the future of how people use phones and listen to music, despite how implausible that future may have seemed back then. As Sir John Hargrave has explained, "Steve Jobs's 'reality distortion field' was a personal refusal to accept limitations that stood in the way of his ideas, to convince himself that any difficulty was surmountable. This 'field' was so strong that he was able to convince others that they, too, could

Learning Objectives

After studying this chapter, you should be able to do the following:

1. Explain how our behavioral choices largely shape the world in which we live and yet are also shaped by the world in terms of factors such as rewards, laws, and rules.

2. Understand how behavior takes place at two levels, an observable physical level and an unobservable mental level, and how self-leadership strategies influence behavior at both levels.

3. Recognize how we as persons, our behavior, and our world are closely related and have important influences on one another.

4. Describe how the practice of self-leadership is affected by our unique tendencies.

5. Recognize that we choose our own behavior.

achieve the impossible. It was an internal reality so powerful it also became an external reality. Whatever you may say about Jobs, he was a master mind hacker."[2]

Elon Musk seems to have a similar vision of the future and the ability to project a similar reality distortion field.[3] "Elon's version of reality is highly skewed," stated an anonymous Internet user purporting to be a SpaceX engineer. "If you believe that a task should take a year then Elon wants it done in a week."[4] Much like Jobs before him, Musk aims to revolutionize how we drive with his electric-car company Tesla and to facilitate travel to Mars with his aerospace manufacturing company SpaceX. As *Wall Street Journal* writer Rolfe Winkler has noted, "Skepticism is the natural response. But each time Mr. Musk delivers a better, less-expensive electric car or launches another rocket successfully, he proves his doubters wrong."[5] The story of Elon Musk is an interesting but cautionary tale of self-leadership. On one hand, Musk is a striking example of how one person can lead him- or herself to do world-changing things. On the other hand, it is also a story that warns us that we need to make sure our deeper values that form the foundation for our self-influence (the "Why?" for our self-leadership) are at least as solid as the personalized strategies we apply to lead ourselves. As of this writing the verdict is still out on Musk's legacy (he recently settled a fraud suit filed by the Securities and Exchange Commission), but it remains clear that Musk has led himself to do things never done before.

A number of years ago, Charles Manz, a member of our author team, worked as a retail clothing salesperson during a Christmas holiday break from college. He recalls the following incident:

> One particularly hectic day, I observed a woman, amid a mob of customers, looking through piles of casual slacks. She was obviously frustrated and grumbled as she worked her way through the piles. I had been straightening the pants between helping what seemed to be an endless onslaught of customers, and I noted that the woman's method of searching was, much to my dismay, essentially to destroy slacks by throwing them on the floor or stuffing them in other piles as she continued her search. Finally, she turned to a customer nearby and commented, in obvious displeasure, that the slacks were in a totally disorganized mess, and she could not find the size she needed. At this point, being a bit tired and irritable myself and having watched her undo a substantial amount of my work, I turned to her and said, "You know why they're a mess, don't you?" She looked at me, obviously surprised, thought for

a few moments, and then said, "I suppose because of impatient, pushy ladies like me."

Many of us practice the same kind of behavior throughout our lives, and, unfortunately, it often concerns considerably more important matters. For example, the way we behave toward others largely determines how they behave toward us. We can alienate people and then complain (just as the woman did in the clothing store) about the mess our relationships are in. It is important to realize, however, that we do have an impact on our world just as it has an impact on us. We change the world just by being alive. We breathe the air, we take up space, we consume limited food resources, and so on.

We may even bring out hostility in others just by being alive. Charles Manz recalls quite vividly another experience that he had when he was about sixteen years old:

> I was walking down a long hall in my high school, thinking of nothing in particular, when I heard an exasperated sigh behind me. I turned around to receive a lethal look from a girl in my class and to hear the words "Would you get out of my way?" snapped at me. It turned out that this young lady wanted to walk faster than I and had tried several times (unsuccessfully, given the crowd of students in the hall) to pass me. By the time I realized that she was competing for my physical space, my existence as a living being had already made her angry.

Most of us probably can offer similar examples of experiences in crowded restaurants or traffic jams.

We have little control over the impact we have on the world in cases such as these. What is of greater importance is the behavior that we freely choose to practice. What we choose to do with our lives and how we go about accomplishing our chosen ends will largely shape the relevant world in which we live. To help you appreciate the importance of this idea, we need to address several issues. We start by examining some of the conceptual foundations of self-leadership before we turn to a discussion of the substantial impact the world has on us.

CONCEPTUAL FOUNDATIONS OF SELF-LEADERSHIP

As we mentioned at the end of Chapter 1, the concept of self-leadership is based on a well-established foundation of research and theory from the field of psychology, including self-regulation theory, social cognitive theory, self-management, intrinsic motivation theory, and positive psychology. In this section, we provide a brief overview of each of these theories and how it relates to the theoretical context in which self-leadership takes place. We then explain how self-leadership goes beyond these basic underlying theoretical contexts to provide a higher degree of individual self-influence.

Self-regulation theory suggests that people regulate their behavior through a process that is quite similar to the way a mechanical thermostat works.[6] A thermostat senses temperature differences relative to a temperature setting and then signals the furnace (or air conditioner) to produce warm (or cool) air to reduce the discrepancy. In much the same way, self-regulation theory suggests that people monitor their behavior relative to a set standard or desired state. If there is a deficit between a person's actual level of performance and the standard, then the person will adjust his or her effort and attempt to change the behavior to improve the performance and eliminate the difference.

Within self-regulation theory, standards are largely taken for granted, and very little attention is paid to where such standards originate. For example, in an organization, standards for employee behavior are often determined and assigned by managers based on existing organizational policies, rules, and procedures. On a continuum ranging from complete external influence to complete internal influence, basic self-regulatory processes tend to fall closer to the external influence end.

Social cognitive theory also proposes a self-regulatory system involving self-monitoring and behavioral reactions.[7] However, in contrast to self-regulation theory, which focuses primarily on processes of discrepancy reduction, social cognitive theory involves a dual-control system of both discrepancy production and discrepancy reduction. This theory assumes that people have greater influence over establishing their own performance objectives. Based on their past behavioral experiences, people set goals in ways that create discrepancies, which then result in behaviors and effort aimed at reducing the discrepancies. After the goals are obtained and the discrepancies are eliminated, people tend to set even higher standards, and the process of discrepancy reduction is repeated.

Social cognitive theory suggests that two important self-influence processes help motivate people to achieve their goals. The first is the *triadic reciprocal model of behavior,* which suggests that human behavior is best explained by external factors relating to the world in which we live, internal personal factors, and the behavior itself. We will discuss these external and personal factors and how they interact to help shape our behaviors in greater detail later in the chapter. The second important self-influence process is *self-efficacy,* which is, in essence, our level of effectiveness in dealing with our world. More specifically, our perceptions of our own ability to deal successfully with and overcome situations and challenges we face in life can have a major impact on our performance. Available evidence indicates that our self-efficacy judgment influences the activities we choose to undertake or avoid, how much effort we expend, and how long we persist in the face of difficult situations. Low self-efficacy judgment (e.g., belief that we lack the ability to deal with a difficult challenge) can lead to mental exaggeration of our own deficiencies and the potential hazards of difficult situations. This, in turn, can lead to anxiety and stress, which can detract from our performance. For example, we can too easily focus on obstacles and potential failure rather than on opportunities and potentially successful alternative courses of action.

Perceptions of self-efficacy can indeed have important influence on our personal effectiveness, but from where do our self-efficacy judgments come? They stem from several sources. One of these is our *observation* of the performance of others and their successes and failures. If we observe others with whom we can reasonably identify as they successfully overcome a particular challenge (e.g., earn a college degree, learn to skydive), our own self-efficacy judgments concerning the type of challenge involved should be enhanced. Another source is verbal *persuasion*. An inspiring speech by an athletic coach or a boss at work sometimes can convince us that we can succeed and move us to execute the action necessary to do so. A third source of self-efficacy judgments is our perception of our *physical reactions* to a situation. If we feel calm and relaxed in the face of a challenge, for example, we are more likely to judge ourselves capable of overcoming the challenge than if we feel anxious and stressful.

All of these sources of self-efficacy perceptions are important, and insight into them provides us with useful knowledge for enhancing our personal effectiveness. If we seek out people with whom we can identify (people we believe are reasonably equal to us in ability), who use their talents well and overcome challenges they face, we provide ourselves with a good source for developing positive judgments of our own self-efficacy. Similarly, purposefully exposing ourselves to constructive verbal persuasion and gaining control over our physical reactions to difficulties can help us improve our self-perceptions, which in turn should facilitate our performance. The most important source of perceptions of self-efficacy, however, is even more basic. It is simply our own *performance history*. If we experience success in difficult situations, our perceptions of our self-efficacy will improve. If we experience failure, they will be undermined.

Although everyone engages in the self-regulatory processes described by self-regulation and social cognitive theories, not everyone is an effective self-regulator. Goal-setting research pioneers Gary Latham and Ed Locke have noted that "although people are natural self-regulators in that goal-directedness is inherent in the life process, they are not innately effective self-regulators."[8] Some researchers have even used the term *self-regulatory failure* to describe extreme dysfunction or breakdown in self-regulatory processes.[9] In response, the concept of self-management has been proposed to help people be more effective self-regulators. *Self-management* is a process through which people apply a set of behavioral strategies in an effort to manage their behaviors in terms of reducing discrepancies from established standards.[10] Self-management, however, generally does not involve any assessment of the standards themselves. Consequently, although self-management is concerned with *how* discrepancy reduction should be approached, it allows for very little self-influence regarding *what* should be done and *why*. On a continuum ranging from complete external influence to complete internal influence, self-management tends to fall in the middle.

Self-leadership, in contrast, provides a broader and more encompassing approach to self-influence.[11] Self-leadership involves not only behavior-focused strategies (discussed in greater detail in Chapter 3) but also cognitive strategies founded on intrinsic motivation theory (addressed in Chapter 4) and constructive thought processes (expanded upon in Chapter 5). Thus, self-leadership encompasses a more comprehensive set of strategies that addresses not only *what* should be done (the standards and objectives) and *why* it should be done (strategic analysis) but also *how* it should be done. On our continuum of self-influence, self-leadership falls more toward the complete internal influence end.

One of the primary ways in which self-leadership extends beyond the basic self-regulatory and self-management perspectives is by incorporating a focus on the natural rewards that result from engaging in a given task or activity. Here self-leadership draws from intrinsic motivation theory and more specifically self-determination theory. *Self-determination theory* suggests that the needs for competence and for self-determination are primary mechanisms for enhancing intrinsic or natural motivation derived from a task or activity itself.[12] The need for competence encompasses the need to exercise and extend one's capabilities. The need for self-determination consists of the need to feel freedom from the pressures often created by contingent rewards. In short, self-determination theory suggests that people will seek out and attempt to overcome challenges in order to increase their feelings of competence and self-determination. We will address the self-leadership concept of natural rewards in more detail in Chapter 4.

Finally, self-leadership is informed by ideas from the growing field of positive psychology. Prior to World War II, the general field of psychology was concerned with three broad areas: treating mental illness, making people's lives more fulfilling and productive, and nurturing exceptional talent. After the war, the field narrowed its focus almost exclusively to the treatment of mental illness, and with impressive results: at least fourteen previously misunderstood or poorly treated disorders can now be cured or relieved with contemporary techniques.[13] More recently, however, another perspective has emerged within the field that has refocused attention on improving people's lives and nurturing individual capabilities. *Positive psychology* is a broad term that refers to the study of positive emotions (including happiness, gratitude, and fulfillment) and positive character traits (such as optimism, resilience, and character strengths).[14] One important finding from the field of positive psychology is that a substantial portion (estimates suggest around 40 percent) of an individual's happiness and well-being is determined by intentional activity—over and above the effects of external circumstances (estimates suggest about 10 percent) and each individual's "set point" or predisposition toward happiness (estimates suggest close to 50 percent).[15] By definition, an individual's set point is a constant and therefore unchanging, and external circumstances are largely beyond the individual's control. This suggests that intentional activity, which can include shaping behaviors and changing cognitive attitudes and processes, is critical in determining a person's happiness and well-being. Self-leadership strategies are designed to result in intentional activities that can help people reshape their behavior and cognitive processes to be more positive and productive. See Figure 2.1 for a visual summary of the conceptual foundations of self-leadership.

Now that we have examined the theoretical contexts in which self-leadership operates, we turn our attention to a more detailed discussion of the external and personal factors that influence how we choose and shape our own behaviors.

Figure 2.1 Conceptual Foundations: The Building Blocks of Self-Leadership

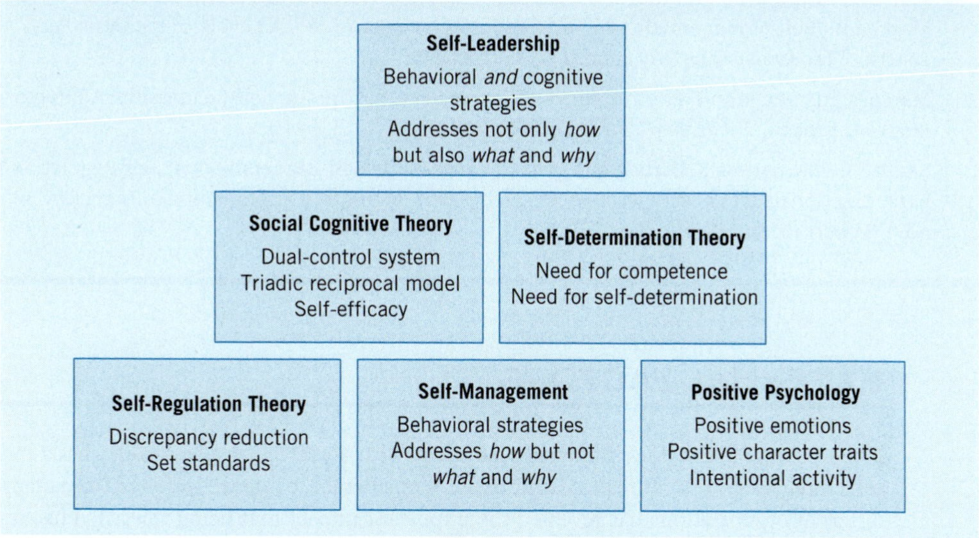

Self-Leadership
Behavioral *and* cognitive strategies
Addresses not only *how*
but also *what* and *why*

Social Cognitive Theory
Dual-control system
Triadic reciprocal model
Self-efficacy

Self-Determination Theory
Need for competence
Need for self-determination

Self-Regulation Theory
Discrepancy reduction
Set standards

Self-Management
Behavioral strategies
Addresses *how* but not
what and *why*

Positive Psychology
Positive emotions
Positive character traits
Intentional activity

Is Self-Leadership a Unique Concept?

As discussed in this chapter, self-leadership is rooted in other established theories of motivation and self-influence, including social cognitive theory, self-regulation, and goal-setting theories. This has caused some researchers to question whether self-leadership is a unique concept relative to personality concepts such as conscientiousness and related psychological processes such as self-regulation.[1] However, in a study of 374 professionals with leadership experience, researchers found that self-leadership was distinct from the related classic motivational concepts of need for achievement, self-regulation, and self-efficacy.[2] Furthermore, this study found that self-leadership predicted job performance over and above the effects of these motivational concepts (i.e., incremental validity). More recently, another study with a sample of 408 full-time working adults yielded similar results,[3] showing that self-leadership predicted unique variance across a variety of job performance dimensions and providing additional evidence that self-leadership predicts job performance beyond the influence of personality and self-regulatory traits. These findings suggest that self-leadership is a unique and valuable concept with the potential for improving individual effectiveness beyond other foundational concepts of motivation and self-influence.

Notes

1. See, for example, R. A. Guzzo, "Leadership, Self-Management, and Levels of Analysis," in *Leadership: The Multiple-Level Approaches—Classical and New Wave*, ed. Fred Dansereau and

(Continued)

SELF-LEADERSHIP RESEARCH

(Continued)

Francis J. Yammarino (Stamford, CT: JAI, 1998), 213–19; Steven E. Markham and Ina S. Markham, "Self-Management and Self-Leadership Reexamined: A Levels-of-Analysis Perspective," *Leadership Quarterly* 6, no. 3 (1995): 343–59.

2. Marco R. Furtner, John F. Rauthmann, and Pierre Sachse, "Unique Self-Leadership: A Bifactor Model Approach," *Leadership* 11, no. 1 (2015): 105–25.

3. Sarah F. Bailey, Larissa K. Barber, and Logan M. Justice. "Is Self-Leadership Just Self-Regulation? Exploring Construct Validity with HEXACO and Self-Regulatory Traits," *Current Psychology* 37, no. 1 (March 2018): 149–61.

EXTERNAL FACTORS

The world we live in does influence what we do with ourselves on a day-to-day basis and can largely shape our ultimate destiny in life. Considerable evidence gathered from many different organizations has revealed the important impact that being rewarded has on chosen actions.[16] In fact, one author has gone so far as to describe "the folly of rewarding A, while hoping for B," suggesting that what we are rewarded for is the type of behavior we are likely to use, even if some other behavior is more desirable.[17] The point is that we respond to what we experience and especially to what we receive for our efforts.

PROFILES IN SELF-LEADERSHIP

Walt Disney

On a cold and dreary late-winter morning in New York City, a twenty-six-year-old businessman sent a telegram to his brother and business partner in California, telling him that all would be well and imploring him not to worry—he would explain everything when he arrived back in California. The short message did not accurately reflect the true situation. The brothers were experiencing a disaster of serious magnitude: Oswald the Lucky Rabbit had been stolen!

The year was 1928, and the businessman was Walt Disney. In 1928, Oswald the Lucky Rabbit was one of the more popular cartoon characters in the United States. Oswald candy bars, stencil sets, and buttons were for sale in many stores. Disney had traveled to New York to ask his distributor, Charlie Mintz, for more money to make Oswald cartoons. Because of Oswald's success, Disney anticipated no problems in securing additional funding. After a friendly lunch at the luxurious Hotel Astor, during which Mintz lavished Disney with praise for his work, the two men returned to Mintz's office, where the mood turned decidedly cold. Mintz informed Disney that there would be no more funding for future Oswald cartoons. He suggested to Disney that without funding the brothers' studio would probably not be able to remain in business. Mintz offered Disney a job working for him making cartoons in New York, but Disney politely refused.

It had always been Disney's dream to have his own cartoon studio, and he believed that with hard work and effort, he could control his destiny and make his dreams a reality. When Mintz went on to explain that he had hired Disney's entire staff of animators to work for him in New York, Disney was devastated. He had hired many of "his boys" right out of high school and had taught them everything he knew about animation. They often came over to his house for dinner. Despite the blow, Disney stood firm. He would not work for Mintz, he would follow his dream—and at least he still had Oswald! It was at this point that Mintz explained that according to the fine print in the Disneys' contract, Universal Pictures, not the Disneys, owned the rights to Oswald. In the future, Charlie Mintz would make all Oswald cartoons.

Disney thought for a few moments about his options, and then he looked Mintz squarely in the eyes and turned him down once more. He quietly walked out of the office to follow his dreams.

During the train ride back to California with his wife, Lillian, Disney took out a sketching pad and pencil. He began doodling to calm his nerves. A character began to emerge. Stick legs and arms, a round body with big eyes and ears. Disney finally turned to Lillian and asked what she thought about his new character . . . he was thinking of naming him Mortimer. She replied that Mortimer was kind of a funny name for a mouse . . . how about Mickey instead? Mickey Mouse was born!

Walt Disney always believed that through his own actions and efforts, he could affect outcomes in positive ways. Throughout his life, he believed in himself and his ideas, and he didn't listen when others around him told him what he couldn't do. By the late 1930s, Walt Disney's cartoon studio was the most successful in the country, but Disney wanted more. He began making plans for a full-length animated motion picture. Nothing like it had ever been done before, and the project was widely criticized. It was thought that no one would sit and watch a cartoon for an hour and a half and that no one would believe the story of a cartoon boy falling in love with a cartoon girl. The project became known as "Disney's Folly." Cost overruns put the final price tag at $1.5 million, a staggering sum at the time and nearly three times the original budget. But on December 21, 1937, *Snow White and the Seven Dwarfs* opened in Los Angeles to rave reviews. The film would go on to become the highest-grossing film up to that time. Once again, Disney had followed his own path to success.

By the 1950s, Disney had one of the most successful film studios in the country, having branched out from animation to include live-action films. But Disney had another vision for his future. When he explained his latest dream, people responded with surprise: You want to go into the carnival business? Why? You're a successful filmmaker! Disney ignored the doubting voices, however, and followed his own way. In July 1955, he opened Disneyland. He had single-handedly created an entirely new form of entertainment: the theme park.

Throughout his life, Walt Disney followed his dreams and convictions to tremendous heights of creativity and success, ignoring all the doubters around him. He truly believed that he could shape his world through the choices he made, that through his own efforts he could make his dreams come true. Disney summed it up best: "If you can dream it, you can do it. Always remember that this whole thing started with a mouse."

(Continued)

(Continued)

Sources/Additional Readings

Greene, Katherine, and Richard Greene. 1991. *The Man Behind the Magic: The Story of Walt Disney.* New York: Viking Press.

Thomas, Bob. 1994. *Walt Disney: An American Original.* New York: Hyperion.

Being rewarded for what we do can influence what we choose to do in the future. This is because rewards provide us with information concerning what leads to positive or negative results and incentive to do what is rewarded. We are more likely to do in the future those things that we anticipate will lead to desirable results and not do those things we expect to lead to negative results. This logic is simple and widely supported by research.[18]

Many influences affect our daily living. Laws place limits on our choices, as do rules that we must follow to function within organizations. If we violate these limits, negative results are likely to follow, such as getting traffic tickets or being dismissed from our jobs. The intention of this book is not to suggest that external influences such as these are not important; rather, it is to emphasize the importance of the role we play in determining the external influences that will be relevant to us, as well as the importance of the influences that we place on ourselves directly. The world does have an impact on our lives, but we are in no way helpless pawns.

PERSONAL FACTORS

Each person is unique. We all possess certain qualities, ways of thinking, and so forth that help determine how we see the world and what we do with our lives. To understand fully our own self-leadership practices, we must recognize the importance of what we are and how we think about things. This book is particularly concerned with our personal differences in terms of the actions we choose. Rather than dealing with abstract concepts such as "attitudes" or "values," a more workable approach is to deal with individual behaviors.

A broad view of the concept of behavior is helpful for an understanding of self-leadership. Behavior takes place at both an observable physical level and an unobservable mental level. In fact, the events that come before behavior and the results of behavior take place at these same physical and mental levels. Thus, complex chains of behavioral influence take place. This idea is represented pictorially in Figure 2.2. For example, imagine a person who thinks about the joys of trout fishing and decides to skip work that day to go fishing but later feels guilty. This example includes a mental event (thinking about fishing) that comes before and influences an actual physical behavior (skipping work). The physical behavior is followed by a mental result (guilt), which is likely to discourage similar behavior in the future.

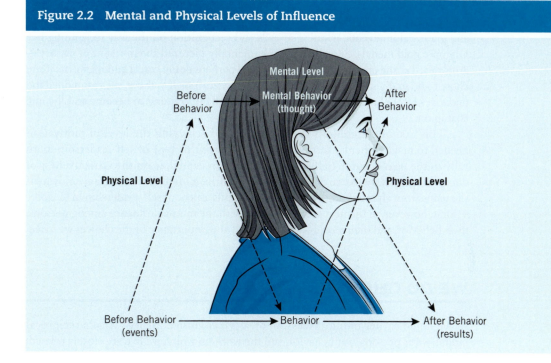

Figure 2.2 Mental and Physical Levels of Influence

Mental Level

Mental Behavior (thought)

Before Behavior

After Behavior

Physical Level

Physical Level

Before Behavior (events) → Behavior → After Behavior (results)

The way we practice self-leadership is affected by our unique tendencies in terms of thinking patterns and physical action. We can lead ourselves to desired accomplishments by combining these two levels of influence.

An athlete's cereal box endorsement serves to illustrate these ideas. Mikaela Shiffrin is an alpine ski racer and a member of the U.S. Ski Team. She is a two-time Olympic, seven-time World Cup, and three-time World Championships champion in the slalom and giant slalom. In fact, she became the youngest Olympic slalom champion in history when she captured her first gold medal at the age of eighteen. Following her victory, Shiffrin's image appeared on the front of a cereal box with the caption "Breakfast of Champions." One might conclude from this statement that Shiffrin's motivation for training centers on winning Olympic gold medals or becoming the world champion women's slalom skier. In actuality, if she had just thrown herself into training through force of will, basing her motivation only on the reward of taking gold at the Olympics or winning a world championship, what she would actually have gotten would have been physical and mental pain, cramps, sore legs, exhaustion, and other consequences that most of us would not view as rewarding at all. Victory in the prestigious Olympic slalom and giant slalom races is a worthy pursuit, but a great deal of self-leadership is needed to carry a person through the sacrifices necessary to reach that final destination.

Physical and mental forces are involved in maintaining such a level of motivation. For example, Shiffrin competed in World Cup and World Championship slalom and giant slalom events, winning awards and recognition on the way to winning her Olympic gold medals. She also probably mentally pictured the moment of victory—arms raised as she crossed the finish line—and perhaps doing cereal endorsements if she chose to do so. By taking actions (mental and physical) such as these, she maintained the necessary level of motivation to complete the difficult training to become an Olympic champion.

This example highlights the importance of achieving the level of motivation needed to make difficult sacrifices. We will discuss this type of self-leadership more fully in the next chapter. Self-leadership also can capitalize on the attractiveness of doing things that we like to do (for Mikaela Shiffrin, it might be the natural enjoyment she gains from alpine skiing). We will address this aspect of self-leadership in Chapter 4. First, however, in the next section we deal with the mutual influence among persons, their behavior, and their world—and especially the importance of the choices we make.

WE DO CHOOSE

As we noted earlier in our discussion of social cognitive theory's triadic reciprocal model, we as persons, our behavior, and the world in which we live are closely related. Each of these factors has important influence on the others. For example, our behavior helps determine what we will be faced with in our world. If our actions generally contribute to the well-being of those with whom we interact, positive forces for a more favorable, relevant world are put into motion. By taking such actions, we can help ensure the personal security and happiness of others and also increase the likelihood of their being supportive of us. On the other hand, if our actions are strictly for our own benefit at the cost of others, we might get what we want in the short run, but in doing so we create a hostile world in which we must live in the longer run. Ebenezer Scrooge creates this sort of hostile world for himself in Charles Dickens's *A Christmas Carol.*

The world's influence on our behavior is also important, as noted earlier in this chapter. Thus, our behavior and our world influence one another. Indeed, Scrooge takes actions that largely create the hostile world he experiences, and this likely brings out more hostility in Scrooge. A vicious cycle of influence is set in motion, and eventually Scrooge's own behavior breaks the cycle only after the appearance of frightening ghosts prompts him to change his behavior.

A final factor that needs to be included to complete the influence picture is ourselves. Because this book is concerned with behavior as a workable focus for improving our own self-leadership, a useful way of viewing ourselves is in terms of behavioral predispositions. That is, the concern is not with elusive ideas like "good attitudes" or "bad attitudes" but instead with our behavioral tendencies (physical and mental). This viewpoint is represented by questions such as "How do we tend to react to certain types of situations?" and "How do we think about problems?" Such tendencies influence how we behave and how we view the world. (The world is probably more a product of the way we see it than what it really is in any concrete sense.) Also, our behavioral tendencies or predispositions are greatly influenced by what we experience, such as praise from our fellow humans for certain types of behaviors. They are also influenced by past behaviors. Most of us, for example, tend to develop habits and patterns in our conduct. In addition, it has been suggested that if we change our behaviors, changes in us as persons (attitudes) will follow.[19]

The mutual influences among these three factors are represented pictorially in Figure 2.3. The illustration suggests that we as persons, our world, and our behavior cannot be fully understood separately. Instead, each factor continually influences and is influenced by the others. We should not expect to have circumstances work out to our optimum liking just because we behave in a favorable way. Other factors are involved in addition to the actions we take. At the same time, we do exercise choices that can have major impacts on what we experience and thus increase our chances of achieving more frequent desirable outcomes.

The choices we make concerning all three parts of the total influence picture are important. First, the world includes potential influences that will not affect us unless we allow them to do so. We do not feel the effects of cold weather unless we leave our dwellings and expose ourselves to the cold. Also, you are not affected by this book unless you choose to read it; it is only a potential influence that is dependent on your choice to pick up a copy and make the effort to read the words it contains.

We also choose the actions we take, which in turn influence the world. For us as authors, the ideas we had on self-leadership were only a potential influence for the world until we took the time and put in the effort to write this book. If our choosing to write this book helps others become more effective and contented, then our world is that much improved.

We also have choices in how we think about what we experience. For example, we can decide to take an optimistic view of the world even though many others take a pessimistic one. In doing so, we accomplish two things. First, our world looks more positive to us, and as a result we find it a more enjoyable place to live. Second, as a result of choosing to take an optimistic view of things, we respond more to the opportunities of life rather than to its constraints. Thus, to the extent that we can choose what we are as persons (or at least the way we practice thinking about things), we can influence what the world is to us and how we behave toward it.

The point is, even though we function within a complex system of influence—involving ourselves, our behavior, and our world—we possess a great deal of choice concerning what we experience and what we accomplish with our lives. We are subject to constraints. These include limitations in our situations (for example, because of Earth's gravity we cannot fly without the aid of equipment of some kind) and the roles in which we find ourselves (such as parents, bosses, citizens). This fact, however, is no reason to feel helpless. Even when faced with the most difficult situations, we lead ourselves by the choices we make. To understand this point, consider the plight of two frogs:

Figure 2.3   The Three Factors of the Influence Picture

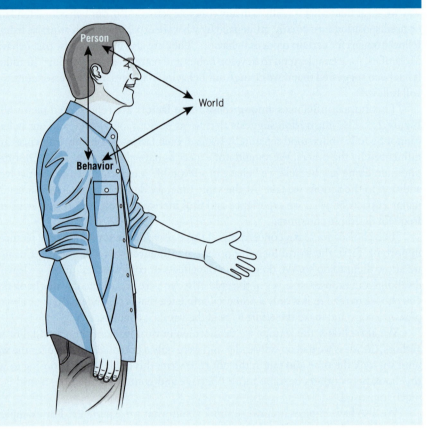

Two frogs fell into a bucket of cream. The first frog, seeing that there was no way to get any footing in the white fluid, accepted his fate and drowned.

The second frog didn't like that approach. He thrashed around and did whatever he could to stay afloat. Soon his churning turned the cream into butter, and he was able to hop out of the bucket.

The point is that both frogs were faced with a challenging situation, and both led themselves by the choices they made. One led himself to his death because he chose to let his "world" control him. The other frog led himself to safety because he adapted to his world; he controlled what he was able to control—himself—and by working hard and not giving up the fight, he was able to reach safety. Both frogs practiced self-leadership; however, only one did it effectively.

Harry Potter and the Chamber of Secrets (2002)

A scene from the second installment in the popular Harry Potter series helps to illustrate our power to choose our own behaviors and, through our choices, to influence what happens to us. Near the end of the movie, Harry is speaking with Hogwarts School of Witchcraft and Wizardry headmaster Albus Dumbledore in his office. Harry is troubled by the fact that he has noticed certain similarities between himself and the evil Lord Voldemort. Dumbledore suggests that Voldemort unintentionally transferred some of his power to Harry in a failed attempt to kill Harry when he was a baby. Harry responds by saying, "Then the sorting hat was right, I should have been in Slytherin!" (the Hogwarts house in which Voldemort himself was a member as a student). Dumbledore replies, "It's true, Harry. You possess many of the qualities that Voldemort himself prizes: determination, resourcefulness, and if I may say so, a certain disregard for the rules. Why, then, did the sorting hat place you in Gryffindor?" Harry pauses to look at the magical sorting hat, which places each new Hogwarts student into one of four distinct houses based on their abilities and characteristics. "Because I asked it to," Harry finally concludes. "Exactly, Harry, exactly!" Dumbledore exclaims, "Which makes you different from Voldemort. It's not our abilities that show what we truly are . . . it is our choices!"

Discussion Questions

1. Consider the three factors of the influence picture: ourselves, our behavior, and our world (see Figure 2.3). Harry's personal abilities and characteristics (i.e., determination, resourcefulness, disregard for rules, etc.) should have resulted in him being placed in Slytherin. How was Harry able to influence the reality of his external world (in this case, the house to which he was assigned) through his choices and behavior?

2. Do we really have the power to choose? Can we, like Harry, alter the world around us through our behavior and our actions?

The importance of choice can be illustrated further with an example that involves a rather troubling situation. Imagine that you are the head of a group—a department in a company, a community organization, or any other kind of group that might seem relevant to you. In this group, you are faced with a troublesome individual. This person always complains at the smallest hint of being slighted. To stop these annoying occasions, you have found yourself giving in to his wishes much as a parent might to a whining child. This might involve giving him special privileges that others do not have, or doing things his way even if his way makes things difficult for everyone else. Over time, you have fallen into a pattern without recognizing it, until finally the situation becomes nearly intolerable. What can you do?

The solution to the problem is simple—the value of presenting it is in its usefulness for illustrating the issue at hand. You simply choose to stop giving in to the complainer. This might lead to rather annoying experiences at first, but gradually the situation (your world) is likely to improve. In the present pattern, you are rewarding this person for complaining and thereby encouraging the situation to continue and even worsen. You are also being rewarded yourself when you eliminate the complaining each time it occurs. Thus, until you make the choice to break the pattern and lead yourself out of the situation, your rewarding behavior is likely to increase, which will make the situation worsen.

To cope with the immediate negative effects of this person's excessive complaining when you stop giving in, you need to motivate yourself to stand firm. You might do this by using methods such as mental support (for example, having such thoughts as "I'm not giving in this time, buster—I know I can stand firm and things are going to improve around here") or by removing yourself temporarily from the presence of the complainer.

Specific approaches that you can use to lead yourself to do what you set out to do are discussed in the following chapters. The lesson at hand is that we do choose. We do not live in a vacuum, free from all external forces. Would life be interesting if we did? We are faced with challenges, obstacles, and many difficult situations. All this makes effective self-leadership that much more important and rewarding. We are self-leaders—why not be the best ones we can be? Travel onward and see if you can lead yourself to this end.

REAL-WORLD SELF-LEADERSHIP CASE

Darrius Simmons

At the relatively young age of seventeen, Darrius Simmons of Warren, OH is already an accomplished musician and composer. Indeed, at the age of just fifteen, Darrius was invited by renowned South Korean pianist and composer Yiruma to join him in playing a piano concert at the legendary Carnegie Hall in New York City. All of this would be impressive enough, but it is even more impressive given the fact that Darrius has only four fingers; three on his right hand, and one on his left. In addition, Darrius had his legs amputated when he was young and uses prosthetics both to walk and to operate the pedals on the piano. And yet he is able to skillfully play the piano in a way that astounds his audiences, from those with no musical aptitude to expert pianists like Yiruma. "It's just amazing. How can you do that? All those jumps, you must find it really difficult?" Yiruma observed after watching Simmons play. "It's not that difficult to me," Darrius replied, "Honestly."

Darrius has never let the world around him define what he was capable of doing or becoming. Despite his physical limitations, from a very young age Darrius has always believed in his abilities to meet and overcome challenges. "He'd say, 'I can do it myself. I can do it myself,' and so I just let him go," his mother Tamara explained. At the age of 10, after watching other people play piano, he sat down at a piano at his elementary school, determined to show that he could play too. "They got ten fingers, but I felt like, I could make four fingers work," Darrius explains, "I like to show people that I can do things that you think that I might not be able to do, and I think that piano was a good way to show that."

Darrius plays both piano and trombone in his high school jazz band, and a video of him performing his original composition "Dreams Are Forever" has gone viral on Facebook where it has been seen by millions. He hopes to pursue a full-time career in music after high school. Darrius sums it up by saying, "I'm just glad I inspired people and made somebody's day. That's all I ever really wanted to do, just share my great music with everybody, and just put a smile on their faces."

Questions for Class Discussion

1. Did Darrius Simmons believe that his own actions and choices would have effects on his life's outcomes?

2. What external factors placed limitations on Darrius' abilities to achieve his dreams?

3. To what extent was Darrius able to shape his world through his behaviors? To what extent did the world around him shape his behaviors?

4. What personal factors have caused Darrius to follow his dreams despite his physical limitations?

Sources/Additional Readings

Jenkins, Beverly L. 2018. "Teen Born With Only 4 Fingers Plays Stunning, Original Piano Piece," *Inspire More*, May 22, 2018. https://www.inspiremore.com/darrius-simmons-pianist-4-fingers/.

Kim, Michelle. 2016. "Self-Taught Teen Pianist Born With 4 Fingers Performs at Carnegie Hall," *NBC New York*, April 28, 2016. https://www.nbcnewyork.com/news/local/Teenager-Four-Fingers-Piano-Carnegie-Hall-377367181.html.

BEHAVIOR-FOCUSED STRATEGIES

Overcoming Rough Roads, Detours, and Roadblocks

Hard work won't guarantee you a thing, but without it you don't stand a chance.

—Pat Riley

"I can't face another—no, not today," she groaned to herself as she looked at her new, formidable challenger.

"You must," she heard from a voice somewhere in the deep recesses of her mind. Only moments before, she had overcome what she thought to be her last adversary of the day and had risen to start the journey she had longed for—only to be challenged again. Looking cautiously at the massive features of the beast, she sighed deeply in dismay. But then a strategy came to her, and her determination returned. She reached swiftly, but with great control, for her weaponry. Touching the appropriate areas on the dark rectangle before her, she awakened it from its slumber. The beast seemed almost to shrink from the bright beam of light that shone forth. Then she reached efficiently, coolly, for the mechanism with the powerfully illuminated panel that she knew could help her overcome the beast. She braced herself . . . then, without warning, she was upon it.

Some hours later she backed away, weary and victorious, from her defeated, now harmless-looking prey. She had won again, but she wondered how much longer she could endure such battles. She sighed, stretching and rolling her shoulders, while

Learning Objectives

After studying this chapter, you should be able to do the following:

1. Employ world-altering strategies such as using reminders and attention focusers, removing negative cues, and increasing positive cues.

2. Demonstrate self-imposed strategies, including self-observation, self-goal-setting, self-reward, self-punishment, and practice.

3. Recognize the importance of the concept of purpose as a catalyst for organizing life and for guiding the self-goal-setting process.

momentarily closing her eyes. Then slowly, with the finished report saved on her hard drive, she returned her touch-screen laptop to its case and rose for her journey to the suburbs.

Let's face it—it's not always easy to do the things that we know we should. Often the sacrifices and effort necessary to reach our desired destinies and to become fulfilled as people present formidable barriers. So how do we lead ourselves over the rough roads of life's journey? How do we motivate ourselves to hang in there when everything seems to be saying, "Give up, you fool—you can't do it"?

Our inner nature might be likened to a constant battle between opposing forces. A part of us seems to say, "Give up; take the easy way out; it's just too difficult; don't even try," while another part says, "I want my life to count for something; I want to become all that I am capable of becoming." So how do we get ourselves to take action and do the things that we believe we should do? How do we get ourselves to face life's hardships and lead ourselves to our own personal victory, to our own chosen destiny? In many ways we experience the inner conflict of a Dr. Jekyll and Mr. Hyde. How do we lead ourselves to win the battle that Dr. Jekyll lost?

This chapter is about leading ourselves to do unattractive but necessary tasks. It's about leading ourselves to face the challenges, make the sacrifices, and take the actions necessary to achieve what we choose for ourselves. In the discussion that follows, we suggest specific strategies for managing our own behavior. These strategies are especially suited for motivating and leading ourselves in the face of difficult and, at least in the short run, unappealing but necessary tasks (undesirable desirables).

Before we begin, take a few moments to assess some of your own self-leadership tendencies. Respond to the items in Self-Leadership Questionnaire 1 by circling the number corresponding to the description (describes me very well, describes me well, and so on) that best reflects your position regarding each of the eighteen statements. Some of the statements might seem a bit redundant, but try not to let this bother you. Respond to each statement and then score your responses according to the directions provided. You might want to indicate your responses and calculate your score on a separate sheet of paper. That way you can reuse this and other questionnaires and exercises included in this book at a later date without being biased by your earlier responses.

INTERPRETING YOUR SCORE

Your scores for A through F suggest your current tendencies concerning six self-leadership strategies that will be addressed in this chapter. Your score for each of these strategies could range from 3 (a total absence of the strategy in your current behavior) to 15 (a very

Self-Leadership Questionnaire 1
Self-Assessment Questionnaire for Dealing With Unattractive but Necessary Tasks

	Describes me very well	Describes me well	Describes me somewhat	Does not describe me very well	Does not describe me at all
1. I try to keep track of how well I'm doing while I work.	5	4	3	2	1
2. I often use reminders to help me remember things I need to do.	5	4	3	2	1
3. I like to work toward specific goals I set for myself.	5	4	3	2	1
4. After I perform well on an activity, I feel good about myself.	5	4	3	2	1
5. I tend to get down on myself when I have performed poorly.	5	4	3	2	1
6. I often practice important tasks before I actually do them.	5	4	3	2	1
7. I usually am aware of how I am performing on an activity.	5	4	3	2	1
8. I try to arrange my work area in a way that helps me positively focus my attention on my work.	5	4	3	2	1
9. I establish personal goals for myself.	5	4	3	2	1
10. When I have completed a task successfully, I often reward myself with something I like.	5	4	3	2	1
11. I tend to be tough on myself when I have not done well on a task.	5	4	3	2	1
12. I like to go over an important activity before I actually perform it.	5	4	3	2	1

(Continued)

Self-Leadership Questionnaire 1   (Continued)

	Describes me very well	Describes me well	Describes me somewhat	Does not describe me very well	Does not describe me at all
13. I keep track of my progress on projects I'm working on.	5	4	3	2	1
14. I try to surround myself with objects and people that bring out my desirable behaviors.	5	4	3	2	1
15. I like to set task goals for my performance.	5	4	3	2	1
16. When I do an assignment well, I like to treat myself to something or an activity I enjoy.	5	4	3	2	1
17. I am often critical of myself concerning my failures.	5	4	3	2	1
18. I often rehearse my plan for dealing with a challenge before actually face the challenge.	5	4	3	2	1

Directions for scoring: Add the numbers you circled for each statement as indicated below to determine your score for each self-leadership strategy.

	Scores
A. Self-observation (add numbers circled for statements 1, 7, and 13)	
B. Cueing strategies (add numbers circled for statements 2, 8, and 14)	
C. Self-goal-setting (add numbers circled for statements 3, 9, and 15)	
D. Self-reward (add numbers circled for statements 4, 10, and 16)	
E. Self-punishment (add numbers circled for statements 5, 11, and 17)	
F. Practice (add numbers circled for statements 6, 12, and 18)	
X. Total score, including self-punishment (add scores for A through F)	
XX. Total score, not including self-punishment (add scores for A through F, except E)	

Source: Adapted from Jeffery D. Houghton and Christopher P. Neck, "The Revised Self-Leadership Questionnaire: Testing a Hierarchical Factor Structure for Self-Leadership," Journal of Managerial Psychology 17, no. 8 (2002): 672–91.

high level of the strategy in your current behavior). Your scores on A through F can be interpreted as follows:

1. A score of 3 or 4 indicates a *very low* level of the strategy.

2. A score of 5 to 7 indicates a *low* level of the strategy.

3. A score of 8 to 10 indicates a *moderate* level of the strategy.

4. A score of 11 to 13 indicates a *high* level of the strategy.

5. A score of 14 or 15 indicates a *very high* level of the strategy.

Evidence indicates that the use of each of these strategies tends to be related to higher performance, with the exception of self-punishment (E). Therefore, high scores on A, B, C, D, and F reflect a high level of self-leadership, which is likely to enhance your performance. A high score on E, however, reflects a high level of self-punishment, which might detract from your performance. Each of these strategies is discussed in more detail throughout the remainder of the chapter.

Your score on X indicates your overall use of the self-leadership strategies, including self-punishment. Your score could range from a low of 18 to a high of 90. Your score on X is not easy to interpret because it includes self-punishment, which might detract from performance. Your score on XX, on the other hand, reflects your score on only the five self-leadership strategies that, in general, are positively related to performance. Your score on XX, which could range from 15 to 75, can be interpreted as follows:

1. A score of 15 to 22 indicates a *very low* overall level of the strategies.

2. A score of 23 to 37 indicates a *low* overall level of the strategies.

3. A score of 38 to 52 indicates a *moderate* overall level of the strategies.

4. A score of 53 to 67 indicates a *high* overall level of the strategies.

5. A score of 68 to 75 indicates a *very high* overall level of the strategies.

A high score on XX usually suggests that you already possess some positive self-leadership tendencies. Regardless of your score, this chapter is designed to help you implement and improve upon several self-leadership techniques that are available. A high score on XX indicates that you believe you are exercising these self-influence methods. Whether you are using them *effectively* is a different matter. The field of psychology has made some interesting discoveries regarding the means we use to control our own behavior. As we explained in Chapter 2, the area of thought concerned with *self-control* or *self-management* is especially insightful.[1] Several useful techniques for getting ourselves to do the "undesirable desirables" are suggested by the work in this area.[2] Some of the strategies that are available are addressed in the questionnaire you have just completed and will be discussed in the remainder of the chapter. These can be classified under two general approaches: strategies that alter the world and the way it affects us in a beneficial way, and strategies that we directly impose on ourselves to influence our own behavior. The remainder of this chapter addresses how you can implement these strategies more fully and effectively into your own self-leadership. It offers guidelines, including checklists that summarize the primary steps involved, as well as exercises to help you get started practicing systematic self-leadership.

WORLD-ALTERING BEHAVIOR-FOCUSED STRATEGIES

We possess the ability to make alterations in our immediate worlds that will help us behave in desirable ways. Many of these alterations are simple, yet they allow us to make a real difference in our actions. Three different strategies are discussed below: using reminders and attention focusers, removing negative cues, and increasing positive cues.

Using Reminders and Attention Focusers

"What's this piece of paper with a big letter A on it doing on your office door?"

"It's to remind me to buy my wife flowers for our anniversary. I forgot last year, and if I forget again she'll skin me alive."

This first strategy involves using physical objects to remind us of, or to focus our attention on, things we need to do. Probably the most well-known example of this strategy is tying a string around one's finger as a reminder of something. Admittedly, if we used this method today we would probably be met with amusement and embarrassing comments from coworkers and friends. But other similar kinds of methods are available that offer practical benefits.

One simple strategy that has been emphasized for improving the effectiveness of time management is to make a list of pending tasks.[3] At the beginning of a workday, for example, we make a list of all the important things that need to be done during the day. If possible, we prioritize the list and keep it handy throughout the day (many effective to-do list apps are available for smartphones).[4] The list not only serves as a reminder and guide but can also provide the basis for a feeling of personal accomplishment and reward as we complete tasks and cross them off the list.

Many additional techniques are available. For example, if we have a top-priority project that needs to be done, we can place the physical elements of it in the center of our work space, so that each time we return to our work area, we have a powerful reminder of our most pressing task. The important point is that we can use physical cues to focus our efforts. The challenge is to find those reminders and attention focusers that work best for us and use them.

Removing Negative Cues

Every time we go to that restaurant, I am overcome by the dessert display. For the good of my diet, can't we go somewhere else for lunch today?

If we wish to eliminate our behaviors that we don't like, one strategy is to eliminate cues that might lead to these behaviors. If we wish to cut down on our consumption of sweets, we can remove the candy dish from the coffee table. Similarly, if we are disturbed about spending excessive time watching television, we can move the TV to another, less frequently used room.

When Ben Carson—renowned surgeon, presidential candidate, and United States Secretary of Housing and Urban Development—was a child, he struggled with his schoolwork. Other kids teased him and told him he was stupid, and he began to believe it himself. And then his mom, Sonya, decided to remove the family's TV. She replaced it with two library cards, requiring Ben and his brother to read at least two books each week and submit written book reports. Ben and his brother would leave their reports on the table each night before going to bed and would find red checkmarks on the papers the next morning, showing their mother's approval. They didn't realize until many years later that their mother could not read herself.[5]

The point is that we are surrounded by physical cues that tend to encourage certain behaviors. If we can identify the things in our world that encourage our undesired behaviors, then we can remove or alter those elements. In addition, we can remove ourselves from their presence. If we need to get some work done, for example, we are well-advised to leave the TV/video game room and put down our smartphones (with all their powerful cues) and go to a study room with fewer distractions. In fact, we can design the layout of the rooms in our home with healthy, constructive living in mind. Similarly, we can design our work space to eliminate cues to destructive, unproductive behavior.

Increasing Positive Cues

I think placing the safety record displays around the plant has had positive results. It keeps our workers thinking about safety, and our accident record has improved.

Another strategy involves increasing the cues that tend to lead to positive behaviors. If we would like to become more knowledgeable on a particular subject but find that we never take the time to read much on that subject, what can we do? We can set up cues that will encourage our reading. We could, for example, place appropriate books on a table next to our favorite chair or download appropriate e-books onto our favorite devices. We might then be faced with a choice between cues for reading and cues for some other activity, such as watching television or texting our friends (if we have not removed the TV set or put down our phone!), but at least we are more aware of the choice.

We can also arrange cues that have impacts on important matters—such as what kind of a person we can become. The workplace, for example, contains many cues for desired and undesired behavior. If our workplace contains more negative cues than positive ones, we can try to alter the cues available, or, if that's not possible, perhaps it's time to make a job change.

Visual cues such as a posted safety record or reminders written on posted sticky notes can be especially effective in shaping our workplace behaviors. Early in his career, a young stock broker named Trent Dyrsmid developed a visual cueing strategy to encourage himself to make sales calls each day. "Every morning I would start with 120 paper clips in one jar," Dyrsmid explained recently, "And I would keep dialing the phone until I had moved them all to the second jar." It was as simple as that: one paper clip, one call, 120 calls each day. Within 18 months of starting his career, Dyrsmid had built a business book of more than five million dollars in assets.[6]

Coworkers can serve as powerful cues. Are their values consistent with ours? Over time, coworkers are likely to influence what we become. If we know ourselves, what we are striving toward, and what we believe in, we should recognize that it is important to surround ourselves with the right people. We are likely to select role models from among our associates. Do our present role models display behaviors that are consistent with the kinds of achievement we have chosen for ourselves? If we work with people whom we view as using unethical means to achieve their ends, we are exposing ourselves to undesirable cues. On the other hand, we can choose to associate with persons who act in ways consistent with our values and who achieve the worthwhile ends we desire. By choosing such an organization and consequently the people who work there, we establish positive cues for our behavior.

The following checklist summarizes the major steps in exercising self-leadership through the use of world-altering (cueing) strategies. In the checklist, the primary objective of the strategy is stated first, followed by a list of the steps involved. This general format is used for all the checklists throughout this book. You can personalize the checklists by adding steps that would be helpful to you. An exercise is also provided here to help you get started in applying these techniques.

CHECKLIST FOR USING CUES

Use cues to help you exercise self-leadership.

- Use physical cues to remind you of your important tasks—for example, make lists to guide your daily activities.

- Establish cues to focus your attention on important behaviors and tasks—for example, place helpful signs around your work area that focus your thinking in desired ways.

- Identify and reduce or eliminate negative cues in your work environment—for example, remove objects you find distracting.

- Identify and increase positive cues in your work environment.

- Wherever possible, associate and surround yourself with people who cue your desirable behavior.

Study how cues affect your behavior. Make notes.

1. How do you use reminders and attention focusers?

    _____
    _____
    _____
    _____

2. What are some ways you could improve on your use of reminders and attention focusers?

    _____
    _____
    _____
    _____

3. List some negative cues in your work or school environment that encourage your undesirable behaviors.

    _____
    _____
    _____
    _____

4. How might you reduce or eliminate these negative cues?

    _____
    _____
    _____
    _____

5. List some positive cues in your work or school environment that encourage your desirable behaviors.

    _____
    _____
    _____
    _____

(Continued)

(Continued)

6. How might you increase these positive cues?

_____

_____

_____

_____

SELF-IMPOSED BEHAVIOR-FOCUSED STRATEGIES

In addition to creating or altering cues in the world around us to influence our behavior, we can exercise control over ourselves directly. The cement that makes up the foundation for this self-imposed control is the information we possess about ourselves—our self-awareness. By observing our own behavior and its causes (for example, why we behave in desirable or undesirable ways), we gain the information we need to manage ourselves effectively. Thus, the first self-imposed strategy is self-observation.

Self-Observation

> That is the third time I've lost my temper and criticized someone today, and I've done it several other times this week. I wonder what's wrong and why I'm behaving like such an ogre?

Self-observation involves determining when, why, and under what conditions we use certain behaviors. For example, if we feel we are not accomplishing enough each day in our work because of wasted time, we can study the distractions we experience. Are we spending too much time engaged in informal conversations? By observing the amount of non-work-related conversing we participate in and the conditions that exist at those times, we can learn more about this behavior. If we spend five hours of the eight-hour workday chatting about matters other than work, we probably have a problem. Furthermore, if most of these conversations begin during visits to the office watercooler, we have useful information to help us cut down on the behavior (we need to reduce the number of trips we make to the watercooler).

Additional power can be added to this strategy if we physically record our self-observations. A handy pen and a three-by-five note card or a notepad smartphone app might be all we need to make brief notes that we can examine in detail later.

One of the things that has made Peyton Manning one of the greatest quarterbacks in NFL history is his ability to observe his own behaviors and adapt those behaviors to the game situations he encounters.[7] Similarly, SpaceX founder and PayPal and Tesla cofounder Elon Musk is a master self-observer. When asked by an interviewer what traits have propelled him to become a successful entrepreneur, Musk replied, "Accurate self-analysis. It's difficult to do so, since you're too close to yourself by definition. People do not think critically enough."[8]

Self-observation can provide the foundation for managing our behavior. Several other distinct strategies build on this foundation. It is important to remember that we already use these strategies in our daily living; the problem is that we often use them unknowingly and ineffectively.

A checklist summarizing the major steps in practicing self-observation and an exercise are provided to help you get started using self-observation.

CHECKLIST FOR SELF-OBSERVATION

Use self-observation as a basis for self-leadership.

- Identify the behaviors that you feel are especially important for you either to increase or to reduce.

- Identify the behaviors that you feel are especially important for you to either increase or reduce.

- Keep a record of the frequency and duration of these important behaviors.

- Note the conditions that exist when you display these behaviors.

- Identify other important factors concerning these behaviors—for example, the time of day or week you tend to display them, and who is present at the time.

- When possible, keep a written record of your self-observations, but try to keep the process simple enough that you will not be discouraged from using it.

SELF-OBSERVATION EXERCISE

Develop your self-awareness by intentionally observing yourself for the next week. Make notes about your behaviors that you see as desirable and undesirable. Include the frequency and duration with which they occur, when they occur, and why you think they occur (the identified reasons for your behaviors should include external world influences as well as directly self-imposed influences). Develop your own self-observation system for future use.

Behavior	Frequency and Duration	When (day/time)	Why (external and internal influences)

Self-Goal-Setting

If you don't have a destination, you'll never get there.

—Harvey McKay

It is futile to exert effort with no direction. Imagine for a moment that you and some friends decide to take a road trip together, so you all pile into a large van and you are selected as the driver. You start the van and head toward the nearest freeway. For a while, everyone in the van is happy and smiling. Then, about an hour later, someone asks, "Where are we going?" You reply, "I don't know." Others in the van just shrug their shoulders. After a few minutes, some bickering erupts among the passengers because someone wants to go to city A but someone else wants to go to city B. Amid the noise and chaos, you think to yourself, "Wow, this mess could have been avoided if we had agreed on a destination before we left."

Every day you "travel" somewhere. In short, your traveling involves working toward success in your personal and professional life. The question that arises is, do you know what you are working *toward?* In other words, do you know your destination, or are you traveling without a clear picture of where you are going—without specifically knowing what you are trying to achieve? The story above illustrates what can happen to you in your daily activities if you fail to set a destination—a personal goal—in terms of what you want to achieve. Consider the definition of *goal* in this case as "the *end* toward which effort is directed."[9] In short, what are your goals?

One way we can provide ourselves direction in our self-leadership is through the use of personal goals. What we strive toward, both in our long-term life achievements and on a daily basis, influences our behavior. Often we are not clear on what our goals are. We might want to achieve a position of importance and influence in life, for example, but we do not determine how we will go about obtaining the position or even what the position will be. The systematic, thought-out, intentional setting of personal goals can influence our behavior positively.

Self-set goals need to address long-range pursuits and short-run objectives along the way. If we decide on a long-range goal of becoming a lawyer, we need to accomplish many shorter-range goals to reach that destination, such as acceptance into law school and passing courses once we are admitted. Our immediate behavior in turn should be aimed at specific, meaningful, short-term goals, such as reading a law journal (or a few pages in a journal) or completing a law brief (or a portion of a brief). For maximum effectiveness, the shorter-range goals should be consistent with the longer-range goals.[10]

When actor Will Smith was 12 years old, his father showed him and his younger brother Harry a large hole, 16 feet high and 30 feet wide, in the front of a building he owned. For reasons Will didn't understand, his father had torn down the old wall and he now told his sons that it was their responsibility to rebuild the wall. Every day, after school, the boys would come home and work on the wall, mixing the cement by hand and carefully placing each brick in place. Smith recalled the seemingly insurmountable task of building the wall: "I remember standing back and looking at that wall and saying, 'There's gonna be a hole here forever!'" But the boys never gave up, and a year and a half later they placed the final brick in the wall. Their father stood back and looked at the wall before telling the boys, "Don't ever tell me that you can't do something." Smith summarized what he learned about goal-setting this way: "I learned very young . . . that you don't try to build a wall. You don't set out to build a wall. You don't say, 'I'm gonna build the biggest, baddest, greatest wall that's ever been built.' You don't start there. You say, 'I'm gonna lay this brick as perfectly as a brick can be laid. There will not be one brick on the face of this earth that's gonna be laid better than this brick that I'm gonna lay in this next ten minutes.' You do that every single day. And soon you have a wall."[11]

Before we can set the goals that we need to reach to achieve our ends, we must first engage in the self-analysis necessary to understand what we want out of life. This process takes effort, and although our goals are likely to change over time, it is important that we try to have current goals for our immediate efforts.

Goals are generally most effective for managing our immediate behavior if they are specific and challenging yet achievable.[12] Classic studies in goal-setting research have involved dividing subjects into varying goal conditions. One group of people would be assigned an easy and specific task goal (for example, solving five word puzzles in five minutes). Another set of people would be assigned a specific and challenging goal (for example, solving twenty word puzzles in five minutes). Finally, a third group of subjects would be assigned a vague and easy or unspecified goal condition (for example, "do your best" or "solve as many puzzles as you can").[13] The findings across multiple studies with a variety of tasks have been the same: specific and challenging goals produce better results than vague and easy goals. There is one important caveat, however: if we set unreasonable goals that we cannot realistically achieve, we are likely to do more harm than good. Realistic and achievable goals tend to be most effective and motivational, and reaching such goals can provide satisfaction.

If we understand what we value in life and what we want to accomplish, then we can set specific, achievable goals (such as reading for one hour each day on a given subject or attending a lecture to improve our skills in a given area). It is often helpful to record in writing our long-term and immediate goals and then modify them as necessary. Kyle Dake is one of the most decorated wrestlers in NCAA history, and his success began with specific and challenging self-set goals. Dake not only set goals for himself, he also wrote them down. And he not only wrote them down, he also wrote them a lot! When he was a freshman he wrote his goal in a spiral notebook twice a day, once in the morning and once in the evening: 2010 141 lb DI NCAA National Champion. As a sophomore, he wrote his goal twice every morning and twice every night: 2011 149 lb DI National Champion. In his junior year, Dake wrote his goal three times each morning and evening: 2012 157 lb DI National Champion. Finally, as a senior he wrote his goals four times each morning and evening: 2013 165 lb DI National Champion. With the help of his specific, challenging, and written goals, Kyle Dake became the first person in NCAA history to win four Division I national titles at four different weight classes.[14]

We spend a great deal of time doing many things in our lives. A little effort expended on setting self-goals can help us have purpose and direction so that we don't waste valuable time. Popular singer-songwriter Taylor Swift understands the importance of self-goal-setting. She has said, "In order to develop and reach goals, I think it's important that you NEVER feel entitled to them. Take it one step at a time, because it's very rare people just get 'discovered.'"[15]

Successful self-leaders like Kyle Dake and Taylor Swift don't travel without specific goals. If you don't have specific goals, you never get anywhere. Take some time to think about your life and what you want to accomplish—set goals. Following are some tips to help you summarize our discussion on goals thus far.

Conduct a Self-Examination

Before you can establish specific goals, you need to decide what's important to you and what you'd like to accomplish (the next section of this chapter should help you conduct this step). You must truly want to accomplish your self-set goals, so you must truly value your final destination. (The goal-setting exercise provided below might help you with this point.)

Avoid Fuzzy Goals—Be Specific

If you say to yourself, "Someday I'll be the best employee in the company," you might have a goal, but you're not likely to reach it. The problem is the word *someday*—it's fuzzy, or unclear and nonspecific. Your goal needs to be specific. *When* are you going to be the best employee? *What* does "best" mean? *How* are you going to do this? If your goals are specific, they paint a vivid picture of your destination and thus make it easier for you to get there.

Set Long-Term and Short-Term Goals

Your goals need to focus on both the long and the short term. If you decide on a long-term goal of becoming the top performer in the company, you need to accomplish short-range goals to get there—for example, learning new skills or improving current skills. Another way of looking at this is to imagine that your long-term goal is to write a book. To do this, you set a short-term goal of writing five pages each day. Short-term goals help you reach your long-term destination—what you truly value in life or your purpose in life. Indeed, we cannot talk about the benefits and importance of long-term goals without discussing the ever-important concept of purpose.

Peaking With Purpose

We are focusing here on how self-leadership can help us in terms of performing necessary but unattractive tasks. In the next chapter, we examine the concept of naturally rewarding tasks and activities. A central component of a naturally rewarding work process is the establishment of a sense of purpose. Thus, in the next chapter we emphasize the concept of purpose as a strong component of such a work process. However, purpose is also a key aspect of self-goal-setting, especially the self-setting of long-term goals. Consequently, we turn now to a discussion of purpose.

Think for a moment about the word *purpose*. What does it mean to you? In this chapter, it refers to our reason for being, our aim in life, our reason for getting up in the morning. In short, our purpose establishes our ultimate long-term goal(s). In his book *The Power of Purpose*, Richard Leider describes purpose as follows:

Purpose is that deepest dimension within us—our central core or essence—where we have a profound sense of who we are, where we came from, and where we're going.

Purpose is the quality we choose to shape our lives around. Purpose is a source of energy and direction.[16]

Leider suggests that having purpose involves asking ourselves three fundamental questions.

- Who am I?

- What am I meant to do here?

- What am I trying to do with my life?[17]

Have you ever pondered these questions? Do you know the answers? The importance of answering these questions lies in the fact that to be truly happy, we must discover our purpose and then live it! For some people, purpose might be spiritual. For others, it might be work related. For many, it is a combination of both dimensions. If we don't live our purpose, we cannot reach full contentment in life—we feel like something is missing. Abraham Maslow stated this point best:

A musician must make music, an artist must paint, a poet must write, if he is to be ultimately at peace with himself. What a man can be, he must be.[18]

Are you happy right now? Do you enjoy your job? If not, perhaps you are in a job that does not help you fulfill your purpose—that does not allow you to use your talents and skills. Are you performing well on your job yet still are not happy? Are you, as someone once said, climbing the ladder to success only to realize that the ladder is propped up against the wrong wall? Have you achieved many short-term and long-term goals in your life yet still find that you are not content? Then perhaps your ladder in life has been propped against the wrong wall. Maybe you have been striving to achieve goals that have nothing to do with what really matters to you—your purpose in life. Those individuals who are truly happy and are "peaking" in their lives are those who are performing jobs and accomplishing goals that indeed reflect their purpose in life.

Blake Mycoskie, founder of TOMS Shoes, serves as an illustration of Maslow's words. When Mycoskie created TOMS in 2006, he had a clear purpose and vision for the company. During a visit to Argentina, he had been invited to accompany a woman who worked for a nonprofit as she distributed shoes to children in poor rural communities. Mycoskie later explained: "In every town we were greeted with cheers and tears. I met a pair of brothers, ages 10 and 12, who had been sharing a single pair of adult-size shoes. Because the local schools required footwear, they had to take turns going to class. Their mother wept when I handed her shoes that actually fit her boys' feet. I couldn't believe that such a simple act could have such an enormous impact on people's lives."[19] Based on this experience, he felt it was his purpose to help. But instead of merely asking people to donate old shoes or make financial contributions, he decided to start a for-profit company based on the idea of "buy one, give one." He called the company Shoes for Tomorrow, later Tomorrow's Shoes, and finally simply TOMS. For every pair of shoes the company sold, it would donate a pair to a needy person. The company was a runaway success, with an annual growth rate of 300 percent for five years in a row, during which time it gave away 10 million pairs of shoes.

By 2012, however, Mycoskie was beginning to feel stagnant. He decided to step away from the company to refocus. "As an organization, we were so focused on protecting what we'd already built that no one was thinking about new possibilities," Mycoskie explained. "I noticed that longtime employees were starting to leave for more-entrepreneurial organizations, and I realized that, secretly, I wanted to follow them."[20] Soon after, Mycoskie read Simon Sinek's book *Start With Why*, in which Sinek argues that movements are built and sustained generally only when their leaders begin with "why."[21] "The more I thought about this idea, the more I realized that TOMS had veered away from its 'why.'" Mycoskie stated. "In the early days we always led with our story: We weren't selling shoes; we were selling the promise that each purchase would directly and tangibly benefit a child who needed shoes. But our desire to sustain the company's hypergrowth had pushed us away from that mission and into competing on the 'what' and 'how,' just as every other shoe company does."[22]

Around this same time, Mycoskie learned from a friend about how important water is in the coffee supply chain. Coffee beans processed with clean rather than dirty water can be sold at dramatically higher prices. This gave Mycoskie a new idea and a new purpose for TOMS: TOMS Roasting. For every bag of coffee sold, TOMS would provide a week's worth of water to a needy person. TOMS Roasting wasn't an attempt to compete with large coffee companies, but rather a way to reconnect with the underlying purpose and vision of the TOMS company: helping people. As TOMS reached its tenth anniversary, Mycoskie summed up the importance of purpose as follows: "The 'why' of TOMS—using business to improve lives—is bigger than myself, the shoes we sell, or any future products we might launch. It took going on a sabbatical to realize the power of what we've created—and the best way for me to move it forward. Now that I have a clear purpose and amazing partners supporting me, I'm ready for the company's next 10 years and the many adventures ahead."[23] Clearly, Blake Mycoskie and TOMS are living their purpose. Are you living your purpose right now?

The Search for Purpose

Purpose is the reason a person was born. From birth to death, each of us is on a quest to discover that reason. Many never do. Yet, our world is incomplete until each one of us discovers our purpose.[24]

Do you know what your purpose is in life? Have you begun your own personal search for your purpose? If you have yet to understand your purpose, you are not alone. As Viktor Frankl points out, "Ever more people today have the means to live, but no meaning to live for."[25] If you connect with Frankl's words and do not feel meaning in your life, then the time to start your search might be right now.

The quest for a purpose in life can be long and difficult, but the effort is worthwhile. The rewards of finding our purpose are immense. They include the satisfaction of living a contented life in which we truly believe we are using our gifts to make a contribution to the world.

To clarify this message, consider the legend of the search for the Holy Grail. Although this story has many versions, a basic synopsis is as follows:

> The Grail was said to be the cup of the Last Supper and at the Crucifixion to have received blood flowing from Christ's side. It was brought to Britain by Joseph of Arimathea, where it lay hidden for centuries.
>
> The search for the vessel became the principal quest of the knights of King Arthur. It was believed to be kept in a mysterious castle surrounded by a wasteland and guarded by a custodian called the Fisher King, who suffered from a wound that would not heal. His recovery and the renewal of the blighted lands depended upon the successful completion of the quest. Equally, the self-realisation of the questing knight was assured by finding the Grail. The magical properties attributed to the Holy Grail have been plausibly traced to the magic vessels of Celtic myth that satisfied the tastes and needs of all who ate and drank from them.[26]

In this story, searching for the Holy Grail was not an easy task. The knights had to undergo "many perils and trials along the way."[27] The Grail was difficult to find, and only a few knights out of many succeeded in the quest. The knights who found the Grail underwent sacrifice and struggle, but they persevered, and in the end they enjoyed much happiness and at the same time were able to help others (e.g., heal the king).

Similarly, the search for one's purpose is not an easy mission. It can take years of trial, error, and self-observation to truly discover who we are and what we are supposed to be doing with our life. Those who discover their mission and purpose in life are those who sacrifice and persevere until they eventually find it. Like the knights who succeeded in their quest for the Holy Grail, those who realize their reason for being not only discover a happier life for themselves but also are able to make a deeper contribution to society (help others) because they are using their talents to make a difference.

Further, successful self-leaders recognize the value of the purpose-related self-leadership concept not only to themselves but also to the people who surround them. As Ben Carson has noted in the context of his position as a surgeon:

> I think one of the keys to leadership is recognizing that everybody has gifts and talents. A good leader will learn how to harness those gifts toward the same goal. Take the Siamese twin operations—when we gather these big teams, it's not because we want a lot of people. It's because this person is particularly good at this and that person is particularly good at that. You could get one person to do both, but why do that if somebody else is so much better at it?[28]

The Importance of Having Purpose in Life

Having purpose is the catalyst for organizing life. Purpose itself can serve as our guide to how to spend our lifetime and how to allocate our resources. If we realize the meaning for our existence (our ultimate long-term goal), then every decision we make can be guided by this realization. To clarify: Recall the last time you went to the grocery store. Did you take a shopping list with you? If not, what happened? If you are like many other people, when you got home you realized you had bought some items that you did not need. Similarly, without a purpose in your life, you can "buy" or accomplish a shopping cart full of goals that don't amount to much or that you don't need or want. In the grocery store of life, purpose helps you buy only that which is truly important to you. It can help you avoid spending time and energy on things that you don't value.

In sum, we suggest that by searching for and finding your purpose, you will be better able to organize your life and thus experience the pinnacle of happiness and productivity. Purpose can serve as your daily guide. It can help you use all of your resources in the most effective manner to reach your ultimate potential. Purpose is an integral aspect of all effective self-leaders, and it can help you attain peak performance in all aspects of your life. The following quotation from Dorothea Brande illustrates the importance of having purpose in your life:

> In the long run it makes little difference how cleverly others are deceived; if we are not doing what we are best equipped to do, or doing well what we

The Shawshank Redemption (1994)

A scene from *The Shawshank Redemption* helps to illustrate the concepts of self-goal-setting and purpose. The movie tells the story of Andy Dufresne (Tim Robbins), a Maine banker who is serving two life sentences in prison after being convicted of murdering his wife and her lover, despite his claims of innocence. The scene begins (approximately 1 hour and 48 minutes into the movie) with Andy putting a ledger into the prison warden's safe and ends with Andy raising his arms in triumph in the rain outside the prison. The scene demonstrates how Andy meticulously planned and executed his escape from prison based on short-term and long-term goal-setting driven by an overarching purpose. Over a nearly twenty-year period, Andy chipped away at the wall of his cell using a tiny rock hammer. He disposed of the small fragments from the wall by dropping them through holes in his pockets each day in the exercise yard. Andy's tunnel through the thick concrete wall eventually reached a space containing a main sewer line. Andy persisted and finally broke into the sewer line, and he has now crawled to freedom through five hundred yards of raw sewage inside the pipe.

Discussion Questions

1. What was Andy's long-term goal? What was his primary purpose in life? How did his purpose help shape his long-term goal?

2. How did Andy use short-term goal-setting to help him achieve his long-term goal? Give specific examples.

have undertaken as our *personal* contribution to the world's work, at least by way of an earnestly followed avocation, there will be a core of unhappiness in our lives which will be more and more difficult to ignore as the years pass.[29]

A checklist for using self-goal-setting follows. We also provide an exercise that includes a guide for conducting an all-important self-analysis and an opportunity to establish your purpose and set related long- and short-term goals.

CHECKLIST FOR SELF-GOAL-SETTING

Use self-goal-setting to establish direction for your efforts.

- Conduct a self-analysis to help you establish your purpose and related long-term goals (see the self-goal-setting exercise).

- Establish long-term goals for your life and career—for example, what do you want to be doing and where do you want to be in ten years? In twenty years?

- Establish short-term goals for your immediate efforts.

- Keep your goals specific and concrete.

- Make your goals challenging but reasonable for your abilities.

- When feasible, let others know about your goals to provide you with added incentive to achieve them.

Answer the following questions, which are intended to help you establish your purpose and set your long- and short-term goals.

Long-Term Goals

1. Who am I?

   _____

   _____

   _____

2. What am I meant to do?

   _____

   _____

   _____

   (Continued)

SELF-GOAL-SETTING EXERCISE

(Continued)

3. What am I trying to do with my life?

_____

_____

_____

4. What do I value most in life (for example, prestige, wealth, acceptance of others, family relations)?

_____

_____

_____

   a. What would I most like to accomplish during my lifetime? (Note: An interesting way to approach this question is to write your ideal obituary, including all that you would like to have accomplished before you die.)

_____

_____

_____

   b. Develop a list of long-term goals.

_____

_____

_____

Goals for Developing Abilities to Reach Long-Term Goals

5. What are my primary strengths and weaknesses that are related to what I would like to accomplish?

_____

_____

_____

6. What do I need to do to prepare myself to accomplish my long-term goals (for example, education, skills that need to be developed)?

_____

_____

_____

Short-Term Goals

7. What do I need to do now (today, this week) to progress toward my long-term goals (for example, read a book, complete a task)? Develop a list of short-term goals and update it as needed.

_____

_____

_____

Rudy Ruettiger

The benefits of goal-setting are well demonstrated by the case of Rudy Ruettiger, widely known simply as Rudy. Effective self-leadership skills paid off for Rudy in the game of football and in the game of life.

While growing up, Rudy had a dream: he wanted to play football for Notre Dame University. However, after he graduated from high school, with no money for college, he spent four years working in a power plant and as a yeoman in the U.S. Navy, serving on a communications command ship. During this time, Rudy never lost sight of his important long-term goal. He applied to Notre Dame but was rejected. Did he quit? Did he complain about how unfair life was? No, he did not. After receiving the rejection, he drove in the middle of the night to Notre Dame. Upon his arrival, he met a priest who counseled him to enroll at Holy Cross, a community college a stone's throw from Notre Dame. Although Holy Cross was not Notre Dame, Rudy decided to view succeeding there as his short-term goal on the way to reaching his long-term goal of playing football for Notre Dame.

Thus Rudy, already in his early twenties, entered Holy Cross in 1972. During each of his first three terms at Holy Cross, he reapplied for admission to Notre Dame but was rejected each time due to his poor academic record. However, Rudy never gave up. He buckled down and put his heart and energy into improving his grades. Although unwelcome at Notre Dame as a student, he started working as a groundskeeper at Notre Dame Stadium, and he boxed in campus charity matches. In 1974, Rudy applied once more for admittance to Notre Dame and was accepted. After he was accepted, he told Notre Dame's head football coach, Ara Parseghian, that he intended to make the team. Rudy's fighting spirit and ability to take punishment from the larger players earned him a spot on the practice squad; he helped the team prepare for each week's game during practice sessions but sat in the stands during the games.

Rudy played on the practice squad for two years. As his second season neared its completion, the now twenty-six-year-old Rudy had yet to play in a real game. For the last game of the

(Continued)

(Continued)

season, the coach finally allowed him to suit up and stand on the sidelines with the rest of the team. With seventeen seconds remaining in the game and Notre Dame leading comfortably, his teammates and fans began to chant, "Rudy, Rudy, Rudy!" Everyone wanted to see Rudy play. Even more, Rudy wanted to play, to finally live his dream. The coach got the message and put Rudy in the game. Was Rudy prepared for this opportunity? Indeed! In fact, he sacked the opponent's quarterback for a five-yard loss. When time ran out, Rudy's fellow teammates carried him off the field on their shoulders.

Rudy's actions show the rewards of effective self-leadership. As self-leaders—directing our own lives by setting long-term goals, setting short-term goals to achieve those bigger ideals, and tirelessly persisting toward reaching our goals—we enjoy personal excellence in life.

Source/Additional Reading

Neck, Christopher P. 1996. "Rudy! Rudy! Rudy! Dreams Do Come True." In Henry P. Sims Jr. and Charles C. Manz, *Company of Heroes: Unleashing the Power of Self-Leadership*, 119–20. New York: John Wiley.

Self-Reward

> After giving her speech she walked as though floating to her chair, sat down slowly, and thought to herself, "Well, I'll be darned, I did a hell of a job."

One of the most powerful methods we can use to lead ourselves to new achievements is self-reward. We can influence our actions positively by rewarding ourselves for desirable behavior.[30] Furthermore, we are capable of rewarding ourselves at both physical and mental levels.

At the physical level, we can reward ourselves with objects or activities that we desire. In our executive development seminars and college courses, people have revealed numerous ways in which they use things they value to reward themselves. Some of the rewards they give themselves for completing tasks include favorite foods like ice cream and activities such as shopping, watching television, listening to music, and going out to eat. By rewarding themselves with desired items and activities such as these, people exert a positive effect on their future work habits. An example is a salesperson who enjoys the self-rewarded gift of a day off or an expensive dinner after making a big sale.

The important point is that we can reward ourselves with things that we enjoy when we accomplish desired objectives. Many of us do this without realizing it. To increase our motivation and effectiveness, the challenge is to identify those things we find rewarding and then use them systematically to reward our behavior. By having an exquisite dinner out after we finally talk to that problem employee we've been avoiding, we are providing incentive for ourselves to use similar desired behavior in the future.

We also can reward ourselves at a mental level. We can do this through internal speech and through our imagination. When a salesperson finally makes that big sale, she may be calm on the outside, but if we could listen inside her head we might hear, "Yahoo! . . . I did it! . . . I'm a genius! . . . I'm the best! . . . Yahoo!" We've often wondered what a professional baseball player is thinking after hitting the game-winning home run in the ninth inning. We all probably engage in self-rewarding internal speech after big successes like these, but why not try this powerful method for less momentous occasions? In fact, we probably could improve our own behavior significantly if we purposefully sought out our desirable behaviors and gave ourselves internal words of praise.

This practice can be especially useful for people who are quick to criticize themselves. We have a choice between focusing on what we've done right, and thus building ourselves up, and focusing on what we've done wrong, and thus getting down on ourselves. The research done in this area indicates that the former strategy is more effective. Guilt and self-criticism may have their place in keeping us from engaging in socially and personally undesirable acts, but to rely on these mechanisms and ignore self-praise is a poor way to lead ourselves. Our self-esteem, enthusiasm, and enjoyment in life are likely to suffer if we are consistently self-critical.

We also can reward ourselves in our imagination. For example, through imagination, we can journey to our favorite vacation spot in an instant. We can close our eyes and see the deep-blue water and the white-sand beach with seagulls overhead and feel the warm sun on our face. Or maybe it's cool air we feel rushing across our face as our skis glide gracefully through pure white, new-fallen snow. Wherever and whatever the place, we can go there in an instant, and we can take the trip as a reward for finally getting that difficult report done or for accomplishing some other task. We might even hang a picture of the place on a wall and keep souvenirs nearby to help us make that mental trip when we choose to make it.

In fact, we can combine the physical and mental levels to exercise a particularly powerful self-reward strategy. We might take short, imaginary trips as we accomplish our tasks throughout the year and then physically enjoy a real vacation after the months of hard work. By doing so we reward both our short-run and our long-run activities. Also, the actual vacation will renew our ability to take especially enjoyable imaginary trips when our mind is called on to reproduce the physical setting once we are back at work.

We can use our imagination to reward ourselves in countless other ways as well. We can picture the success and esteem we will experience and enjoy when we finally get that promotion we are working toward. Enjoyment of such an image after completion of each difficult task can help us maintain the motivation we need as we face our labors. Indeed, the mind is capable of being a powerfully motivating tool. If we are to become truly effective self-leaders, we need to master the use of this tool. In doing so, we can make the effort we expend seem worthwhile, if not truly enjoyable.

A checklist to guide your attempts to master self-reward follows, along with an exercise to help you put the steps in the checklist into practice.

CHECKLIST FOR SELF-REWARD

Achieve self-motivation through self-reward.

- Identify what motivates you (for example, objects, thoughts, images).

- Identify your behaviors and activities that you believe are especially desirable.

- Reward yourself when you successfully complete an activity or engage in desirable behavior. Potential rewards you can use include the following:

    1. Desired physical objects or activities, such as an expensive dinner, a night out on the town, a cup of coffee or a snack, or time reading a good book

    2. Enjoyable or praising thoughts, such as thinking to yourself that you performed well and reminding yourself of future benefits you might receive from continued high performance

    3. Pleasant images, such as imagining yourself in your favorite vacation spot

- Develop the habit of being self-praising and self-rewarding for your accomplishments.

SELF-REWARD EXERCISE

Identify what you find rewarding.

1. What physical objects or events do you find rewarding (for example, a delicious dinner, an evening out)?

   _____

   _____

   _____

2. What thoughts or images do you find rewarding (for example, self-praising thoughts, imagination of your favorite vacation spot, thoughts about future career success and prestige)?

   _____

   _____

   _____

3. Identify behaviors that you would like to increase or improve upon that require special motivation for you to do them (for example, reading a technical book, working on a difficult project). Make a list.

   _____

   _____

   _____

4. Try rewarding yourself for working on the activities you have identified in step 3. Use physical and mental rewards. Keep track of your efforts on these behaviors, the rewards you use, and the results, as well as ideas for future improvement (for example, more effective rewards discovered) stemming from the self-reward process.

Behavior	Rewards Used	Results and Ideas

Self-Punishment

> After giving her speech, she dragged herself to her chair, sat down dejectedly, and thought to herself, "I really did a lousy job."

One way that we lead ourselves is through the application of various self-punishments. Unfortunately, many individuals rely too heavily on this approach. Habitual guilt and self-criticism can impair motivation and creativity.

Self-punishment operates in much the same way as self-reward, in that it focuses on self-applied consequences for behavior. The difference is that it involves negative rather than positive self-applied results to decrease undesired rather than increase desired behavior. A salesperson, for example, might engage in self-punishment after making (in her opinion) a poor sales presentation. Refusing to play that weekly game of golf or to watch the big game on television and instead working endlessly on the next sales presentation is an example of how self-punishment might be carried out at the physical level. At the mental level, self-punishments might take the form of negative internal speech ("I really did a lousy job . . . I should be ashamed of myself") or images of possible negative results of the behavior (imagining loss of one's job and not being able to afford to pay the bills and support the family).

Research has generally indicated that self-punishment is not an effective strategy for controlling behavior.[31] First, if we are applying the punishment to ourselves, we can freely avoid it. If we decide purposefully to use self-punishment to eliminate our undesired behaviors, we are likely to find that we do not use it consistently because it is unpleasant and we can choose to avoid it. Second, those who use self-punishment consistently (often in a habitual manner without realizing it) are likely to become discouraged and not enjoy their work.

At times, however, we need to work on our negative behaviors, so what can we do? Probably a better strategy than self-punishment would be to try to remove any rewards supporting the problem behavior and apply self-reward when we do things right. Self-observation is important for the successful application of this strategy. For example, imagine that we identify our problem behavior as watching too much television. One thing we might do is allow ourselves to watch only our second or third choice of programs on certain days, thus removing some of the reward of watching. Also, we could keep a record of how much television we are watching and reward ourselves when we substantially decrease our viewing time (with, for example, an expensive dinner out or even a free night of endless TV viewing).

We could use similar strategies to deal with many of our problem behaviors. Self-punishment might be useful at times, such as when we experience guilt after doing something we know is obviously wrong. To live without a conscience would perhaps be the same as being inhuman. In most cases, however, we can deal more constructively with our problem behaviors by studying them, removing the rewards that support them, and rewarding related behaviors that are desirable. The goal should be to take constructive action to correct these behaviors, not to demoralize and psychologically paralyze ourselves by dwelling on them.

A checklist for gaining control of your self-punishment patterns is provided, as well as an exercise to help you get started in constructively controlling your undesirable behaviors.

CHECKLIST FOR SELF-PUNISHMENT

Control your self-punishment patterns.

- Identify behaviors that create guilt.

- Identify your actions that result in self-critical feelings.

- Identify your destructive self-punitive tendencies.

- Work on reducing or eliminating habitual, destructive patterns of self-punishment.

- Try alternative strategies to self-punishment for dealing with your negative behavior, such as the following:

  o Identify and remove rewards that support your negative behavior.

  o Establish rewards for behaviors that are more desirable than your negative behaviors and that could be substituted for them.

- In general, reserve self-punishment for only your very wrong, seriously negative behaviors.

Study your self-punishment patterns.

1. What are some of your behaviors that result in feelings of guilt?

_____

_____

_____

2. What are some of your behaviors that result in your feeling critical about yourself?

_____

_____

_____

3. Think about the behaviors you have identified in steps 1 and 2. Are your guilt and self-criticism constructive or destructive?

_____

_____

_____

4. In the next few days, try a different self-leadership strategy for dealing with your undesirable behavior in cases when you think your self-punishment is destructive.

   a. Try to identify and remove rewards that are encouraging your negative behaviors.

   _____

   _____

   _____

   b. Try reinforcing related, more desirable behaviors (for example, rewarding yourself for being calm and dealing rationally with conflicts with others rather than exploding with anger).

   _____

   _____

   _____

(Continued)

(Continued)
Keep track of your progress.

Undesirable Behavior	Strategy Used	Comments

Practice

"Hey, isn't this the third time you've been out here hitting balls this week?"

"Yes, it is. I'm tired of playing golf in the wrong fairway. I'm going to practice until I get rid of this slice."

One way we can improve our behavior is through practice. This point has been stated clearly by Muhammad Ali, former world heavyweight boxing champion and Olympic gold medalist:

The fight is won or lost far away from witnesses—behind the lines, in the gym, and out there on the road, long before I dance under those lights.[32]

Indeed, by going over activities before we are called on to perform them when it counts, we can detect problems and make corrections. In doing so, we can avoid costly errors. For example, suppose we have developed a work plan for our place of employment that we strongly believe will improve profits for the company and working conditions for workers. Also, suppose we have been allowed fifteen minutes to propose the plan to a group of executives who will decide whether or not it is to be adopted. We will want to make those fifteen minutes count, so it is in our best interest to practice the presentation ahead of time.

Practice can take place at both the physical and the mental level. For the situation just discussed, we can verbally practice our presentation in front of a mirror or an audience of willing friends, and we can also go over the key points we want to make in our minds. Olympic athletes often take the same approach: practicing their events repeatedly at a physical level as well as rehearsing them mentally before competing.

Practice can also be paired with self-rewards to increase motivation and self-confidence. In addition to rehearsing our presentation mentally, for example, we might picture praise from our audience and adoption of the plan. An Olympic athlete might picture winning the gold medal and the benefits that go with such an accomplishment.

Practice can be a powerful strategy to improve our behavior. The challenge is to apply it systematically. In essence, we need to practice practicing. The key is to develop the ability to identify the important parts of a given task, practice those parts physically and mentally, and pair the practice with rewards. The more important the activity is, the more important it is to practice. Practice might not make perfect, but it can make better—if we do it.

A checklist for practice is provided, as well as an exercise to get you started practicing.

Self-Concordance and Behavior-Focused Strategies

As explained throughout this chapter, behavior-focused strategies are designed to help people improve their performance through the effective management of necessary but perhaps unattractive tasks. But how and when are behavior-focused strategies most effective at influencing task performance? Research suggests that the answer may be found in a concept known as self-concordance, which occurs when a person's individual values are congruent with the tasks they must perform. A recent study found that self-concordance strategies designed to help people identify connections between their personal values and their routine daily tasks moderated the relationship between specific behavior-focused strategies (self-observation, self-goal-setting, self-reward, and cueing) and key outcomes (effort, creativity, and performance) such that the outcomes were best when the use of both behavior-focused strategies and self-concordance strategies were high.[1] The study authors suggest that self-concordance strategies include building more naturally motivating aspects into required tasks, which should increase alignment between the task activity and a person's values; restructuring the task environment such that non-task values, such as friendship or beauty, may be integrated into the task; and refocusing attention on the pleasant rather than unpleasant aspects of the task. In short, the findings of this study suggest that behavior-focused strategies used in isolation may not always be effective, especially when the task is not intrinsically motivating and lacks congruence with an individual's values, goals, and personal identity. In chapter 4, we will explore in greater depth how natural reward-focused strategies may enhance the self-regulatory processes facilitated by behavior-focused strategies.

Note

1. Kerrie L. Unsworth and Claire M. Mason, "Self-Concordance Strategies as a Necessary Condition for Self-Management," *Journal of Occupational and Organizational Psychology* 89, no. 4 (December 2016): 711–33.

CHECKLIST FOR PRACTICE

Improve your future performance through practice

- Identify especially important upcoming challenges.
- Note the important components of these future challenges.

- Physically practice these key components (for example, practice an important oral presentation, focusing special effort on the key points to be made).

- Mentally practice key components while thinking about possible improvements in the performance plan.

- Pair your practice with rewards (for example, while mentally going over a future challenge, imagine a positive, rewarding outcome resulting from your actions).

Use physical and mental practice to improve your performance. Make notes.

1. Identify those challenges you believe will be most important for you in the next few weeks.

   _____

   _____

   _____

2. What are the important components or steps involved in dealing with the challenges identified in step 1?

   _____

   _____

   _____

3. Practice your performance plan to deal with these challenges. Practice physically and mentally, and pair your practice with rewards. Keep a record of your practices and possible improvements and ideas identified during them.

Behavior Practiced	When Practiced	Ideas and Possible Improvements

This chapter has presented several strategies for understanding and improving self-leadership in the face of difficult challenges and activities. The checklists and exercises provided have been designed to help make these ideas more concrete in terms of your own behavior. We hope that you have taken the time and exerted the effort to try at least some of these exercises. The next chapter focuses on a different aspect of self-leadership: capitalizing on the "natural" rewards that come from performing attractive activities.

Roger Bannister

A dejected Roger Bannister staggered off the track inside Helsinki's Olympic Stadium. A favorite to win the 1952 Olympic gold medal in the 1,500-meter event, Bannister had just faded, along with the hopes of the entire British nation, to a fourth-place finish. Bannister saw his failure as nothing short of a personal disaster. He later said, "A disaster is something which is shared between you and the public which expects something of you and which you cannot or have not fulfilled." Bannister was one of the last great amateur athletes. He trained part-time while in school, with the benefit of very little coaching and no financial support. He was just beginning medical school; his future lay in the medical profession, not in athletics. But as he headed back to the Olympic Village that afternoon, Bannister knew he had to find a way to overcome the failure, to make amends for disappointing his countrymen. Most important, he didn't want to retire from running as a loser. That afternoon, Bannister set a goal for himself—a specific and very difficult goal that, if achieved, would more than make up for his Olympic failures and let the world know the kind of athlete he truly was. He would attempt to break the 4-minute mile.

In 1952, a 4-minute mile seemed impossible. Sweden's Gunder Hägg had set the world record of 4:01.4 (4 minutes, 1.4 seconds) in 1945, and in the intervening seven years a 4-minute mile had begun to appear insurmountable. Some even felt that it was a physiological impossibility—that anyone breaking the 4-minute barrier would die in the effort. But Bannister was undaunted. His quest to break the 4-minute mile would be a textbook application of goal-setting and self-leadership. With his long-term goal in place, Bannister began setting shorter-term goals to help move him toward his ultimate objective. A typical workout consisted of ten 440-yard (quarter-mile) sprints with 2-minute rest intervals in between. He and his training partners,

Chris Chataway and Chris Brasher, set a goal of 60 seconds for each 440. Over several months of training, they were able to lower their 440 times from an average of 66 seconds to 61 seconds. Finally, in late April 1954, the three friends astonished themselves by averaging just 58.9 seconds over ten 440s. Bannister knew he was ready to make his attempt.

That would come on May 6, 1954, at the Iffley Road track in Oxford. Once again, goals would be the key to Bannister's hope of shattering the 4-minute mile. Chataway and Brasher were officially entered in the event, but they would serve primarily to pace Bannister. The group had set some very specific goals for the race. Brasher would set the pace for the first two laps, finishing the first lap in 57 or 58 seconds and the second lap in precisely 60 seconds. At this point Chataway, known for his endurance, would take over and pace Bannister through the third lap, again in 60 seconds flat. Bannister would be on his own for the final lap, and any time around 61 seconds should allow him to break the 4-minute mark.

As Bannister stepped to the starting line, he *knew* that he could break the barrier. Because of his training and the goal-setting processes he had used, he was certain that if he just hit the goals that he and his friends had set he would achieve his ultimate objective. The gun sounded and the trio set out, quickly putting the rest of the competitive field behind them. Brasher led Bannister and Chataway to a 57.5 first lap. Right on target. The three runners passed the half-mile mark at about 1:58. Perfect. Brasher began to fade in the third lap as Chataway surged to the front. When Chataway and Bannister went into the final lap, their time was 3:00.4, slightly off the mark, but close. As Bannister finally edged past Chataway, he realized that he would need to run the final half lap in less than 30 seconds in order to break the record. Bannister willed himself forward, taking longer, more powerful strides. As he drove toward the line, his chin came up and his head tilted back as his body, fully depleted of oxygen, began to shut down. Bannister crossed the line in a state of physical collapse, on the brink of unconsciousness and struggling for breath. "Did I do it?" he gasped. It was very close, and no one on the field knew for certain. Finally, the announcement came over the loudspeaker: "Ladies and gentlemen . . . in the one mile . . . first place, R. G. Bannister . . . with a time which is . . . a new English Native, British National, British All-Comers, European, British Empire and WORLD'S RECORD. The time is THREE . . ." The remainder of the announcement was lost in the cheers of twelve hundred jubilant spectators! Roger Bannister had reached his goal with a time of 3:59.4!

In May 1954, through a process of goal-setting and self-leadership, Bannister rewrote the record books while reaching toward his fullest athletic potential. He also redefined "impossible." Just forty-six days later, Australian John Landy surpassed Bannister's record with a time of 3:58! Since 1954, more than nine hundred runners have broken the 4-minute barrier. On July 7, 1999, Hicham El Guerrouj of Morocco set a world record of 3:43.13 with an incredible average of 55.78 seconds per lap. All of these runners owe a debt of gratitude to Roger Bannister, who helped show them what is possible.

Questions for Class Discussion

1. Explain how Roger Bannister used goal-setting to become the first person to break the 4-minute mile.

2. Do you think Bannister could have been successful in his attempt if he had not used self-set goals? Why or why not?

3. How might Bannister have used other self-leadership strategies mentioned in this chapter, such as cueing, self-observation, self-reward, and practice?

4. What role do you think purpose played in Bannister's goal-setting process?

Sources/Additional Readings

Bannister, Roger. 2004. *The Four-Minute Mile*, 50th anniversary ed. Guilford, CT: Lyons Press.

Bascomb, Neal. 2004. *The Perfect Mile: Three Athletes, One Goal, and Less Than Four Minutes to Achieve It*. Boston: Houghton Mifflin.

4

NATURAL REWARD-FOCUSED STRATEGIES

Scenic Views, Sunshine, and the Joys of Traveling

We need to stop looking at work as simply a means of earning a living and start realizing it is one of the elemental ingredients of making a life.

—Luci Swindoll

One morning a national leader gazed in the mirror and knew his time had passed. He decided that he should select his successor. He believed this to be his most important remaining decision. Under his guidance, his tribe had grown from a small, disorganized, self-defeating people into a powerful nation with much pride and sense of purpose.

So it was that he summoned his two greatest governors to his quarters—one of whom he would choose as his successor. He turned to the first governor, whose accomplishments were great although significantly less than those of the other, and said, "Tell me of your philosophy of leadership and of how you have accomplished what you have."

The first governor responded quickly and simply, "I have learned the skill of getting my people to do what they should do whether they like it or not."

Then the national leader put the question to the second governor, whose physical stature and manner were considerably less impressive but who for some reason had accomplished significantly more.

Learning Objectives

After studying this chapter, you should be able to do the following:

1. Contrast externally administered rewards and natural (intrinsic) rewards.

2. Compare the three primary features of naturally rewarding activities that create feelings of competence, self-control, and purpose.

3. Employ the two primary natural reward approaches or strategies: building natural rewards into our life's activities and focusing on natural rewards.

The second governor had to think for a few moments, and then he answered in a manner that was not so clear and simple. "I'm not really a leader at all," he began.

The great national leader was concerned with this response and was beginning to think that the first governor was a more likely choice.

"There are your leaders," the second governor continued, motioning toward the crowds of citizens outside the building.

Now the great leader was more thoughtful and curious about the second governor's response, although still unsure of its merit. All was quiet for some time, and then the great leader motioned toward the crowds and asked, "Then what is the secret of their leadership?"

The second governor again responded slowly and thoughtfully: "They believe in what they are doing and for the most part enjoy doing it. You see, the secret to leading oneself is doing what one believes is worthwhile and doing so specifically because one believes in it and enjoys doing it. I'm just a coordinator of sorts. I simply try to help them discover what it is they see as worthwhile and the capability, interest, and desire within themselves to do it. I find if I can help them get themselves pointed in the same purposeful, exciting direction, there is an unleashing of a tremendous power for progress."

Now the great leader thought for a while, considering the second governor's response with a sense of awe and wonder. "I have made my decision," he stated after a few moments.

All those inside and outside the chamber within hearing distance grew very silent as they strained to listen.

"For the future leadership of our nation, I have chosen these people!" he proclaimed while motioning with both hands toward the crowds outside. And then, turning to the second governor, he said, "And you shall coordinate them."

This chapter is concerned with a naturally positive approach to self-leadership. The approach is reminiscent of the old joke in which a man says to his physician, "Doctor, it hurts when I do this," to which the doctor responds, "Then don't do that." In this chapter we discuss a principle involving similar logic but with a reversed focus. That is, if you say, "I like to do that," the parallel self-leadership response would be "Then do it." Please don't misinterpret this discussion as a "Do your own thing no matter what" message. Indeed, restrictions on this approach—laws, your own values, and so on—must be addressed. The primary purpose of this chapter, however, is to get across one simple idea: the desirability of using natural rewards (your naturally motivating activities and tasks) toward the pursuit of more effective self-leadership. Hopefully, reading this book is shaping up to be this type of naturally rewarding activity for you, as opposed to a "getting yourself to do a dreaded, unattractive, but necessary" type of task.

Take a few moments to assess your own tendencies regarding the use of natural rewards. Select the number in Self-Leadership Questionnaire 2 that best describes your position in response to each of the fifteen statements listed. These statements might seem similar to those in Self-Leadership Questionnaire 1 in Chapter 3, but you should still respond to each one. Follow the directions provided for scoring your responses.

INTERPRETING YOUR SCORE

Your scores for A through E suggest your current self-leadership tendencies concerning several self-leadership strategies that will be addressed in this chapter. Your score for each of these strategies could range from 3 (a total absence of the strategy in your current self-leadership) to 15 (a very high level of the strategy in your current self-leadership). Your scores on A through E can be interpreted as follows:

1. A score of 3 or 4 indicates a *very low* level of the strategy.

2. A score of 5 to 7 indicates a *low* level of the strategy.

3. A score of 8 to 10 indicates a *moderate* level of the strategy.

4. A score of 11 to 13 indicates a *high* level of the strategy.

5. A score of 14 or 15 indicates a *very high* level of the strategy.

Each of the strategies addressed by the questionnaire should generally contribute to personal performance and effectiveness. Therefore, high scores on A through E suggest a high level of self-leadership, which offers potential to enhance performance. Each of the specific strategies is discussed in more detail throughout the remainder of the chapter.

Your score on X indicates your overall use of the self-leadership strategies. This score could range from a low of 15 to a high of 75. Your score on X can be interpreted as follows:

1. A score of 15 to 22 indicates a *very low* overall level of the strategies.

2. A score of 23 to 37 indicates a *low* overall level of the strategies.

3. A score of 38 to 52 indicates a *moderate* overall level of the strategies.

4. A score of 53 to 67 indicates a *high* overall level of the strategies.

5. A score of 68 to 75 indicates a *very high* overall level of the strategies.

Self-Leadership Questionnaire 2
Self-Assessment Questionnaire for Creating the Self-Motivating Situation

	Describes me very well	Describes me well	Describes me somewhat	Does not describe me very well	Does not describe me at all
1. I try to be aware of what activities in my work I especially enjoy.	5	4	3	2	1
2. When I have a choice, I try to do my work in places (e.g., a comfortable room, outdoors) that I like.	5	4	3	2	1
3. I seek out activities in my work that I enjoy doing.	5	4	3	2	1
4. I spend more time thinking about the good things than about the drawbacks of my job.	5	4	3	2	1
5. I pay more attention to enjoyment of my work itself than to the rewards I will receive for doing it.	5	4	3	2	1
6. I know the parts of my job that I really like doing.	5	4	3	2	1
7. I try to arrange to do my work in pleasant surroundings when possible.	5	4	3	2	1
8. When I have a choice, I try to do my work in ways that I enjoy rather than just trying to get it over with.	5	4	3	2	1
9. While I work, I think less about things I don't like about my job than about things I like.	5	4	3	2	1

Statement					
10. My thinking focuses more on the things I like about actually doing my work than on benefits I expect to receive.	5	4	3	2	1
11. I can name the things I do in my job that I really enjoy.	5	4	3	2	1
12. When I can, I do my work in surroundings that I like.	5	4	3	2	1
13. I try to build activities into my work that I like doing.	5	4	3	2	1
14. I focus my thinking on the pleasant rather than the unpleasant feelings I have about my job.	5	4	3	2	1
15. I think less about the rewards I expect to receive for doing my job than about the enjoyment of actually doing it.	5	4	3	2	1

Directions for scoring: Add the numbers you circled for each statement as indicated below to determine your score for each self-leadership strategy.

	Scores
A. Distinguishing natural rewards (add numbers circled for statements 1, 6, and 11)	
B. Choosing pleasant surroundings (add numbers circled for statements 2, 7, and 12)	
C. Building naturally rewarding activities into your work (add numbers circled for statements 3, 8, and 13)	
D. Focusing on the pleasant aspects in your work (add numbers circled for statements 4, 9, and 14)	
E. Focusing on natural rewards rather than external rewards (add numbers circled for statements 5, 10, and 15)	
X. Total score (add the scores for A through E)	

In general, a high score on X suggests that you possess some positive self-leadership tendencies. Your score on X reflects what you believe are your current self-leadership tendencies. Regardless of your score, the remainder of this chapter is designed to help you implement and improve upon several self-leadership strategies. This chapter will provide you with a basis for better understanding and more effectively using the power of natural rewards.

NATURAL REWARDS

The psychological literature emphasizes an important distinction between two basic types of rewards.[1] One of these is the externally administered reward that we most often associate with work organizations. Examples of this type of reward include praise, pay raises, time off, promotions, awards, and monetary bonuses. In Chapter 3, we noted that we can self-apply many such rewards to influence our own motivation positively.

The second type of reward is generally less recognized and less understood, but it is no less important. This type consists of rewards that are so closely tied to given tasks or activities that the two cannot be separated. For example, an individual who enjoys reading the newspaper and spends a great deal of time doing so is engaging in an activity that could be described as naturally rewarding. No special externally administered or self-administered incentives are necessary to motivate this behavior—the incentives are built into the task itself. Of course, some externally applied rewards might result, such as compliments from others on being well informed. Both types of rewards can be and often are at work at the same time. Still, the importance and power of these natural rewards should be recognized and, where possible, used in positive ways.

In Chapter 2, we suggested that an Olympic athlete might use many strategies to help motivate him- or herself to engage in the difficult training behavior that accompanies success. We also suggested that some of the necessary training might be naturally enjoyable—such as the speed and motion of alpine skiing for an Olympic skier. This chapter will suggest ways of harnessing the power of these naturally rewarding activities. It is intended to help you do what you want to do (and to like it) on your journey toward becoming what you choose for your life. This is important for you as well as for the organizations that may employ you. Indeed, top companies such as Google have shown that they understand the power of natural rewards, as we discuss later in this chapter.

WHAT MAKES ACTIVITIES NATURALLY REWARDING?

Naturally rewarding activities tend to have two primary features: they make us feel more *competent*, and they help us feel *self-controlling* (or self-determining).[2] A recent research study found evidence supporting this relationship, showing that when leaders focus on employee development, employees are more likely to fulfill their basic needs for competence and autonomy (or self-control); employees respond to such leadership with increased task performance, increased positive extra-role (unrequired) behaviors, or both.[3] Another aspect of naturally rewarding activities is the sense of *purpose* we derive from them.[4] The following discussion addresses each of these features separately.

Feelings of Competence

One common aspect of naturally rewarding activities is that they frequently make us feel more competent. We often enjoy tasks that we perform well. People who perform well in a sport often like that sport; persons who do well in school often like school.

If we think of activities we especially like, we probably will find that many or most of them contribute to our feelings of competence in some way. For example, people often enjoy talking about their work, hobbies, and other areas in which they possess knowledge and skill. If we find that a conversation we're having with another person is lagging, we might begin asking about his or her work or hobbies—the likely result being an increase in interest and enjoyment of the discussion for that person. It can be argued that talking about a person's area of expertise contributes to that person's feelings of competence and is therefore naturally rewarding. Perhaps you have noticed increased interest on your own part when you talk to others about your skill areas. Similarly, as we improve our performance in an activity, we often find it becomes more enjoyable. A couple of good shots on the golf course, for example, can go a long way toward enticing us to play again in the future.

Activities that tend to make us feel more competent are often tied to external rewards of some kind. Compliments from others on our display of knowledge in a conversation and "oohs" and "aahs" for spectacular shots on the golf course will motivate us to continue these activities. The focus here, however, is on the naturally rewarding aspects of the activities themselves. The feeling of strength and power for a runner who is in good condition can contribute to feelings of competence and be rewarding in itself, apart from trophies won and praise received for effort. The same logic applies to our activities in general.

Feelings of Self-Control

A second common characteristic of naturally enjoyable activities is that they frequently make us feel more self-controlling. Humans seem to have a natural tendency to want to control their own destinies. From toddlers whose favorite activities seem to be the off-limits "no-no's" to adults who dream of being their own bosses and independently wealthy, the desire for personal control as opposed to external control is readily apparent.

We tend to want to be a major force in determining what happens around us. For example, most of us would prefer to make the important decisions that directly affect us, such as where we will live, where we will work, and whom we will marry, rather than have someone else dictate these things to us. In a more general sense, we prefer to control aspects of our world rather than have them control us. Those of us who have been in situations where our every move seemed to be dictated by someone else, some rule or regulation, or some other external source know the helpless feelings that come with a lack of self-determination. Conversely, projects, hobbies, and other activities that we choose to undertake and in which we choose the method by which they will be performed contribute to our feelings of self-control.

Our desire for feelings of competence and self-control often results in a pattern in our behavior in which we search for challenges that we are capable of overcoming and then expend effort to overcome them. Increasing our running distance by an extra half-mile, cutting a stroke off our golf game, and striving to achieve a reasonable increase in our performance rating at work all potentially reflect this kind of pattern. Grappling with reasonable challenges can be naturally rewarding because overcoming them can contribute to our feelings of competence and self-control. Activities that accomplish this result are prime candidates for us to try to increase or build into our tasks to make them more enjoyable. In essence, we use the potential effects of different activities on our feelings of competence and self-control as a guide for selecting the features to build into our tasks, or to focus our thoughts on while performing them, to make our effort

SELF-LEADERSHIP RESEARCH

Job Autonomy, Self-Leadership, and Work Outcomes

As we describe in this chapter, activities tend to be more naturally rewarding when they lead to feelings of self-control. Yet many work environments restrict the control that individuals have over their work tasks with procedures, policies, and work structures that allow employees little autonomy in choosing their work-related behaviors. Although workplace controls can be useful in positively shaping employee behaviors, self-leadership research suggests that these types of controls may also limit the ability of employees to engage in natural reward strategies, resulting in less motivation and lower job satisfaction. For example, a recent study of 407 supervisor–subordinate dyads sampled from various organizations in Hong Kong and the People's Republic of China found that job autonomy moderated relationships between the use of self-leadership strategies, including natural reward strategies, and a number of work outcomes, including supervisor performance ratings, an objective performance measure, and job satisfaction.[1] In other words, job contexts involving high autonomy intensified the positive effect of self-leadership on these work outcomes. The findings of this study suggest that a less structured work environment characterized by job autonomy may provide employees with the freedom to apply natural reward strategies and engage in other self-leading behaviors, resulting in higher levels of performance and job satisfaction at work.

Note

1. Jessie Ho and Paul L. Nesbit, "Self-Leadership in a Chinese Context: Work Outcomes and the Moderating Role of Job Autonomy," *Group & Organization Management* 39, no. 4 (August 2014): 389–415.

more naturally rewarding. These features often take the form of personal challenges of some sort that we are capable of overcoming.

Feelings of Purpose

One additional important feature of naturally rewarding activities needs to be considered: the tendency of such activities to provide a sense of purpose. Even if a task makes us feel more competent and more self-controlling, we still might have a difficult time naturally enjoying and being motivated by it if we do not believe in its worthiness.[5] As we discussed in Chapter 3, most of us yearn for purpose and meaning. The troubling emergence of the phenomenon of the "midlife crisis" accents this idea. When we look back on our life and look ahead to the future, we have a basic need to feel that what we are doing is of value. The best vacuum cleaner salesperson in the world (who is obviously competent, has freely chosen the profession, and is otherwise self-determining) still might not enjoy the work if he or she has no self-confidence about the job. From where, then, do feelings of purpose and meaning emerge?

One aspect of naturally rewarding activities that many would argue provides a sense of purpose involves helping or expressing goodwill toward others.[6] The term *altruism* often is used in connection with this idea.[7] Endocrinologist Hans Selye has suggested that the way to enjoy a rewarding lifestyle, free of disabling stress, is to practice "altruistic egoism."[8] In essence, this idea involves helping others and "earning their love" while at the same time recognizing one's own needs and enhancing oneself (egoism). Selye explains that the natural biological nature of humankind drives people toward self-preservation, or what might be described more bluntly as *selfishness*. The philosophy suggests that only by marrying this innate, self-centered nature with an attitude of winning the goodwill and respect of others through altruistic efforts will we achieve a happy, meaningful life. In support of this idea, researchers recently developed a model to explain how egoism and altruism are both likely to occur in teams.[9] This model explains which teams will be more altruistic and which will be more egoistic. In contrast, after analyzing evidence from biology and psychology, Martin Hoffman has concluded that an altruistic motive might exist in humans apart from egoistic motives.[10] The evidence suggests that altruism might be a part of human nature that is not entwined with any selfish motive.[11]

Regardless of why altruism can potentially add purpose to a task or, more generally, to one's life, it should not be overlooked. It could be the key to achieving feelings of purpose and meaning. We might never fully understand the altruistic urge, let alone human nature, but the essence of purpose might be centered in the simple idea of helping our fellow humans (and possibly ourselves in the process).

We can identify many pursuits that provide people with a feeling of purpose and that at least appear to exist apart from altruistic motives. A scientist whose life purpose is the advancement of pure scientific knowledge exemplifies this idea, but then doesn't the advancement of science potentially serve an altruistic end—the betterment of all people? Whether scientists are significantly motivated by this aspect of their work may vary from person to person. The challenge is for each of us to search inside ourselves to find what provides us with a feeling of purpose. Altruism might well be at the heart of this search for most of us.

A checklist to guide your attempts to discover the natural rewards in your life is provided along with an exercise to help you get started in identifying your natural rewards.

CHECKLIST FOR DISCOVERING YOUR NATURAL REWARDS

Discover your natural rewards.

- Identify tasks or activities that you naturally enjoy—in which the rewards for doing them are built into, rather than separate from, the tasks themselves.

- To find these naturally rewarding tasks, look for activities that do the following:

  o   Help make you feel competent

  o   Help make you feel self-controlling

  o   Provide you with a sense of purpose

DISCOVERING YOUR NATURAL REWARDS EXERCISE

Discover your naturally rewarding tasks. Make notes.

1. List some of the activities that you naturally enjoy doing—those for which the incentive for doing them is built in rather than separate from the activities

   _____

   _____

   _____

2. Classify the above activities and expand your list by identifying activities that provide you with a sense of

   a.   Competence

   _____

   _____

   _____

b. Self-control

_____

_____

_____

c. Purpose

_____

_____

_____

3. Identify activities that accomplish all three (provide you with a sense of competence, self-control, and purpose). Note that activities that do not accomplish all three might not be true naturally rewarding activities.

_____

_____

_____

TAPPING THE POWER OF NATURAL REWARDS

Below we discuss two primary approaches to using natural rewards to enhance our self-leadership: building more naturally enjoyable features into our life's activities and intentionally focusing our thoughts on the naturally rewarding aspects of our activities.

Building Natural Rewards Into Our Life's Activities

The blizzard hit the forest with tremendous force, leaving a deep layer of new-fallen snow. The beaver was in a bad mood as he struggled toward the river. The snow made it hard to move, and he was irritable as he trudged along. Then he noticed the whistling of the otter, who was sliding and rolling playfully over the snowy slopes on his way to the river. "Why are you whistling on this horrible day?" snapped the beaver, obviously irritated. "Why, it's a great day!" the otter sang out. "The best day I've had since yesterday—which was great, too." The beaver sneered at this response and continued to complain as he trudged forward. The otter continued to slide and roll along playfully, whistling as he went. They both reached the river.

The logic of the first approach to using natural rewards in exercising self-leadership involves identifying aspects of our endeavors that we naturally enjoy and trying to increase these as much as reasonably possible. For example, a business meeting can be held in an appealing location. The same matters addressed in a formal conference room of an office building can take on a different flavor when they are addressed in a relaxed meeting room at a beautiful resort. Similarly, persons who like direct conversations with fellow employees can enjoy communicating face-to-face if they choose to do so rather than struggling to write formal memos. The point is that we usually can identify several ways to accomplish many of our activities. By choosing to accomplish tasks in more enjoyable ways, we are building in natural rewards for our efforts.

We can illustrate this idea further with an example of a person who runs or jogs regularly. This individual might run to obtain benefits such as increased endurance and strength, weight control, and reduced stress. On the other hand, this person might run for the sheer enjoyment of the activity. We know an individual who has been a runner for many years—he takes his running seriously yet finds a way to make it fun. Although he has trained hard and performed well in organized races, including marathons, he does not understand those who choose running as a form of leisure or exercise but pursue it in a dull and monotonous way. A person who runs around a track day after day, probably through some force of will to get in shape, exemplifies this dull approach.

Natural rewards can be built into the activity of running to make it more enjoyable and more naturally rewarding. One way a person might do this is by running in enjoyable places. Running along an ocean shore while listening to the peaceful rhythm of powerful white-crested waves and watching graceful seagulls overhead can be an exhilarating experience. Alternatively, a person could run on a forest trail while listening to the singing of birds and the rushing of streams, and perhaps see an occasional squirrel, deer, or other wildlife. A person might run in the early morning or at dusk while enjoying a brightly colored horizon. Running can be an enjoyable experience for those who choose to make it so.

Google provides a good example of a company that builds natural rewards into its work environment. Google's campuses and work locations around the world demonstrate the company's basic philosophy, "to create the happiest, most productive workplace in the world," as stated by Google spokesman Jordan Newman.[12] The Google work spaces include a dizzying array of play areas, cafés, coffee bars, and gourmet cafeterias serving free breakfast, lunch, and dinner. Theatrical-themed conference rooms featuring velvet drapes are juxtaposed with conversation spaces that have the feel of vintage subway cars. Lego play stations, ladders connecting floors, and secret rooms behind swinging bookcases in cozy libraries are not uncommon. Dogs roam the corridors with their employee owners, and software engineers are encouraged to design their own desks using giant Tinkertoy-like materials. "We're trying to push the boundaries of the workplace," Newman explains.[13] In contrast, another modern corporate behemoth, Amazon, was recently criticized for creating an extremely demanding work environment where employees are held to standards that the company boasts are "unreasonably high."[14]

Such a highly demanding and extrinsically motivated work environment has the potential to create high levels of stress for some employees: "You walk out of a conference room and you'll see a grown man covering his face," said Bo Olson, a former employee. "Nearly every person I worked with, I saw cry at their desk."[15] Nevertheless, despite their vastly differing cultures, both Google and Amazon have been highly successful thus far.

Our emphasis up to this point has been on the obvious aspects of making activities more naturally enjoyable—that is, by choosing a pleasant context for the task, which is, in essence, part of the task. Another approach involves following the guidelines suggested earlier: we can search for features of our activities that provide us with feelings of competence, self-control, and purpose, which are prime factors in making tasks more naturally rewarding. For a runner, this might involve undertaking a reasonable challenge, such as a slightly longer run than usual over challenging terrain. The task is all the better if it provides the runner with a sense of purpose based in the belief that he or she is setting a positive example and being an inspiration for others or the run is part of a fund-raising drive for charity, for example. Similarly, our work and lives can be more naturally rewarding if we take them seriously enough to play at them and make them more enjoyable.

Mary Poppins (1964)

A scene from the well-loved Disney classic *Mary Poppins* helps to illustrate the power of natural rewards. The movie tells the story of a no-nonsense nanny named Mary Poppins (Julie Andrews) who teaches the Banks family how to enjoy life. The scene begins (about 31 minutes into the movie) just after Mary Poppins, newly employed, has met the Banks children, Jane and Michael. Mary Poppins says, "Our first game is called 'Well begun is half done,' otherwise entitled 'Let's tidy up the nursery.'" Michael reacts by telling Jane, "I told you she was tricky!" Mary Poppins proceeds to sing the song "A Spoonful of Sugar" as she shows the children how to focus on the naturally rewarding aspects of the task in order to turn work into play: "In every job that must be done / There is an element of fun / You find the fun and snap! / The job's a game." The scene ends with Mary Poppins saying, "Hats and coats everyone—it's time for our outing in the park," and Michael replying, "But I don't want an outing, I want to tidy up the nursery again!" Even though we can't simply snap our fingers or use magic to accomplish our tasks as Mary Poppins does in the scene, we can find the fun elements in nearly any task and transform it into a game.

Discussion Questions

1. How does Mary Poppins help the children learn about focusing on the naturally rewarding aspects of the task of cleaning up the nursery?

2. What are the "elements of fun" involved in cleaning up the nursery, and how are Mary Poppins and the children able to transform these elements into a game?

3. Are there elements of fun in every task or activity?

SELF-LEADERSHIP IN THE MOVIES

Charles Manz, a member of our author team, recalls the following experience:

One of my first experiences in my academic career was at a conference I attended shortly after I began my doctoral studies. I was excited about the opportunity to listen to some of the most esteemed and respected faculty from across the country. At one of the first meetings of this gathering, doctoral students from dozens of universities (myself included) listened to perhaps the foremost scholar at the meeting present a rather bleak message: we (the listening students) would never again have as light a workload as we had at that time. We were told by the speaker—and his comments were later supported by other speakers—that we should be prepared for long and demanding work hours (perhaps fifty, sixty, seventy, eighty or more hours per week) in our future careers. The listening students, many of whom already felt overworked, were obviously less than enthusiastic about this crystal-ball view of their futures. Although some of the rewarding aspects of our profession were discussed, the underlying message seemed to be that if we really wanted to be successful, we should be prepared to work our tails off. I have thought back to that experience many times. I was impressed with the speakers and believe they were competent people. For this reason, I am all the more disturbed by the message conveyed and the effect it had on the audience.

Our problem with the philosophy presented in this story (a philosophy that we believe is all too common) is that it suggests that the path to a successful career and the ultimate achievement of our life's goals is an agonizing, uphill climb. We do agree that sacrifices and intense effort are often integral parts of achieving our goals (hence the considerable value of self-discipline-oriented self-leadership strategies such as those presented in Chapter 3). Our underlying philosophy concerning achievement and success, however, is different.

In essence, we would argue that the road to success, although often rocky and challenging, should be made as naturally rewarding as possible. To the extent that a person pursues worthwhile challenges that are naturally enjoyed, a built-in motivation is established. We can explore our present work and life for the activities we enjoy that help us make progress toward our goals. We can build enjoyment into our work. We can plan our careers so that we enjoyably progress toward our desired destinies.

Although we believe the accredited speakers at the meeting described above would agree with much of this logic, their message conveyed, intentionally or unintentionally, a less-than-pleasant view of work. Here's a better message:

Fellow students, don't work your tails off. Instead, work as little as possible, for when you are doing what you naturally enjoy, work is no longer work. As Confucius said, "Choose a job you love, and you will never have to work a day in your life." If you enjoy what you do, it will not seem like work. Apple co-founder Steve Jobs had this to say in his Stanford University Commencement Address in June 2005: "You've got to find what you love. . . . Your work is going to fill a large part of your life, and the only way to be truly satisfied is

This exercise involves a difficult mental climb to the peak of your own personal mountain. This climb will be a journey of self-discovery that will help you identify qualities that make you unique—that make you a special human being.

Taking the First Step

The first step is to make an inventory of your life's experiences. Specifically, contemplate the years of your life. Consider the times in your life when you have experienced a "majestic moment" (MM)—the times when you felt an ultimate flow of all your energies; when you enjoyed a sense of accomplishment, exhilaration, happiness, and self-pride; when you became aware of the purpose of your life and felt like you were where you belonged. Further, these times include those when you really stretched yourself—making full use of your abilities. Your MMs could be related to work, school, a sport, a hobby, or anything in which you played a meaningful role. It is important to note that what constitutes a majestic moment for you does not have to be a majestic moment for someone else. Your MMs are defined by you alone. What someone else thinks is not important. Finally, try to think of MMs that are majestic not because you won something or finished first (focusing on an outcome) but because of the actual tasks (processes) involved.

List four of your majestic moments:

1. _____
   _____
2. _____
   _____
3. _____
   _____
4. _____
   _____

You have just completed the first part of your journey. Remember that the longest journey begins with the first step.

Second Step: The Climb

Think carefully about the events you listed in step 1. Recall each experience as vividly as possible. Try to picture the details of the experience. What were your feelings and thoughts? Mentally relive each experience.

Note several aspects of each of your majestic moments using the following cues:

- What skills did you utilize while achieving your MM (e.g., physical, mental, writing, speaking, helping, nurturing)?

- What were the conditions that surrounded or led to your MM (e.g., activity was important, challenging, high autonomy, high accountability, involved teamwork)?

Third Step: Enjoy the View

Recall the quote from Confucius about choosing a job you love. Wouldn't it be wonderful to have a majestic moment every day of your life—every time that you perform your job? If you select a job that allows you to utilize the skills you observed in step 2 and/or involves the surrounding conditions you noted, chances are good that you will experience MMs during performance of your job and, thus, truly enjoy what you do.

(Continued)

(Continued)

Are you currently employed in a job that you don't find enjoyable? Are you majoring in a field that you won't enjoy working in upon graduation? If you answered yes to either of these questions, then try to identify a position in your organization or in another field that would utilize your MM skills and that would match your MM environment. Another approach is to find ways in your current job to use your MM abilities and change the environment to resemble more closely the MM environment identified in this exercise. It might not be easy to find a new job or alter your current one to fit these MM criteria, but if you persevere, you can make it happen. If you are determined, then you can find a job that doesn't seem like work.

to do what you believe is great work. And the only way to do great work is to love what you do. If you haven't found it yet, keep looking. And don't settle. As with all matters of the heart, you'll know when you find it."[16] Expend the effort and put in the necessary hours, but build in natural rewards and work on what you believe in, in the way you most enjoy. When possible, take part in worthwhile activities that you naturally like. Self-leadership strategies focusing on self-discipline can help us overcome formidable obstacles when they arise, but when we have a choice, we should use the power of natural rewards. We can truly reach the pinnacle of success (and create a better world in the process) if our work is inspired.

CHECKLIST FOR BUILDING NATURAL REWARDS INTO YOUR ACTIVITIES

Build natural rewards into your tasks.

- Examine the nature of your current activities.

- Identify pleasing contexts (places) in which you could perform your work to make it more pleasant and naturally rewarding.

- Identify activities that you could build into your tasks (different ways of accomplishing the same things) that would make your work naturally rewarding (that would provide you with a sense of competence, self-control, and purpose).

- Redesign your tasks by working in the contexts and building in the activities that make them more naturally enjoyable.

Follow these steps to build natural rewards into your activities. Make notes.

1. List some tasks you need to do that you do not particularly enjoy doing.

   _____

   _____

   _____

   _____

2. Try to identify different, more pleasant contexts in which you could perform these tasks.

   _____

   _____

   _____

   _____

3. Identify activities you find naturally rewarding (that provide you with a sense of competence, self-control, and purpose) that you could possibly build into the tasks you listed in step 1. Refer to the list that you developed in the "Discovering Your Natural Rewards Exercise" as a starting point, and identify additional activities.

   _____

   _____

   _____

   _____

4. Redesign your tasks. Use your ideas from steps 2 and 3 as a basis for redesigning some of your tasks. Specify plans for redesigning tasks, including contexts and activities that could make your work more naturally rewarding.

   _____

   _____

   _____

   _____

BUILDING NATURAL REWARDS INTO YOUR ACTIVITIES EXERCISE

Dwayne "The Rock" Johnson

A "majestic moment" is a time when you feel an ultimate flow of your energies, when you enjoy a sense of accomplishment, exhilaration, happiness, and self-pride. Few people are fortunate enough to experience majestic moments in their work life, but by following his heart and focusing on what he enjoyed doing, actor Dwayne "The Rock" Johnson successfully transformed himself from a failed football player into one of the highest-paid entertainers in the world. Johnson was born in 1972 in Hayward, California, the son of Rocky "Soul Man" Johnson, a member of the first African American tag-team professional wrestling champions. Although he would later follow in his father's footsteps and become a professional wrestler, Johnson first excelled at football. He played college football for the Miami Hurricanes, appearing in 39 games and making 77 tackles as a member of the 1991 national championship team. He dreamed of playing in the NFL, but instead found himself playing for the Calgary Stampeders of the Canadian Football League for $250 per week.

Two months into the season, he was devastated by getting cut from the team and was left struggling with depression. "The dreams I had, they're dashed," he recalled. "There is no more football. My relationship was crushed. That was my absolute worst time." A month and a half later, the Calgary coach called and said, "Hey, I know we cut you, but I'd like you to come back." Johnson told the coach he would think about it and hung up the phone. His dad said, "You're gonna do it, right?" Johnson replied, "No, I don't think so. I think I'm done with that. My gut tells me I'm done." His dad said, "What are you going to do?" Johnson took a deep breath and said, "I'd like to get into the business." His dad asked, "What business?" Johnson replied, "The wrestling business." Clearly not pleased, his dad responded, "You are throwing it all away! It is the worst mistake you will ever make—you are ruining your career." Johnson looked at his father and said, "Maybe I'll be no good, but I feel like in my heart, I have to do this."

After spending some time in World Wrestling Entertainment's (WWE) minor leagues, Johnson debuted in 1996 in WWE's Survivor Series and quickly became a fan favorite. Johnson won the WWE heavyweight title six times along with five tag-team titles and is considered by many to be the greatest professional wrestler of all time. Johnson's big break into the wider world of entertainment came when he was invited to host the iconic Saturday Night Live (SNL) show in New York City. Johnson's SNL performance was a hit and showed Hollywood that he had legitimate acting ability. His film debut came as the villain in "The Mummy Returns" and was quickly followed by other roles, including his performances in the popular "Fast and the Furious" series and most recently a starring role in the hit HBO TV series "Ballers." Through it all, Johnson has maintained that his successes have been grounded on simply being himself and doing things he loves to do. Although his acting career has been going strong, he often returns to the wrestling ring for special events like WWE's Wrestlemania. "I'm back, not for money, not because I like being on the road, but because I love the business," Johnson once explained. "I've always loved the showmanship of professional wrestling. While I love making movies, I love that platform, too." By applying his diverse talents as an athlete, showman, actor, and entertainer in such a way as to create a naturally rewarding work life, Dwayne Johnson has discovered the secret to experiencing majestic moments in his everyday life.

Sources/Additional Reading

Acuna, Kirsten, Jason Guerrasio, and Carrie Wittmer. 2017. "How The Rock Went From Failed Football Player to the Highest-Paid Actor in Hollywood." *Business Insider*, April 14, 2017. https://www.businessinsider.com/the-rock-career-2016-7.

Banks, Alec. 2016. "How The Rock Went From Depressed Football Player to Hollywood Mogul." *Highsnobiety*, May 19, 2016. https://www.highsnobiety.com/2016/05/19/dwayne-the-rock-johnson-biography/.

"How a Bout of Depression Led to Dwayne Johnson's Career-Defining Moment." 2015. *Oprah's Master Class | OWN*, November 12, 2015. https://www.youtube.com/watch? v=y_T9Jg0U2DA.

Wete, Brad. 2011. "Dwayne 'The Rock' Johnson Talks About His Return to the WWE on the Eve of WrestleMania XXVII." *Entertainment Weekly*, March 24, 2011. https://ew.com/article/2011/03/24/dwayne-johnson-the-rock-wrestlemania-27/.

Furthermore, making your work more enjoyable can provide benefits beyond your work success. Did you know that when you can honestly say, "I love my work," you reduce your risk of heart disease? In a study by the Massachusetts Department of Health, Education, and Welfare that investigated the causes of heart disease, participants were asked two questions: "Are you happy?" and "Do you love your work?" The results suggest that those who can answer yes to both have a better chance of not getting heart disease.[17] By working on what you believe in (by living your purpose) and by building natural rewards into your job to make it more enjoyable, you could greatly improve both your health and your job performance.

Would you like to experience more enjoyment and natural rewards while performing your job? If so, the checklist and exercise on pp. 78 and 79 should help you identify a job that is filled with naturally rewarding activities for you, or help you alter your current job so that it becomes more naturally rewarding.

Focusing on Natural Rewards

The three men were all called crafters, and they worked side by side using the same tools and crafting the same items. The first man thought the sun was too hot and his tools were too old, and his arms got too tired. He frowned and grumbled as he worked. The second man thought of the money he would receive on payday, the praise that would be bestowed on him for his good work, and the promotion to chief crafter he hoped for one day. He did not think about his work much—only of his better future ahead. The third man thought of the pure, clean air that fed his lungs, the feeling of power and strength he enjoyed as he worked his tools, and the admiration he felt for the finely shaped item he was creating with his own hands. He smiled, for he was not working at all.

A second approach to tapping the power of natural rewards centers on the focus of our thoughts while we perform tasks. We can choose to think about, talk about, and, in general, focus on the parts of our work that we don't like—and thereby feel bad about our work. We also can choose to direct our focus toward the rewards we expect to receive from performing our labor (money, praise, recognition) and thus be motivated by our images of the future. Or we can choose to focus on the naturally enjoyable aspects of our work and enjoy the activity for its immediate value. We will argue here that this last approach is the key to gaining natural rewards from our present endeavors.

Most of our activities have both pleasant and unpleasant characteristics. A runner, for example, can think about heat and sweat, sore muscles, exhaustion, blisters, and a score of other things most people would consider unpleasant, or she can think about praise from others for her excellent physical condition, a potentially longer life due to improved health, and the feeling of power and strength that accompanies a conditioned runner's stride. Both types of thoughts are available to the runner, and the type she chooses will significantly affect her enjoyment of the activity.

This simple logic can be applied to our major activities in life. If we think for a moment about the various aspects of our work, we probably can identify several pleasant and unpleasant features. To bring these ideas to life, try the following exercise.

This exercise may appear overly simplistic, but it emphasizes a crucial aspect of the importance of choice in self-leadership. Perhaps the most critical aspect of self-leadership concerns the way we choose to think about our tasks. We consider the importance of our thinking patterns in more detail in the remainder of this chapter and in Chapter 5. Suffice it to say here that if we believe we have freedom to choose our thoughts (if we do not possess freedom in our thoughts, it would seem that we possess no freedom at all), then choosing to focus on the pleasant aspects of our work rather than on the unpleasant appears to be a logical strategy for helping us experience natural enjoyment.

Another issue that should be addressed centers on this question: Does it make any difference what pleasant features of our activities we focus on? Our position is that it does. Recall that we can distinguish between rewards that are separable from a task and natural rewards that are built into a task and that derive largely from effects on our feelings of competence, self-determination, and purpose. When we focus on the former type of reward, our incentive for doing the task comes from the expectation of future rewards. When we focus on the latter, our reason for doing the task is the task itself. This latter focus is the key to natural enjoyment of our work. These ideas suggest another simple exercise, which follows.

If you are not able to identify naturally rewarding activities such as those suggested in the exercise, you are probably in the wrong job or you are not sincerely trying to identify them. Focusing on rewards that are separate from the work should lead to motivation based on future expected benefits. Focusing on rewards that are part of the work should result in enhanced enjoyment of your present activities for their own sake.

Follow the steps below. Note that the logic of this exercise is simple—you will experience the power of the exercise only by trying it, so it is important that you take the time and exert the effort to do so.

1. Identify and list several aspects of your work under the following two categories.

Aspects of My Work	
Pleasant	Unpleasant

2. Later, when you're at work, focus your thoughts on the pleasant features you have identified. You might even try focusing your conversations with others on these features. Then switch your focus to the unpleasant features while you work. Make notes here about how this process makes you feel.

_____

_____

_____

3. Comment on the results of this exercise. How did you feel while you focused your thoughts on the pleasant aspects of your work? The unpleasant aspects? How did your focus affect your motivation and satisfaction with your work?

_____

_____

_____

1. List the rewarding aspects of your work under the following two categories. In the first category, list things such as monetary incentives (salary and bonuses), praise and recognition received from superiors and fellow workers, possible promotion, and awards. In the second category, list things that are part of performing the work, such as feelings of skill you experience while working, enjoyable interactions with people who help you accomplish tasks, fascinating learning that accompanies your performances, and challenges overcome.

Rewarding Aspects of My Work	
Separate From the Work	Part of the Work

2. While at work, focus your thoughts on the rewards listed under the category "separate from the work" for a while, and then focus on the rewards listed under the category "part of the work." Make notes here about how this process makes you feel.

_____

_____

_____

3. Comment on the results of this exercise. How did you feel while you focused on the rewards that are separate from the work? Those that are part of the work? How did your focus affect your motivation concerning your present efforts? Your future efforts? Your enjoyment of the task itself?

_____

_____

_____

What we are suggesting, then, is that we should not only focus our thoughts on the rewarding aspects of our work but also be selective about the kinds of rewards we focus on. Research evidence indicates that when external rewards are increased for work that workers like, the workers might be motivated subsequently by the rewards rather than by natural enjoyment of the task.[18] It might be that people reevaluate their reasons for doing enjoyable work when external rewards are emphasized. Receiving the rewards might consequently take precedence over natural enjoyment of the activities. Although this viewpoint has been controversial among researchers, a fairly substantial body of evidence exists to support it. The significance of this viewpoint for the present discussion is that focusing our thoughts on expected external rewards could undermine our immediate enjoyment of the task. Although such a focus might be useful for some tasks that do not possess many naturally enjoyable qualities, focusing on natural rewards is preferable because it optimizes our enjoyment of our present activities.

The following checklist will help guide your efforts toward achieving motivation through focusing on the natural rewards. Take a moment to look over this checklist and reflect on how you can take advantage of the power of natural rewards in your future activities.

CHECKLIST FOR FOCUSING ON NATURAL REWARDS

Focus your thoughts on the natural rewards of your tasks.

- Identify the pleasant, enjoyable aspects of your tasks.

- Distinguish between the rewarding aspects of your work that are separable from the work itself and those rewarding aspects that are part of (built into) your work.

- Focus your thoughts on the pleasant rather than on the unpleasant aspects of your tasks while you work.

- When possible, focus your thoughts on the rewards that are part of (not separate from) the actual tasks to obtain motivation and satisfaction for your immediate efforts.

- Work toward developing the habit of distinguishing and focusing on the natural rewards in your work.

(*Note:* The intention of this strategy is not to ignore problems and concerns. Important negative issues regarding our work must be considered. Although we exert effort, focusing our thoughts on the naturally rewarding aspects of our tasks can provide motivational and emotional benefits, including on those occasions when we must deal with problems and concerns that are part of the job.)

COMBINING EXTERNAL AND NATURAL REWARDS

Another thing to consider is the relationship, and perhaps the seeming contradictions, between the ideas presented in this chapter and those presented in Chapter 3. This chapter has emphasized the natural rewards built into a task, whereas Chapter 3 suggested several self-applied techniques, including the use of self-applied rewards that are separable from the task. We have presented both approaches as ways to achieve more effective self-leadership. The strategies discussed in the two chapters can complement each other well. Strategies such as those offered in Chapter 3 can be used in especially difficult situations that are lacking in natural rewards. The intention is to maintain the self-leadership necessary to work through the difficult and unattractive but necessary tasks on the way to activities and future job positions that we can naturally enjoy. However, as we highlighted in the Self-Leadership Research box in Chapter 3, recent research suggests that the behavior-focused strategies of Chapter 3 may combine interactively with natural reward strategies outlined in this chapter to result in better outcomes, including effort, creativity, and performance.[19] Consequently, we should make an effort to build in natural rewards and focus on those that are available. To the extent that we can accomplish this, we can find greater enjoyment in our present moments.

The inspirational writer Norman Vincent Peale, who has been read by and has affected the thinking and living of millions of people, made a statement in one of his books that parallels the major thrust of this chapter closely: "Do your job naturally, because you like it, and success will take care of itself."[20] If we practice a self-leadership style that allows us natural enjoyment of our activities, we can indeed derive the motivation we need to be successful—especially at enjoying life.

REAL-WORLD SELF-LEADERSHIP CASE

The NashTrash Sisters

Sisters Brenda Kay Wilkins and Sheri Lynn Nichols had been in show business for years. Brenda Kay was pursuing a career in Nashville, while Sheri Lynn was working in Los Angeles. Frustrated with being so far apart and with "trying to make it," the pair brainstormed on what they could do together. They wanted to continue performing, make a living, and be their own bosses. That's when the idea of NashTrash Tours was conceived and the Jugg Sisters were born.

For more than twenty years, NashTrash Tours has conducted guided tours of Nashville, Tennessee, in the most irreverent and unorthodox manner imaginable. The rolling musical comedy NashTrash tour starts when the Jugg Sisters, Brenda Kay and Sheri Lynn, board their Big Pink Bus sporting spandex pants, leopard-print blouses, and lots of accessories in shades of pink (a color for which they have a passion). The Jugg Sisters epitomize "Southern trashy-chic," complete with big hair, over-the-top makeup, and smooth-as-honey Southern accents.

Star sightings are guaranteed: Brenda Kay leans out the bus window to yell, "Hey, Garth!" at a random pedestrian on a Nashville street; on the next corner, Sheri Lynn screams, "Shania Twain!" as a middle-aged brunette woman looks up, bewildered. As the Big Pink Bus roams the city streets, the Jugg Sisters, drawing from their theatrical experience, entertain passengers with a campy musical comedy show, singing and dancing their way through loads of risqué tales about local country music stars and other Nashville luminaries. The sisters note all the changes and construction that have taken place since they first started the tour. "Well, that used to be the jail right there," Brenda Kay explains, pointing out some rubble and debris along 2nd Avenue. Sheri Lynn jumps in and says, "Yeah, they just told all the prisoners to come back when they was ready to open again." The entertainment is dished out with "fancy cheese hors d'oeuvres" (Cheez Whiz on crackers) and beverages that guests bring themselves (yes, alcohol is permitted although bachelorettes and other rowdy customers have recently been banned!). Finally, the sisters choose one guest to receive a NashTrash "makeover," which includes makeup tips and information on how much hair spray to use to achieve and maintain a mile-high 'do.

The wacky NashTrash tour is so popular that it is normally sold out for weeks in advance, and the sisters have had to purchase a bigger bus. The tour has been featured in *Southern Living*, *Reader's Digest Travel Guide*, *Frommer's Guide* to Nashville, and the *American Airlines Destination Guide*, and it has been ranked by TripAdvisor.com as a top Nashville attraction. Brenda Kay and Sheri Lynn have appeared on the BBC and ITV in England, the Food Network, several shows on CMT, the Discovery Channel, Tech TV, CNN, ESPN, Sirius Radio, and even *The Today Show* on NBC—Al Roker took the tour on the original Big Pink Bus, and the sisters were live on national television the next morning.

When the tour is over, the drippy-sweet Southern accents disappear as the sisters step back out of character. "The whole show—the making fun of the people on the bus and of Nashville—is just an act," says Brenda Kay. "In truth, we love the city and we know the people on our tours understand what we're doing. I don't know of another job where I'd get to call somebody names for two hours and then they'd come back and send their mom and dad and sisters and cousins to come see me." These smart, sassy women have created their own way to spend time together, entertain, and run a very successful business.

Questions for Class Discussion

1. Confucius said, "Choose a job you love, and you will never have to work a day in your life." Do you think the Jugg Sisters love their jobs? Do you think that the way they make their living seems like "work" to them?

2. What specific features of the Jugg Sisters' work environment make it naturally rewarding? What types of feelings do these features create?

3. What self-leadership strategies have the sisters used to make their jobs more naturally rewarding?

4. Do you think the sisters experience "majestic moments" in their work? Explain.

Source/Additional Reading

Haggard, Amanda. 2017. "NashTrash Celebrates 20 Years of Raunchy Tours." *Nashville Scene*, September 11, 2017. https://www.nashvillescene.com/news/pith-in-the-wind/article/20974935/nashtrash-celebrates-20-years-of-raunchy-tours.

NashTrash Tours, accessed August 20, 2018. http://www.nashtrash.com.

5

CONSTRUCTIVE THOUGHT-FOCUSED STRATEGIES
Developing a Travel Mind-Set

The mind is its own place, and in itself can make a Heaven of Hell, a Hell of Heaven.

—John Milton

The traveler physically collapsed and groaned with relief as he gazed upon the white-haired old man who sat before him. He paused for a moment to peer cautiously over the sheer cliff he had just climbed to reach the top of the mountain. He looked out at the thick jungle beyond that had been his home for many days. "Old man," he gasped, "I have traveled for days to speak to you because many have said you are among the wisest of all the living. I must know the true nature of life—is it good or is it bad?"

The old man responded with a question of his own: "Tell me first—how do you see life, my son?"

The traveler looked away, frowning, and said slowly and sadly, "I believe life is bad—people are selfish and basically cruel, and fate always seems anxious to deliver a disheartening blow." Then he turned to the old man and asked, with obvious anguish in his voice, "Is this the nature of life?"

"Yes," responded the old man. "This is the nature of life, my son."

The traveler dropped his gaze, his face going blank. He then pulled himself to his feet and solemnly began his descent back down the cliff.

Learning Objectives

After studying this chapter, you should be able to do the following:

1. Recognize that we create our own unique psychological worlds by choosing what to think about and how to think about it, and that our psychological worlds help to shape our behaviors.

2. Employ the concept of self-talk to identify and replace negative internal dialogues with more positive ones.

3. Explain the importance of beliefs relative to behaviors and apply this mental strategy by challenging and replacing irrational

and dysfunctional beliefs and assumptions with more positive and rational ones.

4. Describe and use mental practice techniques following the specific steps outlined in the chapter.

5. Contrast opportunity thinking with obstacle thinking and apply the self-leadership strategies of positive self-talk, challenging beliefs and assumptions, and mental practice to foster habitually opportunistic thinking.

A few moments later another traveler pulled himself up over the edge of the cliff and collapsed at the feet of the white-haired old man. "Tell me, old man of much wisdom," he gasped, "what is the nature of life? Is it good or is it bad?"

The old man again asked the question, "Tell me first—how do you see life, my son?"

At this question the traveler looked hopefully into the old man's eyes. "Life can be hard, and the way is often difficult," he started, "but I believe the nature of life is basically good. People are not perfect, but I see much value in the heart of each I meet—even those that would be called the most lowly. I believe life is challenge and growth, and offers a sweet victory for those who try and endure. Is this the nature of life?" he asked as he continued his hopeful stare into the old man's eyes.

"Yes," responded the old man. "This is the nature of life, my son."

The emphasis of this chapter is on our unique psychological worlds. We begin from the viewpoint that, because of the way we think, each of us experiences a psychological world that is different from the psychological worlds of all others, even when we are faced with the same physical situations. Our senses (sight, hearing, touch, taste, and smell, and perhaps other, more mystical senses) are constantly bombarded with stimuli. Right this minute you likely have a potentially overwhelming number of things to focus on. What sights and sounds are available to you, both near and distant? By the way, how do the bottoms of your feet feel? Are they tired, sore, comfortable? What kinds of things have you thought about lately? Have you spent more mental energy thinking about your problems or about your opportunities?

The point is that we usually have a choice regarding what we focus on and what we think about. We can't deal with every possible stimulus we come in contact with, nor can we deal with every possible thought. Of course, we don't have much of a choice about some of our thoughts, such as those we experience when struck by unexpected physical pain, but we do have a choice regarding what we think about much of the time. In addition, we can think of the things we choose to think about in different ways. That is what this chapter is all about: what we choose to think about and how we choose to think about it. This might sound a little silly, but it is probably the most important part of self-leadership.

This chapter is thus devoted to providing a foundation for increasing your understanding of and improving your psychological world. Several strategies will be suggested that can help you develop more desirable patterns of thought through which to see and deal with the world. Take a few moments to assess your own tendencies regarding the use of constructive thought strategies by responding to the statements in Self-Leadership Questionnaire 3. For each of the nine statements, select the number that best describes your position. Follow the directions provided for scoring your responses.

INTERPRETING YOUR SCORE

Your scores for A through C suggest your current tendencies concerning several constructive thought-focused self-leadership strategies that will be addressed in this chapter. Your score for each of these strategies could range from 3 (a total absence of the strategy in your current self-leadership) to 15 (a very high level of the strategy in your current self-leadership). Your scores on A through C can be interpreted as follows:

1. A score of 3 or 4 indicates a *very low* level of the strategy.

2. A score of 5 to 7 indicates a *low* level of the strategy.

3. A score of 8 to 10 indicates a *moderate* level of the strategy.

4. A score of 11 to 13 indicates a *high* level of the strategy.

5. A score of 14 or 15 indicates a *very high* level of the strategy.

Each of the strategies addressed by the questionnaire should generally contribute to personal performance and effectiveness. Therefore, high scores on A through C suggest a high level of self-leadership, which offers potential to enhance performance. Each of the specific strategies is discussed in more detail throughout the remainder of the chapter.

Your score on X indicates your overall use of the self-leadership strategies. This score could range from a low of 9 to a high of 45. Your score on X can be interpreted as follows:

1. A score of 9 to 16 indicates a *very low* level of the strategy.

2. A score of 17 to 24 indicates a *low* level of the strategy.

3. A score of 25 to 31 indicates a *moderate* level of the strategy.

4. A score of 32 to 39 indicates a *high* level of the strategy.

5. A score of 40 to 45 indicates a *very high* level of the strategy

In general, a high score on X suggests that you possess some positive constructive thought tendencies. Your score on X reflects what you believe are your current

Self-Leadership Questionnaire 3
Self-Assessment Questionnaire for Constructive Thought-Focused Strategies

	Describes me very well	Describes me well	Describes me somewhat	Does not describe me very well	Does not describe me at all
1. I think about my own beliefs and assumptions whenever I encounter a difficult situation.	5	4	3	2	1
2. Sometimes I find I'm talking to myself (out loud or in my head) to help myself deal with difficult problems I face.	5	4	3	2	1
3. I visualize myself successfully performing a task before I do it.	5	4	3	2	1
4. I try to mentally evaluate the accuracy of my own beliefs about situations I am having problems with.	5	4	3	2	1
5. Sometimes I talk to myself (out loud or in my head) to work through difficult situations.	5	4	3	2	1
6. Sometimes I picture in my mind a successful performance before I actually do a task.	5	4	3	2	1
7. I openly articulate and evaluate my own assumptions when I have a disagreement with someone else.	5	4	3	2	1

8. When I'm in a difficult situation I will sometimes talk to myself (out loud or in my head) to help myself get through it.	5	4	3	2	1
9. I often mentally rehearse the way I plan to deal with a challenge before I actually face the challenge.	5	4	3	2	1

Directions for scoring: Add the numbers you circled for each statement as indicated below to determine your score for each self-leadership strategy.

	Scores
A. Evaluating beliefs and assumptions (add numbers circled for statements 1, 4, and 7)	
B. Self-talk (add numbers circled for statements 2, 5, and 8)	
C. Mental practice (add numbers circled for statements 3, 6, and 9)	
X. Total score (add scores for A through C)	

Source: Adapted from Jeffery D. Houghton and Christopher P. Neck, "The Revised Self-Leadership Questionnaire: Testing a Hierarchical Factor Structure for Self-Leadership," *Journal of Managerial Psychology* 17, no. 8 (2002): 672–91.

constructive thought tendencies. Regardless of your score, the remainder of this chapter is designed to help you implement and improve upon several constructive thought-focused self-leadership strategies. This chapter will provide you with a basis for better understanding and more effectively using the power of positive thoughts.

OUR PSYCHOLOGICAL WORLDS

What each of us experiences in life is unique. No one else in the world can experience exactly what we do. We create our own psychological worlds by selecting what enters our minds (where the essence of human experience takes place) and what shape it takes after it does. The content of our unique psychological worlds determines the way we behave, and our behavior helps determine the nature of our physical worlds.[1] All of these things together determine our progress toward our personal destinies. These ideas are represented pictorially in Figure 5.1.

Figure 5.1   The Role of Our Psychological Worlds

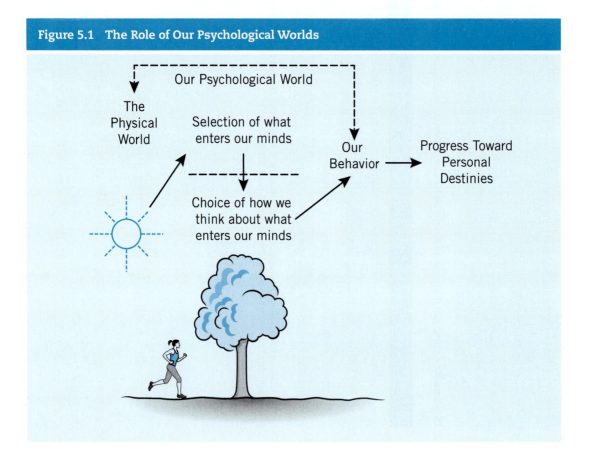

We carry in our minds a world that is more real to us than the physical one within which we live. A winter blizzard has a different meaning to an avid skier than it does to an avid golfer. Identical physical conditions can result in joyful exultation for one person and depression and gloom for another. In fact, we are capable of turning potentially joyful, motivating situations into circumstances of demoralizing gloom through our thoughts and resulting actions. For example, if we are invited to a social gathering of some kind, we can experience the event as an unhappy one by being overly self-conscious about our appearance and what we say. In essence, by doing so we are choosing to focus our mind on negative aspects of a potentially positive situation. In general, we can look for the positive or negative in people and situations, and as a result we create the psychological atmosphere in which we live and experience life. The following story reinforces this point.

The Vision

Do you have a grand idea

To which some might laugh and smile?

They think it can't be done;

They call it a "someday I'll."

Then consider this story of two men;

Their business was selling shoes.

They were confronted with the same situation,

But each had differing views.

Both were sent to a far-away island

To test if their abilities were elite.

And they discovered, upon arrival,

The natives had nothing on their feet.

The first sadly called his boss

With a very large case of despair,

Relayed that there was no hope for business

Because everyone's feet were bare.

The second was filled with much elation;

Told his superior the good news.

Said he was going to make a million.

No one *yet* was wearing shoes.

The meaning in these few words

Is your thoughts can help you advance

Because what to some might spell disaster

Could be for you, your one big chance.

The secret to creating opportunities

Isn't money or political pull.

Simply, it's your attitude—

Is the glass half-empty or half-full?

A different real world example

Might help reveal this story's key.

It's a lesson of a pollinating insect,

The plight of the bumble bee.

According to the laws of science,

The bee should not be able to fly.

But this creature didn't acknowledge this

And instead gave flight a try.

So remember what history reveals

As you pinpoint your dreams with precision;

The primary keys to greatness

Are your attitude and your vision.[2]

Because our actions help shape the physical world where we live, our psychological worlds ultimately have an impact on the physical world itself. In fact, the way we think about the physical world can be self-fulfilling. If we attend a social gathering worrying that we will not be accepted or liked by those present, we can make this fear come true. If we are withdrawn and closed off to others, these others are likely to reciprocate with similar behavior.

   The remainder of this chapter will address different ways of analyzing and dealing with the way we think and how this affects our own self-leadership. The intention is to increase our understanding of and ability to deal with our psychological worlds. We can change our psychological worlds and our resulting behavior and experiences if we choose to do so. This viewpoint is consistent with psychological perspectives that place the responsibility for our actions and self-improvement where it belongs: on ourselves.[3]

If we wish to achieve effective self-leadership and obtain personal effectiveness, we need to take responsibility for what we think and do. This approach is in direct contrast to the common tendency to place the responsibility for our actions on external sources such as authority figures or traumatic experiences from our childhoods. The focus is on dealing with and improving our immediate thinking and behavior rather than on looking for reasons (excuses) to explain why we can't become what we wish to become and are capable of becoming.

IS THERE POWER IN POSITIVE THINKING?

In the 1950s, the concept of more effective living was a topic widely written about. This viewpoint, which can be called *positive thinking*, was introduced by the Reverend Norman Vincent Peale, who published several books on the subject, including the well-known best-seller *The Power of Positive Thinking*.[4] In support of his ideas, Peale subsequently reported numerous cases in which persons overcame challenges and obstacles with the aid of positive thinking.[5] Peale's work, however, was never subjected to what authorities in the fields of psychology and human behavior would describe as scientific research. In fact, until recently, most academics in these areas would likely have considered Peale's work with some amusement. Nevertheless, as a result of the work Peale gained widespread public notoriety and attention such as few authors ever receive. More recently, evidence has been accumulating in support of the many benefits to be gained from positive thinking.[6]

The idea of positive thinking is a useful reference point from which to consider improvement of our psychological worlds. Several different elements that offer the potential to help explain how our thinking can have an impact on our behavior and experience of life will be addressed in this chapter. These include our beliefs, our imagined experiences, our self-instruction (self-talk), and our thought patterns. The underlying logic is that if we make systematic efforts to change our thinking in beneficial ways, then we can improve our self-leadership. Beneficial thinking (or positive thinking, if you prefer) offers the potential to help us improve our personal effectiveness just as beneficial *behaving* does. In fact, as mentioned earlier, our behavior and our unique ways of thinking (mental behavior) are two primary, interrelated features in the total influence picture.

Self-Talk

Puff, puff, chug, chug, went the Little Blue Engine. "I think I can—I think I can—I think I can—I think I can—I."

Up, up, up. Faster and faster the little engine climbed, until at last they reached the top of the mountain.

And the Little Blue Engine smiled and seemed to say as she puffed steadily down the mountain. "I thought I could. I thought I could. I thought I could. . . . "[7]

As children, many of us heard these words spoken by the Little Blue Engine: "I think I can, I think I can, I think I can." These same words can benefit you today! The well-known phrase uttered by the Little Blue Engine is an example of a mental strategy known as self-talk.[8] The way in which the Little Blue Engine talks to herself clearly affects her performance (getting over the mountain). In the same way, we believe that the mental technique of self-talk (what you say to yourself) can help you perform better on the tasks that you are responsible for completing. In fact, if you are at this moment not doing well at school, on the job, or in your personal life, then it could possibly be related to what you are saying to yourself.

For example, consider for a moment if you have ever told yourself any of the following:

- It's going to be another one of those days!

- I don't have the talent.

- My roommate just doesn't like me.

- I can't seem to get organized.

- It's going to be another blue Monday.

- I hate working within a team.

- If only I were a little smarter, then I could do this job well.

- If only I were taller.

- If only I had more time.

- If only I had more money.

- I'm too old to work that hard.

- I never get a break.

- I'll never be as good as the other students in class.

- Nothing ever seems to go right for me.

- Today just isn't my day.

If you are like most of us, you have told yourself negative things similar to these examples. These statements are negative in that they are "sappers"—types of self-talk that sap your energy, your self-confidence, and your happiness. Sappers are destructive self-talk: they prevent you from achieving your goals and feeling good about yourself. They serve as self-fulfilling prophecies, because what you tell yourself every day usually ends up coming true. If you tell yourself that you won't have a good day, you won't. If you tell yourself that you can't lose weight, you can't. If you tell yourself that you won't enjoy your job, you won't. It is that simple.

The story of the Little Blue Engine's sister should reveal the impact of sapper self-talk on performance:

Puff, puff, chug, chug, went the Little Blue Engine's twin sister. "I can't do this—I can't do this—The mountain is too big—I'm tired—I'm hungry—I'm irritable. This is impossible—I can't do this."

Up, up, up. Slower, slower the little engine climbed until it just conked out.

The Little Blue Engine's twin sister just frowned, and all depressed . . . she fell down the mountain. "I knew I couldn't do it—I knew I couldn't do it—I knew I couldn't do it."[9]

These stories represent the utilization of two different styles of the mental strategy self-talk—with two different outcomes. The Little Engine That Could uses positive self-talk to make it over the huge mountain, and the children receive their toys. Her twin sister does not make it over the mountain because her negative self-talk saps her energy and attitude. Rumor has it that the twin sister of the Little Blue Engine (the Little Engine That Couldn't) is roaming around the country from train station to train station holding a sign that reads "Will Work for Fuel."

These two stories reveal the power that our self-talk can have on our success and happiness. As leading psychologist Pamela E. Butler writes,

We all talk to ourselves. What we say determines the direction and quality of our lives. Our self-talk can make the difference between happiness and despair, between self-confidence and self-doubt. Altering your self-talk may be the most important undertaking you will ever begin.[10]

The life of Olympic decathlon gold medal winner Dan O'Brien serves as a real-world example of Butler's words. In 1992, O'Brien failed even to qualify for the U.S. Olympic team, despite being a favorite to win the gold medal. In the 1996 Olympic Games, he returned to win the gold medal that had eluded him four years earlier. What was the difference for O'Brien between the 1992 Olympic trials and the 1996 Olympic Games? Why did he fail in 1992 and then crush the field in the decathlon events in 1996? Quite simply, O'Brien altered his self-talk. As O'Brien explained,

Now I know what to do when I feel panic, when I'm nervous and get sick to my stomach. . . . Instead of telling myself I'm tired and worn out, I say things like, My body is preparing for battle. This is how I'm supposed to feel.[11]

For O'Brien, changing his self-talk pushed him to Olympic glory. In the same way, changing your self-talk can enhance your life at work, school, home—everywhere.

Much like Dan O'Brien before her, Serena Williams uses a form of self-talk to help her stay focused during a tennis match. "Usually, I'm singing a song in my head," Williams says. "Then if I stop singing, I usually start losing, then I go back to singing. It's crazy up there."[12] As Steve Jobs once said, "Your time is limited, so don't waste it living someone else's life. Don't let the noise of others' opinions drown out your own inner voice."[13] The question you might be asking at the moment is: How do I change my self-talk so that I can get over my own personal mountain to achieve my goals and dreams? The following exercise should help you change your sapper self-talk to self-talk that can help you achieve maximum performance.

After answering the questions in the exercise, take a close look at your responses. Do your self-talk examples contain a lot of destructive sappers, or is your self-talk supportive and motivating? If the former is true, that should be a signal to you that what you are telling yourself is causing many of the negative events and emotions that you are experiencing within your life. In other words, you are the person responsible for sapping yourself. The good news is, now that you know you are talking to yourself in a negative way, you can change your self-talk.

After you have completed the exercise, examine what you have written in the negative self-talk and positive self-talk columns. Do you see a pattern? Do you see that your negative self-talk is demotivating and negative, and that it seems to sap energy,

DISCOVERING YOUR NEGATIVE SELF-TALK EXERCISE

This exercise will help you discover your negative self-talk during the course of a day. Respond to the following questions, each of which will require a significant amount of thought. Fully relive the situations you are writing about so that your answers are as accurate as possible.

1. List a project or activity that you have begun or considered beginning. What did you tell yourself as you started or failed to start it?

    _____

    _____

    _____

2. Think of a time when you were feeling lonely. What were you telling yourself at this time?

    _____

    _____

    _____

3. Think of a day when you were feeling stressed and overwhelmed at work. What were you telling yourself during this chaotic time?

    _____

    _____

    _____

4. Think of a criticism you recently faced from a coworker, fellow student, boss, or teacher. What were you telling yourself at this time and after the criticism?

_____

_____

_____

5. Think of a recent compliment that you received from a coworker, boss, teacher, or fellow student. What were you saying to yourself at this time and after the compliment?

_____

_____

_____

6. Think of a day when you were feeling negative about yourself. What were you saying to yourself at this time?

_____

_____

_____

7. Think of a day when you were experiencing some symptoms of illness, such as a headache or achy bones. What were you telling yourself during the time when you were experiencing these symptoms?

_____

_____

_____

Following the examples below, write down some of the instances of negative self-talk you've listed above, and then, opposite them, write what you could have told yourself if you wanted your self-talk to be positive rather than sapping.

Negative self-talk	Positive self-talk
1. I hate working within a team.	1. Although this is a new experience for me, I know that if I make a good effort toward cooperating, we will make a much better product than if we were working by ourselves, and it will be fun getting to know each other.

(Continued)

(Continued)

Negative self-talk	Positive self-talk
2. I'll never lose this extra weight.	2. I will lose this weight. It will take a lot of determination and willpower. I will achieve my goal of losing one pound per week.
3. I'll never be able to earn a good grade on one of Dr. Neck's exams.	3. Someone once said, "If you always do what you have always done, you will always get what you have always got." I need to find out what I'm doing wrong and correct my mistakes in terms of how I study and how I take tests. With effort and persistence, I will get an A on Dr. Neck's exam.
4. I am nervous about this job interview. I'm probably not as qualified as the other applicants.	4. I am prepared for this interview. I have done my homework. This company needs my skills.
5. She [he] will never go out with me. She [he] is out of my league. Why should I even bother asking her [him] on a date?	5. Seize the day! If I don't ask her [him] out, how will I ever know if she [he] would go out with me? Once she [he] gets to know me, she [he] will love me!
6.	6.
7.	7.
8.	8.

Source: Adapted from Charles C. Manz, Christopher P. Neck, James Mancuso, and Karen P. Manz, *For Team Members Only: Making Your Workplace Team Productive and Hassle-Free* (New York: AMACOM, 1997).

happiness, and self-confidence? Conversely, do you notice that your positive self-talk is motivating and supportive? Wouldn't you rather give yourself an advantage in all aspects of your life by making your self-talk positive in the future? Now that you are aware that your self-talk might be negative and have practiced changing it to be positive, you are well on your way.

Finally, you should create situations so that your positive self-talk becomes a habit for you. Try to be aware of what you are telling yourself over the next several weeks. From the moment you get up in the morning until the moment you go to sleep at night, remind yourself to talk to yourself in positive ways. Repeat the exercise above daily, until you start to notice that you are having difficulty identifying any negative self-talk and have chased all the sappers away.

EVALUATING BELIEFS AND ASSUMPTIONS

One of the greatest weight lifters of all time was the Russian Olympian Vasily Alexeev (sometimes transliterated as Alekseyev). Evidently, he was trying to break a weight-lifting record of 500 pounds. He had lifted 499 pounds but couldn't for the life of him lift 500 pounds. Finally, his trainers put 501.5 pounds on his bar and rigged it so it looked like 499 pounds. Guess what happened? Alexeev lifted it easily. In fact, once he achieved this feat, other weight lifters went on to break his record. Why? Because they now knew it was possible to lift 500 pounds. Alexeev created a new mental outlook for weight lifters. Once people believed it was possible to lift 500 pounds, a major barrier to that accomplishment was removed.

The idea that we can achieve what we believe is possible to achieve is not new. The amazing fulfillment of many predictions made in books that have attempted to describe the future, such as *Future Shock*, *Brave New World*, and *1984*, suggests that what we believe can happen *can* happen.

One recently developed perspective in the field of psychology suggests that life problems tend to stem from dysfunctional thinking.[14] In short, mental distortions form the basis for ineffective thinking that can hinder personal effectiveness and even lead to depression. These distorted thoughts are based on some common dysfunctional beliefs that are activated by potentially troubling or disturbing situations. Based on the work of David Burns, we can specify eleven primary categories of dysfunctional thinking:[15]

1. *Extreme thinking*: Seeing things as black or white (e.g., if total perfection is not achieved, then a perception of complete failure results)

2. *Overgeneralization*: Generalizing a specific failure or negative result as an endless pattern

3. *Mental filtering*: Emphasizing a single negative detail, thus distorting all other aspects of one's perception of reality

4. *Disqualification of the positive*: Mentally disqualifying positive experiences from having any relevance or importance

5. *Mind reading*: Drawing negative conclusions regarding situations despite a lack of concrete evidence to support these conclusions

6. *Fortune-telling*: Arbitrarily predicting that things will turn out badly

7. *Magnifying and minimizing*: Exaggerating the importance of negative factors and minimizing the importance of positive factors related to one's situation

8. *Emotional reasoning*: Interpreting reality based on the negative emotions one experiences

9. *Use of should statements*: Using terms such as *should* and *shouldn't*, *ought*, and *must* in one's self-talk to coerce or manipulate oneself into taking actions

10. *Labeling and mislabeling*: Describing oneself, others, or events with negative labels (e.g., "I'm a failure," "He is a cheat")

11. *Personalization:* Identifying oneself (blaming oneself) as the cause of negative events or outcomes that one is not primarily responsible for causing

Burns argues that individuals need to confront these dysfunctional types of thinking and replace them with more rational thoughts (beliefs). For example, imagine an aspiring entrepreneur who freezes up during his presentation of a business plan to a venture capitalist (VC). The entrepreneur stumbles when asked about his valuation method even though he was an investment banker for eight years. Additionally, the VC claims the entrepreneur's pro forma statements are exaggerated given market conditions. Rather than defending his position, the entrepreneur agrees with the VC. The end result is zero financing from the VC. As the entrepreneur leaves the presentation, he thinks to himself, "I am the worst presenter. I'll never be able to get funding for this venture. Never."

This scenario presents an example of the distorted belief of extreme thinking, which, as noted above, takes place when an individual evaluates his or her personal situation in extreme black-and-white terms. The entrepreneur is not recognizing the fact that some of the most successful entrepreneurs present to more than twenty venture capitalists before receiving financing. He is evaluating his personal qualities in extremes of black and white.

To alter this destructive belief, the entrepreneur must identify the dysfunction and then change his thinking to be more rational in nature. The entrepreneur could challenge thoughts of himself as a complete failure and revise his beliefs regarding himself by reversing his thoughts and saying to himself, "Some of the most successful entrepreneurs have to talk to close to two dozen venture capitalists before receiving financing. I shall learn from this mistake. It's not the end of the world; I will do better next time."[16]

An exercise designed to facilitate your attempts to examine and improve your self-talk and beliefs follows.

"You can't control the wind, but you can certainly adjust the sails."

1. Think of a recent time when you were feeling a negative emotion(s) (e.g., stress, anxiety, depression). List the negative emotion(s) you were experiencing.

   _____

   _____

   _____

2. What was the problem or task that you were facing at the time (e.g., job interview, relationship problem, test)?

   _____

   _____

   _____

3. List some of the things that you were telling yourself at this time.

   a. _____

   b. _____

   c. _____

4. Can you identify mental distortions (e.g., extreme thinking) in the self-talk you noted in step 3? If so, what are they?

   a. _____

   b. _____

   c. _____

5. How could you change (reword) your self-talk to rid your internal speech of any mental distortions?

   a. _____

   b. _____

   c. _____

The Power of *Negative* Thinking?

Throughout this chapter we have extolled the virtues of positive thinking. Indeed, self-leadership theory and research suggest that the constructive thought strategies of positive self-talk, evaluating beliefs and assumptions, and mental practice outlined in this chapter can help to shape more positive and optimistic thought patterns that in turn may enhance positive attitudinal and performance outcomes.[1] In contrast, some researchers have suggested that a strategy known as *defensive pessimism* may be effective in shaping our behaviors in positive ways.[2] Defensive pessimism involves setting unrealistically low performance expectations for oneself in advance of a difficult or risky performance situation in order to harness the anxiety associated with the looming potential failure as motivation to increase one's efforts aimed at avoiding that failure. Although we agree that pessimism may have beneficial effects on motivation and performance outcomes in some situations, perhaps in part by prompting individuals to engage in proactive threat assessment and contingency planning, we also are quick to caution that when taken to the extreme, too much pessimism could have negative impacts on one's psychological and physical well-being.[3] For that matter, optimism and positive thinking, if taken to the extreme (like taking toxic

(Continued)

(Continued)

levels of vitamin C or almost any health supplement) without regard to anticipating possible setbacks and obstacles, would likely not yield good results either. In short, we suggest that balance is the key—perhaps something like a 4 to 1 ratio (i.e., 4 doses of opportunity thinking and 1 dose of potential obstacle-based contingency planning)—to effectively harnessing the power of *both* positive and negative thinking.

Notes

1. See, for example, Jeffery D. Houghton and Darryl L. Jinkerson, "Constructive Thought Strategies and Job Satisfaction: A Preliminary Examination," *Journal of Business and Psychology* 22, no. 1 (September 2007): 45–53; Nikolaos G. Panagopoulos and Jessica Ogilvie, "Can Salespeople Lead Themselves? Thought Self-Leadership Strategies and Their Influence on Sales Performance," *Industrial Marketing Management* 47 (May 2015): 190–203.

2. Maria Cohut, "Can Pessimism Be Beneficial?" *Medical News Today*, October 27, 2017, https://www.medicalnewstoday.com/articles/319899.php?utm_source=newsletter&utm_medium=email&utm_campaign=daily-us; Julie K. Norem, "Defensive Pessimism as a Positive Self-Critical Tool," in *Self-Criticism and Self-Enhancement: Theory, Research, and Clinical Implications* (Washington, DC: American Psychological Association, 2008), 89–104; Julie K. Norem, *The Positive Power of Negative Thinking: Using Defensive Pessimism to Manage Anxiety and Perform at Your Peak* (New York: Basic Books, 2001).

3. See, for example, Dusti R. Jones, Barbara J. Lehman, Julie A. Kirsch, and Katherine G. Hennessy, "Pessimism Moderates Negative Emotional Responses to Naturally Occurring Stress," *Journal of Research in Personality* 69 (August 2017): 180–90.

MENTAL PRACTICE

Mary was gliding cautiously across the shimmering ice when one of her skates struck a hard lump on the otherwise smooth surface. Her weight shifted quickly forward, and she found herself flying through the air. She landed hard on her shoulder and right cheek and felt pain go through her body. Her collarbone had been severely fractured, and she noticed blood trickling from a cut on her cheek. Then she heard a loud crack, and the ice began to separate underneath her. A moment later, she could scarcely breathe because of the icy cold water that enveloped her body. The extreme pain in her shoulder made it impossible for her to swim. She gulped water in an attempt to breathe. A desperate sense of panic swept over her, and . . .

"Mary, are you going to put your skates on, or do I have to do it for you?" asked Bill impatiently.

Mary stood up nervously and, turning to walk away, said, "I don't think I want to learn to skate today; maybe some other time."

Would you believe us if we told you that a technique is available that can help you perform better on the job? Would you believe us if we told you that you can access this technique without spending a penny? The only cost to you is a relatively small amount of your time. In fact, athletes have used this technique for years to enhance their performance: golfers, basketball players, gymnasts, and ice skaters employ this technique to golf better, shoot better, tumble better, and skate better. The good news is that this technique is useful not only for people participating in sports but also for you in your job or school.

This technique is called *mental practice*.[17] It involves imagining successful completion of an event before you physically begin the event. For example, consider an NBA basketball player who, before a game, pictures himself making all of his free throws. Because he has performed successfully in his mind, he should experience increased confidence in the real-game situation and thus have a better chance of making his free throws.

Consider another example involving two new salespersons about to make their first sales call. Suppose one salesperson experiences images of a muddled presentation that results in humiliating rejection from the client. This imagined experience could potentially block effective performance. In fact, such self-defeating images can promote corresponding negative results. The resulting lack of confidence and unconvincing presentation could lead to the failure that was imagined. Suppose the second salesperson imagines a positive experience resulting in a sizable sale to the client and a worthwhile experience for both parties. In this case, the individual would likely possess a higher level of confidence going into the presentation and a higher probability of success.

The point is that we are capable of creating a unique world within ourselves. The essence of our experience of life is centered within the inner world we create. Many would agree that the pain and suffering we imagine in anticipation of a visit to the dentist is often, and perhaps usually, much worse than the actual event. The imagined negative experience could last for days prior to the actual appointment, which is over within minutes. Also, our imagined positive experiences can be more striking and powerful than the corresponding experiences in the physical world. Anticipated events are often disappointing when they finally take place because they do not live up to our expectations. A party might not be as enjoyable as we imagined it would be; a vacation we planned for months might not be perfect. Films based on classic novels often fall short of the original works because the richness we can add to books with our imaginations can rarely be achieved in visual form by filmmakers.

Symbolic, imagined experiences are an important component of the psychological worlds in which we interpret and experience life. If we can discover the effects they have on our lives, we can gain a better understanding of ourselves. We might find, for example, that before undertaking new challenges, we usually imagine negative results. To

The Martian (2015)

A scene from the movie *The Martian* provides examples of both positive and negative self-talk. While on a manned mission to Mars, astronaut Mark Watney (Matt Damon) is injured during a sandstorm. His crew presumes that he is dead and leaves him behind. Watney finds himself all alone and fighting for his very survival on the cold, red, inhospitable planet. Throughout the ordeal, Watney uses self-talk to solve problems and maintain a positive attitude. It will take four years for a rescue mission to reach him and, using self-talk, he quickly realizes that his most pressing survival need is a food supply: "Let's do the math. Our service mission here was supposed to last 31 sols [the duration of a solar day on Mars]. For redundancy they sent 68 sols worth of food. That's for six people. So for just me that's gonna last 300 sols, which I figure I can stretch to 400 if I ration. So, I gotta figure out a way to grow three years' worth of food here. On a planet where nothing grows. Luckily, I'm a botanist. Mars will come to fear my botany powers!"

Later, Watney uses more self-talk as he solves the problem of how to grow potatoes on Mars: "I've created one hundred and twenty-six square meters of soil. But each cubic meter needs forty liters of water to be farmable. So, I gotta make a lot of water. Fortunately, I know the recipe. You take hydrogen. You add oxygen. You burn. I have hundreds of liters of unused Hydrazine from the MDV. If I run the Hydrazine over an iridium catalyst, it'll separate into N_2 and H_2. Then I just need to direct the hydrogen into a small area and burn it. Luckily, in the history of humanity, nothing bad has ever happened from lighting hydrogen on fire [chuckling to himself]. NASA hates fire. Because of the whole 'fire makes everyone die in space' thing. So everything we brought with us is flame retardant. With the notable exception of . . . Martinez's personal items. Sorry, Martinez. If you didn't want me to go through your stuff, you shouldn't have left me for dead on a desolate planet." Watney continues his preparations and soon ignites his fire, resulting in a large explosion that literally blows him across the room like a limp rag.

He continues his self-talk in the next scene: "So. Yeah. I blew myself up. Best guess? I forgot to account for the excess oxygen that I've been exhaling when I did my calculations. Because I'm stupid. I'm gonna get back to work here. Just as soon as my ears stop ringing. Interesting side note: this is actually how Jet Propulsion Laboratory was founded. Five guys at Cal Tech were trying to make rocket fuel and nearly burned down their dorm. Rather than expel them . . . banished them to a nearby farm and told them to keep working. And now we have a space program."

Discussion Questions

1. How does Watney use self-talk to help shape his behaviors and his attitudes?

2. What are some specific examples of both negative and positive self-talk in these scenes?

3. How does Watney use the story of the Jet Propulsion Laboratory to help himself recover from the setback of the explosion?

deal with this habitual negative thinking, we could intentionally imagine positive results before we take action. Imagining a receptive, appreciative audience rather than a critical, hostile one before giving a speech, for example, might significantly help us overcome a fear of public speaking. By exercising greater choice and control over our imagined experiences, we can improve the quality of our psychological worlds and, potentially, our personal effectiveness.

To repeat, your mind is a powerful tool. You can use this tool to achieve great success. Just as a hammer is of no benefit to you if you don't know how to use it correctly, the tool of mental practice works only if you know how to use it correctly. Listed below are steps to help you use this mind tool to enhance your performance. By following these steps repeatedly, you can enjoy the benefits of mental practice.

Steps for Successful Mental Practice

1. **Close your eyes.**

2. **Relax, concentrate, and focus**. Feel all the stress leaving your body. Start at your feet . . . feel all the stress leaving . . . go to your chest, then to the top of your head . . . feel all the stress leaving your body. Concentrate all of your energy on this mental practice exercise. Rid your mind of all distractions.

3. **Focus on a specific challenging situation** in which you would like mental practice to help you perform well.

4. **Talk positively to yourself**. Tell yourself several times that you are confident and that you have the power to perform well in this situation.

5. **Mentally picture yourself** right before you are to begin this task, event, or project.

6. **Continue to concentrate, staying relaxed and focused.**

7. **Mentally rehearse** successful performance of this challenging situation several times. It is important that you see yourself in your mind as an active participant and not as a passive observer. For example, if you imagine that you are shooting a basketball during a game, make sure you are standing on the court shooting rather than watching yourself from the stands.

8. **Repeat step 7.**

9. **Open your eyes. Smile. Praise yourself.** You were successful in your mind. Now you should have a greater feeling of confidence that you will perform this event successfully in real situations.

The following are a few more tips to ensure that mental practice works for you:

- Make sure you visualize your actions in normal motion as opposed to slow motion.

- To help you relax (step 2 above), it might be helpful to mentally picture a calming scene, such as a beach, a mountain, a forest, or a pond.

- Repetition of mental practice is critical—make sure you repeat the steps above over and over to gain mental practice perfection.

- Space your practice sessions over several days rather than mentally practicing an event in one lengthy session.

A checklist is also provided to help you make improvements in your imagined experiences. The short exercise that follows will help you get started making the changes that you see as desirable.

CHECKLIST FOR IMPROVING YOUR IMAGINED EXPERIENCE TENDENCIES

Use your imagination to facilitate desirable performance.

- Analyze your current imagined experience tendencies. Ask yourself questions about your imagined experiences:

  o Do they focus on positive or negative outcomes of challenging tasks?

  o Do they generally facilitate or hinder my confidence and performance of tasks?

  o Are they realistic? Reasonable?

- Identify your destructive imagined experience tendencies, such as the tendency to habitually and unrealistically imagine negative results for your actions.

- Work to eliminate these destructive thought patterns by choosing to think about other things.

- Purposefully choose to imagine sequences of events and outcomes that help clarify and motivate (rather than hinder) your efforts—for example, once you have chosen a course of action and are committed to it, motivate yourself by imagining positive rather than negative results.

Follow the steps below.

1. Think about some recent challenges you have faced that especially provoked your imagination regarding the different actions you could take and the likely consequences of these different actions. Also, check yourself throughout the next few days as you face new challenges such as these.

_____

_____

_____

2. Explore the nature of your imagined experiences on these occasions. Were they realistic? Did they tend to focus on the positive or the negative? Were they constructive?

_____

_____

_____

3. Analyze the specific instances you identified in step 1 regarding the effect your imagination is having on your performance. What effect is your imagination having on your decisions (such as your willingness to take risks)? How is your imagination affecting your confidence and motivation?

_____

_____

_____

4. Purposefully use your imagined experiences to enhance your performance when facing new challenges. When facing problems that provoke your imagination, choose to keep your images constructive, reasonably realistic, and positive. This will take work, because it will likely mean changing ingrained, habitual ways of thinking—here the practice of self-leadership (e.g., using the strategies presented in Chapter 3) becomes important as you work to achieve further improvements in your self-leadership abilities.

_____

_____

_____

Mary Lou Retton

In 1984, a ninety-four-pound girl with a mega-watt smile and boundless enthusiasm captured the heart of America. That girl was sixteen-year-old Mary Lou Retton. Standing no taller than four feet nine inches, Mary Lou overcame amazing odds to become the first American-born woman to capture the all-around gold in Olympic gymnastics history.

Mary Lou had studied gymnastics in her hometown of Fairmont, West Virginia, since early childhood, but at the age of fifteen, she got the chance to train under the legendary coach Béla Károlyi in Houston, Texas. Károlyi helped the young gymnast develop her talent, and Mary Lou qualified to be on the 1984 U.S. Olympic gymnastics team. However, six weeks before the Olympics were to begin, she was told that she had to have arthroscopic surgery on her knee to remove torn cartilage and that she would not be able to compete. "She was declared out of the Olympics," said Károlyi, "declared out of any hard landing." But Mary Lou would not accept it. She wanted to compete, and she was determined to do just that.

Mary Lou did not focus on the setback the surgery would represent. Instead, she engaged in opportunity thinking. She focused on what was possible: a gold medal. Following her surgery, she went through physical rehabilitation and then went back to the gym. During the three weeks leading up to the Olympics, she followed a routine of both physical and mental practice. Each night before bed, Mary Lou went through each of her routines in her head. In her mind she performed each routine perfectly, over and over again. As she mentally practiced, she associated the word stick with the perfect vault she was visualizing. In gymnastics, to stick means to land so solidly that your feet stick to the mat without the slightest hint of a wobble.

When the Olympics began, Mary Lou was ready. In fact, she performed so well that she earned a chance at the all-around gold medal. Going into her final event—the vault—she trailed Romania's Ecaterina Szabo by just 0.05 points. When Szabo scored 9.90 in her final event, Mary Lou realized that if she could perfectly stick her vault and score a perfect 10, she would win the all-around gold medal by 0.05 points. But she also realized that if she wobbled at all, the gold would turn to silver.

In the final moments before her vault, Mary Lou engaged in positive self-talk, telling herself that she is at her best when she is under pressure—that pressure just makes her fight and scrap all the harder. She told herself that all she needed to do was stick, and she would win the gold. "I kept thinking 'stick, stick, stick,'" she would say later. "I knew I had to get a 10." Károlyi called Mary Lou over to give her some encouragement, but before he could give her any advice, she looked up at him and said quite simply, "I'm going to stick it," causing Károlyi to break into a giant grin.

The partisan crowd of more than nine thousand spectators jammed into Los Angeles's Pauley Pavilion fell silent as Mary Lou stood statue-like, waiting for the green light signaling permission for her to attempt her vault. Then suddenly, with a slight smile, she sprang into motion, sprinting seventy-three and a half feet to the board and launching herself twenty-two feet through the air, twisting and turning in midair before landing rock solid on the mat—no wobbles, no movement, just perfection! A perfect stick and a perfect 10! The sellout crowd went crazy, screaming, "USA! USA!" and "Mary Lou! Mary Lou! Mary Lou!"

America fell in love with this amazing athlete and her ability to deliver a flawless performance under pressure. In 1993, nearly ten years after her big win, a national survey by the Associated Press named Mary Lou Retton the "Most Popular Athlete in America." Mary Lou is an example of the power of mental practice and self-talk and their influence on successful performance.

Source/Additional Reading

Weinberg, Rick. 2004. "Mary Lou Gets the Gold in Olympic All-Around." ESPN.com, June 30, 2004. http://sports.espn.go.com/espn/espn25/story? page=moments/70

THOUGHT PATTERNS

Our life is what our thoughts make it.

—Marcus Aurelius

The discussion above has addressed several factors that help shape our unique psychological worlds. One way of picturing these ideas is to view our internal psychological selves in terms of thought patterns. That is, we tend to develop certain ways of thinking about our experiences. We might say that just as we develop habitual ways of behaving, we develop habitual ways of thinking. These thought patterns involve—among other things—our beliefs, our imagined experiences, and our self-talk. Figure 5.2 shows how our beliefs, our imagined experiences, and our self-talk influence one another and help shape our thought patterns. Of course, these factors are also influenced by external forces such as our past experiences. The primary idea, however, is that we each construct a unique concept of life in our minds that influences our actions and how we feel about things.

Notice also in Figure 5.2 that behavior is included as an influence and a result of our thought patterns. Considerable debate and controversy have occurred recently over, essentially, a "chicken-or-egg" issue: Does our psychological makeup (e.g., attitudes, beliefs) cause our behavior, or does our behavior cause our psychological makeup? The logical answer is a bit facetious, but it is yes, they cause each other. Thus, an optimal approach to improving our self-leadership includes a focus on both. Indeed, considerable evidence suggests that if we change our behavior, we change ourselves psychologically. If we behave in a more courteous and friendly manner toward others, for example, we are likely to change psychologically into more courteous and friendly people.

So let's spend a little more time thinking about how we think. Take a moment to complete the short self-assessment exercise starting on page 115.

Figure 5.2 Our Psychological Worlds

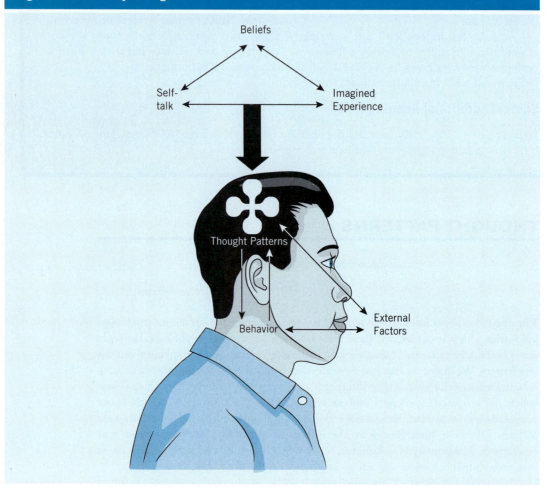

OPPORTUNITY OR OBSTACLE THINKING

Among the different types of thought patterns that a person could adopt are two that might be called opportunity thinking and obstacle thinking. Opportunity thinking involves a pattern of thoughts that focus on the opportunities and possibilities that situations or challenges hold. Creative, innovative individuals who contribute to the major breakthroughs and advances in our world most likely possess this pattern of thinking. Their beliefs, imagined future experiences, and self-talk probably spur them on to undertake new opportunities. Obstacle thinking, in contrast, involves a focus on the roadblocks and pitfalls of undertaking new ventures. Such a mental pattern fosters

Choose the letter of the statement (a or b) that you agree with more for each of the ten pairs presented, and write the letter in the space in the right-hand column.

1. a. A real opportunity is built into every problem.
   b. Anything that can go wrong, will.

2. a. A bird in the hand is worth two in a bush.
   b. Real opportunities are worth sticking your neck out for.

3. a. Most people cannot be counted on.
   b. Every person is a valuable resource in some way.

4. a. Difficulties make us grow.
   b. Difficulties beat us down.

5. a. The world is full of impossibilities.
   b. Nothing is impossible that we can conceive of.

6. a. When half of the days in an enjoyable vacation have passed, I still have half of my vacation to enjoy.
   b. When half of the days in an enjoyable vacation have passed, my vacation is half over.

7. a. The best approach to dealing with energy shortages is conservation.
   b. The best approach to dealing with energy shortages is to develop new energy sources.

8. a. Life after death.
   b. Death after life.

9. a. Failure is an opportunity to learn.
   b. Failure is a negative outcome to effort.

10. a. Happiness is the absence of problems.
    b. Problems are the spice of life.

Directions for scoring: Circle the choice you made (a or b) for each pair of statements (1 through 10). Total the number of letters circled in each column.

	I	II
1.	a	b

(Continued)

(Continued)

2.	b	a
3.	b	a
4.	a	b
5.	b	a
6.	a	b
7.	b	a
8.	a	b
9.	a	b
10.	b	a
Total		
	opportunity thinking	obstacle thinking

Interpreting Your Score

The short exercise you have just completed is designed to help you assess your current pattern of thinking. It focuses on two distinct types of thinking patterns discussed later in this chapter: opportunity thinking and obstacle thinking. The scores that you recorded for column I and column II (the maximum possible total for either is 10) suggest your current thinking tendencies. If your column I total is higher than your column II total, this indicates that your current thinking patterns tend to reflect opportunity thinking more than obstacle thinking. (The reverse is true if your column II total is higher than your column I total.) The greater the difference between the two totals, the more you tend toward one pattern or the other. In general, a higher score in column I than in column II reflects some desirable self-leadership tendencies, and a higher score in column II might indicate some fundamental problems.

As was the case for your scores on the self-assessment questionnaires presented earlier, your results on this exercise should be interpreted cautiously. The way you score might reflect your current mood or outlook as opposed to any long-term tendencies. On the other hand, an exercise such as this is useful for helping you reflect on the pattern of thought that you tend to adopt in thinking about and approaching situations.

avoidance of challenges in favor of more secure actions, often with substantially lesser potential payoffs.

Skiwear mogul Klaus Obermeyer is a classic example of an opportunity thinker. Obermeyer is founder of Sport Obermeyer, a ski apparel company that earned more than $30 million in 1995 despite the fact that Obermeyer went skiing every day of the ski season. He has said that his company originated when he saw an opportunity:

> It's very simple . . . I was making $10 a day teaching skiing, but people kept canceling because of the cold. If I wanted to keep my class, I had to make them comfortable.[18]

Obermeyer clearly viewed the fact that his students were "canceling because of the cold" as an opportunity and not an obstacle. Indeed, in 1950, he made history by tearing up his bed comforter and using it to make the world's first quilted goose-down parka. He also marketed the first turtleneck in the United States and the first mirrored sunglasses. As Obermeyer reasoned,

> People skied in knickerbockers and neckties back then. It was cold as hell. They got frostbite. They got sunburned. And their feet hurt because boots didn't fit. But all these problems were opportunities.[19]

Another example of the benefits of opportunity thinking involves a woman named Helen Thayer. In March 1988, Thayer was on a journey that few believed a woman could accomplish: a solo trek to the North Magnetic Pole. She had only one week left in her grueling expedition when an unexpected storm developed, blowing most of her remaining supplies away; all she had left were seven small handfuls of walnuts and a pint of water. Thus, she would have to adjust from living on about five thousand calories a day to surviving on one hundred calories. Did she make it to her destination? Yes, she certainly did! How did she manage to finish her incredible feat? Her will to win and the power of her mind were her strategic weapons against the brutal elements and other dangers—the wind, the cold, the man-eating polar bears. As Thayer remarks in her book *Polar Dream*,

> I found it to be a decided advantage to accept what I had and feel grateful for it rather than wish I had more. Wishing only made me feel even more hungry and thirsty, whereas acceptance and gratitude allowed me to channel my energy into moving ahead at a good pace.[20]

Thayer practiced opportunity thinking to accomplish her goal. Instead of viewing her loss of supplies as an obstacle that could prevent her from completing her trek, she viewed the loss as an opportunity that enabled her to focus her energy to finish the journey.

College football quarterback Tim Tebow's classic postgame speech after his team's loss to the University of Mississippi—the only loss of his junior year—is another great example of opportunity thinking. At the press conference following the game, Tebow had this to say about the heartbreaking loss:

I promise you one thing, a lot of good will come out of this. You will never see any player in the entire country play as hard as I will play the rest of the season. You will never see someone push the rest of the team as hard as I will push everybody the rest of the season. You will never see a team play harder than we will the rest of the season. God Bless.[21]

Tebow's team, the University of Florida Gators, ended up winning the national championship that year, and "The Promise" has now been memorialized on a plaque displayed at the university's Ben Hill Griffin Stadium.[22]

Each of us can possess both opportunity and obstacle thinking at different times and when faced with different situations. Some undertakings pose too much personal risk and should be avoided. On the other hand, we often find ourselves caught up in difficult situations unexpectedly. When avoiding such a situation is no longer a choice, the issue becomes how we deal with it. We probably tend to rely on certain thought patterns more than others in dealing with life's challenges. For example, should we seek worthwhile challenges because they help us grow, or should we do our best to avoid problems of any kind? Should our thoughts be that the world is cruel and unfair, or that the world is basically good and honest effort is rewarded? The pattern of our thinking influences our actions, our satisfaction with life, and our personal effectiveness.

Even presidents of the United States can benefit from seeing challenging situations as opportunities. On March 30, 1981, President Ronald Reagan was wounded in the chest by a would-be assassin's bullet. The horror of the situation was a shock to millions around the world. Logically, one would think President Reagan would condemn the violent act and display a negative outlook in its wake. Instead, he was said to have smiled through surgery. Numerous optimistic and humorous remarks the president made soon after the shooting reached the public, and this gradually helped relieve the nation's tension. The victim seemed to be trying to support the safe onlookers rather than the seemingly more logical reverse. Among the verbal and written quips made by the wounded president were "Honey, I forgot to duck" (to his wife); "Please, say you're Republicans" (to the doctors); the attempted assassination "ruined one of my best suits" (to his daughter); and "Send me to L.A., where I can see the air I'm breathing" (to the medical staff).

The results? President Reagan's popularity rose to an all-time high. Programs he had been working hard to push through Congress gained momentum. A short time after the incident, the president achieved his first major political triumph since taking office—Congress approved his budget. This accomplishment could be attributed largely to his admirable conduct in the wake of the assassination attempt.[23]

Regardless of whether you are in agreement with this president's political views or approve of his subsequent actions in office, it is difficult to deny that his reaction to the assault on his life is little short of amazing. He was able to transform the would-be tragedy into a powerful opportunity. The public feeling surrounding this distressing event and the president's inspiring behavior is reflected in a view expressed by one television commentator who said, in essence, "I hope President Reagan feels better because of how bad we feel. I know how I feel. I wish I would have voted for him."

Opportunities can be found in even the most unlikely of situations if only we let ourselves see them through the patterns of our thinking. Consider one final example of opportunity versus obstacle thinking involving Thomas Edison. Edison's laboratory was virtually destroyed by a fire in December 1914, and the buildings were insured for only a fraction of the money that it would cost to rebuild them. At the age of sixty-seven, Edison lost most of his life's work when it went up in flames on that December night. The next morning, he looked at the ruins and said, "There is a great value in disaster. All our mistakes are burned up. Thank God we can start anew." Three weeks after the fire, Edison delivered his first phonograph.[24] Edison truly was an opportunity thinker in this case—he viewed the fire as a chance for a fresh start rather than as an excuse to quit. The question for you is, how do you view "fires" or problems in your life—as obstacles or as opportunities?

THE POWER OF FAILURE

Only he who does nothing makes no mistakes.

—French proverb

The self-leadership strategies outlined in this book are designed to help you be successful in achieving your goals and objectives. This leads us to pose an interesting question: Would you like to be successful throughout the remainder of your life? Would you like to enjoy meaningful success, where you learn, grow, and contribute in significant ways, so that your life is full, counts for something, and makes a difference? If your answer is yes, then you must fail. There is no exception to this rule. *Significant success requires failure*, but failure in a whole new light.

Failure is one of the most dreaded words in the English language. The very idea of failing is enough to stop most people in their tracks. It can cause the majority to simply pack up, turn around, and retreat without even trying.

Success, in contrast, is a nearly magical idea for most people. The possibility of succeeding or becoming a success is an almost mythical challenge. People love to be labeled as successful and often sacrifice greatly to achieve this end.

Although most people hate to be labeled a failure and love to be labeled a success, the fact is that only through seeming failure are most of life's greatest successes achieved. Usually, failure and success are almost entirely in the eye of the beholder. Perhaps this reflects an ultimate truth about what we call failure. The perception of failure is very often simply a misperception about difference—difference from what already exists or from what was expected. Of course, sometimes failure is tied to a lack of competence to perform in the face of a specific challenge, but seeming failures can offer us a powerful way to learn—they are almost always the fruitful stepping stones to life's greatest breakthroughs and successes. We can learn to accept that what most people view as failures are usually only temporary setbacks in relation to some arbitrary standard and that they are an essential part of life. They are usually just *challenges in progress*. And when we learn this important lesson, we come to understand that the only real failure is to back away from worthwhile challenges without even trying.

The traditional Japanese art of repairing broken pottery in a way that restores its usefulness while making it even more beautiful and valuable provides a powerful illustration of how failures can often be transformed into success. Kintsugi (literally golden "kin" repair "tsugi") uses precious metals such as liquid gold, liquid silver, or lacquer sprinkled with powdered gold to re-join the shards of a broken ceramic bowl or vase.[25] Because of the random way in which ceramic objects break, each repaired piece has unique and irregular patterns of precious metal that add beauty and refinement to the piece.[26] Similarly, the wounds and scars that we experience as the result of our failures may be transformed into stunningly beautiful golden lines of success.

The book *The Power of Failure* by Charles Manz, a member of our author team, provides simple yet profound self-leadership strategies for turning seeming failures into successes, including practical prescriptions for successfully meeting some of life's most common setbacks.[27] It is helpful to think of the book's various specific lessons in relation to a larger whole—more general guidelines for failing successfully. Most of the book's "success based on failure" prescriptions relate to eight primary themes, which are summarized here. We can think of these themes as offering a new view or vision of how we can transform failure so that it contributes positively to more successful living.

A New View of Failure: Some Primary Themes

1. **Redefine failure.** Failure is a natural part of life that can affect us positively or negatively, depending on how we define it.

2. **Redefine success.** The best measure of success is based on our own deep knowledge of what's right for us rather than on the approval or disapproval of others.

3. **Learn from failure.** Failure presents an opportunity for continued learning and growth, whereas success can lead to complacency and stagnation.

4. **View failures as stepping stones to success.** Success and failure are not incompatible—most failures are simply *challenges in progress* that can provide a foundation for success.

5. **Find the opportunities of failure.** Setbacks or short-term failures can contribute to future success if we focus on the opportunities they contain rather than the obstacles.

6. **Use negative feedback to your advantage.** Negative feedback can provide positive information for improvement and may even suggest that you are onto something new and different—a sign of a pending breakthrough success.

7. **Look beyond yourself.** As you learn to focus outward, on helping others succeed, you become less vulnerable to what otherwise might appear to be personal failures.

8. **Persist.** Keep on trying and trying. *Sustained Effort + the Lessons of Failures* is a powerful formula for success.

Among the many lessons offered by *The Power of Failure* is that we can live more successfully if we understand the following:

- Challenges are disguised opportunities.

- Differences are gifts.

- Mistakes are learning opportunities.

- When we try our best, we always succeed even if we don't achieve the results hoped for.

- The only way we can really fail is if we refuse to learn from our setbacks.

Real success that is sustainable over a lifetime is built on a solid foundation of learning and benefiting from every setback and shortfall, and is forged with the courage and strength that come from a commitment to harness the power of failure.

Jacques Wiesel once wrote, "Bloom where you are planted."[28] What does this mean? As we conclude this chapter, consider how the story of Jacques-Yves Cousteau illustrates both the power of failure and the ultimate message of this quote. From a young age, Cousteau dreamed of becoming a pilot. In pursuit of that dream, in 1930, when he was twenty years old, he passed the highly competitive examinations to enter France's Naval Academy. He subsequently served in the navy and entered naval aviation school.

A near-fatal car crash at age twenty-six denied him his wings, and he was transferred to sea duty. Did Cousteau whine because he could no longer fly an airplane? Did he gripe about life being unfair? Did he complain about the new situation in which he was "planted"? No, he did not. In fact, he decided to use his new position (sea duty) to his advantage. He swam rigorously in the ocean to strengthen his arms, which had been badly weakened by the car accident. This therapy had some unintended yet beautiful consequences. As Cousteau noted in his 1953 book *The Silent World*, "Sometimes we are lucky enough to know that our lives have been changed, to discard the old, embrace the new, and run headlong down an immutable course. It happened to me . . . when my eyes were opened on the sea."[29]

Think about this for a moment. Cousteau's passion, and his claim to fame, was his life as an underwater explorer. His oceanographic expeditions set numerous milestones in marine research and led to Cousteau's role as a spokesperson for the protection of the underwater environment. None of this—his expeditions, his documentary films and television shows, his books, the impact he had on many people's lives—probably would have happened if Cousteau had not "bloomed where he was planted." In other words, if

Cousteau had not embraced the change in his life due to his tragic accident, the world might never have heard of him. If he had cried about not being able to fly and had refused his new assignment, we would be saying "Jacques who?"

How many times in our own lives when we are confronted with change do we say, "I wish I were back home," "I wish I were with my old friends," "I wish I were still doing my old job"? If right now you are living in the past and wishing you were back in a situation from years gone by, consider the story of Jacques Cousteau. Then ask yourself: Am I trying to bloom where I am now planted? If you answer in the negative, you could be missing out on something magical in your life. You could be missing out on discovering something about yourself that could dramatically enhance your life's direction. Cousteau's near-fatal accident led to his being planted somewhere else, somewhere new, somewhere unfamiliar to him. Rather than focusing on the life that he had to leave, he chose to bloom in his new environment—the ocean. This choice resulted in his discovery of who he was and what his life's passion would be. If he had chosen differently—chosen to complain about not being where he used to be and about what could have been—his life probably would have been less fulfilling and his impact on the world less substantial. If you have recently been "replanted" in your life, perhaps because of a new job, a new relationship, a family crisis, or any type of change, what decision have you made or will you make? To bloom or not to bloom is indeed the question. It is our hope that Cousteau's life will show you the correct answer: choose to bloom where you are planted.

REAL-WORLD SELF-LEADERSHIP CASE

Gift Ngoepe: We Have Made History!

When Gift Ngoepe heard the announcement on the loudspeaker that he would enter the game as the Pittsburgh Pirates' second baseman, he quietly said some words to his mother, who had passed away a few years earlier: "This is it, Mom," he said. "We did it. We have made history!" After spending nearly nine years in the minor leagues, Ngoepe would become the first African-born player to appear in a Major League Baseball game. Ngoepe, who grew up in the South African town of Randsburg near Johannesburg, gives his mom much of the credit for his success in baseball. She told him to never give up on his dream of playing major league baseball.

But part of his success no doubt stemmed from his ability to use constructive thought-focused strategies to shape his mental approach to the game in positive ways. In an article featured in *The Players' Tribune*, Ngoepe described his mental approach to his first at-bat in the major leagues:

I led off the bottom of the fourth, and prior to my very first at bat as a big league player, walking up to the batter's box, I was a nervous wreck. I tried my best to get control of my emotions. It was not easy, let me tell you. I had to focus heavily on my breathing, because there was so much adrenaline running through me. I worked hard to control my nerves, but I was in my own head the entire time. "You gotta calm down, Gift. You gotta calm down. Control your emotions. It's just another baseball game. Just go out there and do your thing." That's easier said than done, believe me. When I stepped into the box, I took a very deep breath, and then I looked out at Jon Lester. "O.K. Gift," I said to myself, "This is really happening. You are up against Jon Lester. He has three World Series rings. He's one of the best pitchers in the game. And he's facing you. He's facing Gift Ngoepe!"

My plan was to swing at the very first pitch. I was looking for one pitch, in one zone. The idea was to hit the ball back up through the box. When Lester went away with his first pitch for a ball, it meant that I wouldn't be able to go with my plan, but it also really helped to calm me down. I saw the pitch well. "Stay focused, Gift. You can do this. Look for your pitch." Then another ball. "Alright Gift, you're in a 2–0 count now." At that point, in my mind, I thought about whether I should try to get the bat head out on the next pitch and see if I could pull the ball to left field. I paused for a second. "No! That's not the approach that got you to this place. Stick with the plan, Gift: line drive back up the middle."

The next pitch was a fastball right over the plate. I tried to inside out it, and I didn't barrel it up. I just fouled it off into the stands, and I was not happy about that. "This is not good, Gift. This is a terrible AB right now, man. You were 2–0. You should've gotten

the bat head out and not gotten beat by a fastball. Come on, Gift!" When Lester took me to 3–1, I started to feel better. I relaxed myself. "Gift, you're in a real good hitter's count right now. Do what you know how to do."

Then I got my wish. He threw me a 3–1 fastball over the heart of the plate. I was able to use my hands and hit it back up the middle for a single. It wasn't a cheap hit either. It was solid. It was a real hit. A major league hit. And you better believe I'm smiling as I write that. You should see my smile right now. Gift Ngoepe, from Randburg, South Africa, is a major league baseball player, and he got a hit in his very first at bat in the big leagues. Never let anyone tell you that dreams don't come true.

Questions for Class Discussion

1. In what ways did positive thinking help Ngoepe to be successful in his life and career?

2. Explain how Ngoepe used self-talk to be successful in his first at-bat in the majors.

3. How do you think Ngoepe may have used the strategies of evaluating beliefs and assumptions and mental practice during his rise to the major leagues?

4. During nine years in the minor leagues Ngoepe experienced many failures and setbacks to his career. How was he able to overcome those failures and realize his dream of playing major league baseball?

Sources/Additional Readings

Kepner, Tyler. 2017. "First African to Play in the Major Leagues Is a 'Pinnacle' for Baseball." *New York Times*, May 8, 2017. https://www.nytimes.com/2017/05/08/sports/baseball/gift-ngoepe-south-africa-pittsburgh-pirates.html.

Ngoepe, Gift. 2017. "We Have Made History." *The Players' Tribune*, May 1, 2017. https://www.theplayerstribune.com/en-us/articles/gift-ngoepe-pittsburgh-pirates-south-africa.

6

TEAM SELF-LEADERSHIP

Sharing the Journey

When spiderwebs unite, they can tie up a lion.

—Ethiopian proverb

If we were to end the book at this point, we would be short-changing you.[1] You might decide to return the book to your bookstore and ask for your money back. The good news is that there is more to conquer.

Up to this chapter, our discussion on self-leadership has focused on you as an individual. We understand, however, that much of the work you do on a daily basis is not done by you alone. We realize that to accomplish many of your goals, you need to work with other people. A large majority of the work today in schools and businesses is done by teams of people as opposed to separate individuals.

The use of teams—self-directed teams, self-managing teams, and high-performance teams—is a work design innovation that has swept across the country and the rest of the world over the past few decades. This fact of business life continues to gain in popularity, as estimates suggest that 80 to 90 percent of all North American organizations have at least some type of self-managed teams.[2] Thus, chances are good that right now you are a member of a team—as a student in a university, as an employee in an organization, or even as part of a personal relationship (e.g., boyfriend, girlfriend, husband, wife).

The introduction of empowered work teams into the workplace represents one of the most important new organizational developments since the Industrial Revolution. Teams have demonstrated their ability to make major contributions to

Learning Objectives

After studying this chapter, you should be able to do the following:

1. Explain why team members accomplish more together than they can as individuals.

2. Describe how team self-leadership is the application of mental and behavioral self-leadership strategies at the team level.

3. Demonstrate behavioral team self-leadership practices within a team, including team self-observation, team self-goal-setting, team cue modification, team self-reward and self-

punishment, and team rehearsal.

4. Employ mental team self-leadership strategies within a team, including evaluating team beliefs and assumptions, team self-talk, team mental imagery, and team thought patterns.

5. Recognize the importance of balancing the "me" with the "we" in a team setting by applying teamthink concepts and avoiding groupthink.

organizations in a variety of industries. Increased productivity; higher product and service quality; better quality of work life for employees; and reduced costs, turnover, and absenteeism are among the more salient payoffs.

Usually members of teams, in comparison with individual workers, have increased amounts of responsibility and control. Teams perform many tasks that previously were the responsibility of management, such as conducting meetings, solving technical and personal problems, and making a wide range of decisions on many issues, including performance methods and assignment of tasks. Successful teams are those that possess the skills, equipment, and supplies they need to perform the work well.

The best teams tend to have capable and committed members who successfully combine their skills and knowledge for the good of the team. The challenge for teams is to accept and appreciate the unique contributions that each member can make while effectively combining individual member contributions for the good of the team. The key to team success is the creation of synergy—the condition whereby team members together accomplish significantly more than they could if they acted on their own.[3] (Team synergy might be expressed mathematically as 1 + 1 + 1 = 5.) This definition fits well with the widely used acronym TEAM, for "together everyone achieves more." An interesting recent study compared the individual performance of professional golfers on the PGA tour to their performance when playing in two team-based competitions: the Ryder Cup and President's Cup golf tournaments. The findings showed synergy in the performance of the golfers playing in small groups relative to their play as individuals.[4] Teams work best when their members have strong individual skills and strong group skills. How can a team obtain synergy? We argue that self-leadership plays an integral part in the answer to this question.

SELF-LEADERSHIP AND TEAMS

You might be thinking, "Don't the terms *self-leadership* and *teams* contradict or oppose each other?" In other words, what does leading oneself have to do with working as a member of a team? Actually, the two concepts are quite closely related. Self-leadership is just as important when you are working in a team as when you are working alone. To reach your individual potential while working within a team, you still must lead yourself. In fact, only by effectively leading yourself as a team member can you help the team lead itself, reach its potential, and thus achieve synergy. The act of the team leading itself describes the concept of team self-leadership, which can be defined as follows:

The application of mental and behavioral self-leadership strategies that enable team members to provide themselves with self-direction and self-motivation, and ultimately to become effective, personally empowered contributors to their team.

According to this definition, team self-leadership is similar to individual self-leadership in that both involve the use of behavioral and mental strategies. Next we will examine some of these team-based self-leadership strategies.[5]

BEHAVIORAL ASPECTS OF TEAM SELF-LEADERSHIP

Specific behavioral team self-leadership practices include team self-observation, team self-goal-setting, team cue modification, team self-reward/self-punishment, and team rehearsal (practice).

Team Self-Observation

At the team level, self-observation represents the team's collective effort to purposefully observe (and record) team behavior and performance, as well as the team's attempt to understand the antecedents and consequences associated with those actions. Self-observation should be done by the team. Thus, team self-observation encompasses group members working collectively to measure and understand the team's behavior. An example is a group seeking the information needed to compare the group's performance with its production goals.

Team Self-Goal-Setting

Individuals on a team can have personal goals that are coordinated with and necessary for achieving the team's goals, but the focus for the team is to achieve the shared goals of the team as a whole. Team self-goal-setting accordingly requires the group as a collective (rather than an individual leader) to establish the goals. Goal-setting by the group thus represents an element of self-leadership for the team that encompasses, but is not defined by, individual goals of team members or leaders.

Team Cue Modification

Teams can remove things that cue undesirable behavior and increase exposure to elements that cue desirable behavior. When a team changes environmental conditions that affect behavior, team self-leadership occurs. Attempts to change the environment are collectively performed by the team and are not synonymous with individual attempts to modify antecedents that cue behavior. An example is a team deciding to alter the configuration of its work space.

Team Self-Reward and Self-Punishment

Teams can reinforce their own desirable behaviors by providing rewards—to individual members and to the group as a whole—that strengthen or increase those behaviors. These rewards may be tangible or intangible. Tangible rewards might include monetary bonuses, time off, or the purchase of new equipment. Intangible rewards might include increased satisfaction, joy from working as a team, or a feeling of respect for the work accomplished by the team. Punishment involves applying negative consequences to reduce undesirable behaviors. An example of team self-punishment is a team deciding that all members must work late to make up for time spent in excessive socializing. For team self-influence to take place, the group must administer and receive rewards and sanctions collectively. It is important to note that as with individual self-leadership, team self-punishment is neither the preferred nor the most effective method for influencing a team's behavior.

Team Rehearsal

As discussed, rehearsal or practice is another step associated with the self-leadership process. Teams may conduct rehearsal either overtly or covertly. An example of rehearsal might be several team members practicing a presentation their team must make to the rest of the organization. To be considered team rehearsal, this practice must be initiated and directed by the team as a whole rather than by an individual team member.

MENTAL ASPECTS OF TEAM SELF-LEADERSHIP

An underlying assumption of the discussion of mental team self-leadership strategies involves the emergence of a group pattern of thinking, which is more than the simple collection of the thinking of separate individual minds. This notion of a "group mind" has been addressed by various researchers.[6] For example, W. R. Bion asserted that a group's mind-set exists beyond that of the individual group members in that the group's mind-set connects group members through an unconscious implied agreement.[7]

Accordingly, the basic premise of mental team self-leadership is that, similar to self-leading individuals, teams can enhance their performance through the collective application of specific mental strategies that result in a team mode of thinking. These collective mental strategies include evaluating beliefs and assumptions, self-talk, and mental imagery. As with our representation of individual mental self-leadership, these components of collective mental strategies interact reciprocally to influence thought patterns (in this case, the thought patterns of the team).

Team Beliefs and Assumptions

Recall our earlier discussion of individual beliefs and assumptions. We suggested that distorted thoughts are based on some common dysfunctional beliefs and assumptions that are activated by potentially troubling situations. Most of these types of individual-level beliefs have analogues at the group level. For example, recall the individual-level dysfunctional assumption known as extreme thinking, in which individuals evaluate things in extreme categories, as black or white. Similarly, a group can develop extreme beliefs. To illustrate, if a risk does not seem overwhelmingly dangerous, the team as a whole might be inclined to minimize its importance and proceed without further preparation to meet the risk instead of developing contingency plans in case the risk materializes.

Team Self-Talk

Earlier we described individual self-talk as what we tell ourselves, and we suggested that a person's self-talk can affect his or her effectiveness. In the same manner, group self-talk might significantly influence group performance. For example, within a cohesive team there is a tendency for members to put social pressure on any member who expresses opinions that deviate from the group's dominant form of dialogue. The group members exert this pressure to ensure that the deviant member does not disrupt the consensus of the group as a whole. This tendency toward group-enforced conformity dialogue (group self-talk) might lead to defective decision making on the part of the group (see the discussion of groupthink later in this chapter).

Team Mental Imagery

A team could potentially enhance its performance by utilizing group mental imagery to establish a common vision. Given that members of successful groups tend to share a common vision, self-managing teams faced with strategic decisions should benefit from interactively creating an image regarding what they want to accomplish, as well as visualizing effective means for doing so. Jeff Bezos, CEO of Amazon.com, has commented on the importance of positive team mental imagery:

> My own view is that every company requires a long-term view. If you're going to take a long-term orientation, you have to be willing to stay heads down and ignore a wide array of critics, even well-meaning critics. If you don't have a willingness to be misunderstood for a long period of time, then you can't have a long-term orientation. Because we have done it many times

Constructive Thought-Focused Strategies in Self-Managing Teams

We have suggested in this chapter that self-leadership strategies are just as important for people working in teams as for people working alone. It is easy to understand how behavior-focused strategies applied at the team level, such as team self-goal-setting and team self-reward, could have a positive impact on team effectiveness. But are the mental aspects of self-leadership also effective at the team level? Is there really a "group mind" through which self-leadership's mental strategies can be applied within teams? A recent study of 103 self-managing teams comprised of 453 individuals found that the constructive, thought-focused strategies applied equally well across levels of analysis (i.e., for both individuals and teams).[1] More specifically, the findings suggest that the thought self-leadership strategies of team self-dialogues, team evaluation of beliefs and assumptions, and team mental imagery result in a higher level of team collective efficacy, which involves collective feelings of competence shared among team members, and ultimately in higher levels of team performance and team viability. Although more studies examining constructive, thought-focused self-leadership at the team level are needed, this study provides compelling initial evidence in support of the effectiveness of the mental team self-leadership strategies described in this chapter.

Note

1. Pedro Marques Quinteiro, Ana Passos, and Luís Curral, "Thought Self-Leadership and Effectiveness in Self-Management Teams," *Leadership* 12, no. 1 (February 2016): 110–26.

and have come out the other side, we have enough internal stories that we can tell ourselves. While we're crossing the desert, we may be thirsty, but we sincerely believe there's an oasis on the other side.[8]

Team Thought Patterns

Like individuals, teams can develop thought patterns. In other words, a team can be an opportunity or obstacle thinker. An example of team opportunity or obstacle thinking can involve the group's perception of its ability to overcome a particular challenge. If a team is faced with a technical problem that affects the quality of its product, it can view this as an opportunity to focus the group's energies and utilize the decision-making and technical skills of the team, or it can see the problem as an obstacle that will prevent the team from producing a product of high quality. If the team believes that this technical problem is an insurmountable obstacle, then it is practically assured that the product's quality will suffer. On the other hand, if the team feels that the problem is an opportunity to improve the product further, the probability of the team's producing a high-quality product is enhanced. Thus, if a team believes problems are opportunities to overcome challenges rather than obstacles that will lead to failure, the team's performance should be enhanced.

TEAM SELF-LEADERSHIP STILL MEANS INDIVIDUAL SELF-LEADERSHIP

Now that we have briefly described specific team self-leadership strategies, we return to an important point mentioned earlier in this chapter: you must effectively lead yourself as a team member if you want to help the team lead itself, reach its potential, and thus achieve synergy. To explore this concept more fully, consider the following story:

> A French scientist, Jean-Henri Fabre, had a very interesting passion in life—the study of caterpillars. At one point in his research, he conducted an experiment that involved processionary caterpillars, wormlike creatures that travel in long, unwavering lines, at the same pace and cadence. Fabre placed a group of processionary caterpillars onto the thin rim of a large flowerpot, forming a circle of caterpillars, so that the leader of the group was nose to tail with the last caterpillar in the slow, nonending procession. Even for Fabre it was difficult to figure out who was the leader and who were the followers. For an entire day Fabre watched the caterpillars endlessly circle the rim of the flowerpot. He then went home for the night, and in the morning when he arrived at his laboratory he noticed that the caterpillars were still circling the pot. Then, Fabre placed a supply of food in the center of the flowerpot, but this did not detour the caterpillars. They never stopped circling—not even to eat. Day after day, night after night, the caterpillars paraded around and around and around and around. After seven days of parading the rim, the caterpillars finally stopped because they died of starvation and exhaustion. Not for one moment did a single caterpillar stop to look up, eat, or interrupt the circle of travel. Instead, they all put their heads down and blindly followed the caterpillars ahead of them (instead of thinking maybe some other way was better) until they died.[9]

LeBron James

Despite being one of the greatest individual players in the history of the NBA, LeBron James learned at a very early age the importance of balancing the "me" with the "we" as an essential component of team success. Unsurprisingly, back in 1993, in 9-year-old LeBron's first year playing competitive basketball, his team went undefeated and won the Akron Recreation Bureau's youth league championship. Equally unsurprisingly, James was named the team's Most Valuable Player (MVP). But his teammates Frankie Walker Jr., Willie McGee, and one young lady, Lavette Wilborn, were also named team MVPs. In fact, *everyone* on LeBron's team received an MVP trophy! "That's still fair," his former youth basketball coach Frank Walker Sr. noted recently. "He still got MVP." Coach

Walker's decision to give MVP trophies to everyone on the team had a profound influence in shaping young LeBron's development as a basketball player. Given his limited experience playing the sport, he didn't understand what an exceptional gesture it was to make every player an MVP—he simply thought this was how the game of basketball was played. "Right then I knew that this is a team game," James said in a recent interview. "It's not about one individual and how much one individual can do in order to win championships. In order to win, you have to have a full team."

Another lesson in balancing the "me" with the "we" came courtesy of the Akron Recreation Bureau youth league's rule that no player on a team with ten or more players could play more than two quarters of a game. Young LeBron sat on the bench for half of every game, learning the value of trusting and relying on teammates. "It's just been instilled in me since I was 9 years old, when I first started playing, of what it means to be in a situation where your teammates rely on you," James said. One of those early teammates was an undersized 7-year-old named Sonny Spoon. "Nobody could pass him the ball without him falling over," teammate Willie McGee recalled. But in one of the final games of the season, LeBron decided to find a way to get the ball to Sonny so he could score a basket. "He rolled him the ball on the ground," McGee explained. Sonny scooped up the unconventional pass and heaved it toward the rim with all the strength he could muster. The ball swished through! Assist, LeBron James!

Reliance on teammates has always been important for LeBron. The game-winning shot made in overtime that won that first championship game was made not by James, but by teammate Brandon Weems. Later in high school, LeBron won his first state championship by passing the ball repeatedly to Dru Joyce III, a 5-foot-2-inch, 95-pound freshman who had barely played all year. Joyce made seven three-point shots in a row, and because of LeBron's unselfishness, his team won yet again. James made a similar decision to trust a teammate in Game 1 of the 2018 NBA Finals. With five seconds left in the game and the score tied, LeBron opted not to take the final shot of the game and instead passed the ball to teammate George Hill, who had a better shot under the basket. Hill was fouled and went to the free throw line. Hill missed the attempt and another teammate, J.R. Smith, inexplicably grabbed the rebound and dribbled away from the basket as regulation time expired. This time, his team lost in overtime, but LeBron's unselfish pass demonstrated his belief that basketball should never be solely about one individual player. He was only doing what he learned as a 9-year-old playing youth basketball and has been doing ever since: trusting his teammates and balancing the "me" with the "we."

Source/Additional Reading

Cohen, Ben. 2018. "Why LeBron James (Still) Trusts His Teammates." *The Wall Street Journal*, June 6, 2018. https://www.wsj.com/articles/why-lebron-james-still-trusts-his-teammates-1528211656?ns=prod/accounts-wsj.

This story might parallel a challenge you have faced or will face as a member of a team. The challenge involves not acting like Fabre's caterpillars and blindly following the members of your team. By doing this, you are not practicing effective team self-leadership. To practice effective team self-leadership, you must concurrently maintain your own unique belief system and viewpoint and work together with others as a team. If you give up your own uniqueness and way of looking at the world by failing to tell the group your position on topics, then your group could end up like the helpless caterpillars. In other words, if all the members of your group blindly follow each other, then they will continue to circle, never progressing and thus never performing well. This does not mean that you should not try to cooperate with team members; rather, all members should work together in an effective manner. When a team works together, it is productive for members to disagree and constructively discuss different views. Only by considering differing views can your team develop the ideal way to approach a task or problem. Only by maintaining your individual viewpoint can you add to the team self-leadership of your group.

By now, you might have recognized that team self-leadership involves balance between a focus on yourself and a focus on the team. We refer to this as a balance between the "me" and the "we." By successfully maintaining this balance, you will prosper within your group and help yourself and your team members avoid acting like caterpillars.

BALANCING THE "ME" WITH THE "WE"

A well-known proverb states, "The best potential in 'me' is 'we.'" The underlying message in this adage is a critical aspect of team self-leadership: to reach your ultimate potential as a member of a team, you must work *with* your team and not *against* it. If team members are focused only on themselves and the credit they receive rather than on the success of the team as a whole, the individual members' performance and the team's overall performance will suffer. The following story illustrates this critical point:

> Two geese were about to start southward on their annual migration, when they were entreated by a frog to take him with them. The geese expressed their willingness to do so if a means of conveyance could be devised.
>
> The frog produced a long stalk of pond grass, got the geese each to grab an end with their beaks, while he clung to it by his mouth in the middle. In this way the three began their journey. Some farmers below noticed the strange sight. The men loudly expressed their admiration for the travel device and wondered who had been clever enough to discover it. Whereupon the vainglorious frog opened his mouth to say, "It was I," lost his grip, fell to the earth, and was dashed to pieces.[10]

One moral to this story could be, "When you have a good thing going, keep your mouth shut!" Although truth and humor can be found in this interpretation, a moral more applicable to an understanding of team self-leadership is as follows:

> Effective team self-leadership will not occur when team members place too much emphasis on themselves and worry too much about who is going to get

the credit. This approach will bring poor performance to the team members and to the team as a whole.

Conversely, team members who are committed to team self-leadership, who recognize that the best potential in "me" is "we," and who recognize that team success requires a total group effort whereby team members strive unselfishly to complete their task or project, eventually will achieve their individual goals and those of the team. Consider an additional example written by organizational consultant Dr. Bruce H. Jackson regarding the importance of balancing the "me" with the "we" in teams:

> For more than three decades I have studied the lives of high performers to identify the principles and practices that make them great.
>
> In the study and practice of self-leadership we often speak of vision, goals, values, attitude, perspective, grit, discipline, commitment, physical strength, and hundreds of other factors designed to produce individual results. But in my personal journey to excel as an athlete, student, and professional, and to help others do the same, I have discovered that to achieve your best you often have to help others discover their best. This great secret seems counter-intuitive. But it's true.
>
> Case in point: I recently spoke to a former Olympic gold medalist (rower) to better understand what it took to make the final cut. We spoke of his personal journey to make the team from more than 30 exceptional athletes. Through our conversation a significant principle emerged.
>
> You might think, as I did, that making the team had everything to do with proving your speed, strength, and technical prowess. But that wasn't it at all. . . .
>
> This rower explained that there are 3 mindsets a team can choose when rowing together: Mindset 1: Row your best and hope your teammate does the same. Mindset 2: Seek to bring out the best in your teammate with your own performance taking a secondary focus. The hope is that your selfless efforts will buy the team a few seconds. And Mindset 3: Where both rowers focus on bringing out the best in each other to maximize the synergy of the pair.
>
> Recognizing that Mindset 3 is pretty rare, especially when everything is on the line (think Prisoner's Dilemma), this rower knew that if he could bring out the best in every member he rowed with during the trials, that this philosophy might make the difference—however small. But small is all you need when a hundredth of a second is the difference between winning a medal— and not.
>
> While not the fastest or the strongest amongst his colleagues, this rower knew the strengths and weaknesses of every other rower seeking a spot on

the team. Whoever he was paired with he devised unique ways to tap into their deepest reservoirs of motivation and energy to bring out the best in each partner. This philosophy landed this rower, and whomever he was rowing with, the best time in each heat.

With his name amidst every #1 pair, he ultimately made the Olympic team and the rest is history. To this day he retains this winning philosophy, recognizing that achieving greatness does not come solely from physical and technical gifts, nor a focus on self, but instead on helping the other members of his team tap into their greatness—for their greatness carried his greatness—making 1 + 1 = 3.

I've had similar conversations with former and current NAVY SEALs, Rangers, and other Special Forces units. While each member of the team is an extraordinary performer, no mission is accomplished alone without the support and encouragement of the other team members. Each member is more dedicated to the lives of their teammates than to themselves. That is why they are the best at what they do.

Whether you seek to be a great basketball, football, or hockey player, law enforcement officer or fire fighter, actor or surgeon, discovering one's best self is never a solo act.

In a world where "selfie" is now a registered word (heaven help us), this secret principle puts much needed attention on the value of bringing out the best in others—giving us all something to think about as we seek to make, and be an indispensable member of, our own version of the gold medal team![11]

One of the more powerful self-leadership strategies that can be used in relation to teams is that of shared leadership. Shared leadership is a dynamic, interactive influence process in which team members lead one another to accomplish team goals successfully.[12] With shared leadership, leadership comes from, and is received by, all team members such that all members actively engage in the leadership of the team. The idea behind shared leadership is that everyone involved is a leader at least some of the time, and all members share in the overall leadership process.

If leadership is to be shared by the team, what is the point of self-leadership? Shared leadership and self-leadership are inextricably linked in that team members incapable of self-leadership also are incapable of shared leadership. For instance, effective shared leadership requires all team members to trust that each will follow through with his or her specific responsibilities; in other words, all team members need to be capable self-leaders. Equally important is the fact that capable self-leaders have the self-confidence and self-awareness to know their abilities as well as their limitations. This clear self-knowledge enables them to (1) lead others when they possess the relevant knowledge and (2) be led by others when it is others who possess the relevant expertise.

Miracle (2004)

Two scenes from *Miracle*, the story of the 1980 U.S. Olympic hockey team, help to demonstrate the importance of balancing the "me" with the "we" in a team setting. The first scene begins just after the opening credits with U.S. Olympic hockey team coach Herb Brooks (Kurt Russell) in a meeting discussing his vision and goals for his team. Brooks explains that he wants to adopt a new style of hockey, based on the Soviet style, for his team that takes the talents of the individual and uses those talents inside a system that is designed for the betterment of the team. He further states that his goal is to beat the Soviets at their own game. One of the participants in the meeting replies, "Beat the best team in the world? Gold medalists in '64, '68, '72, and '76? That's a pretty lofty goal, Herb." Brooks responds simply, "That's why I want to pursue it."

The second scene (about 38 minutes into the movie) begins with Coach Brooks saying, "Get a whistle." His team has just tied the Norwegian national team in a halfhearted effort. Brooks is seeing too much individualism in his players. When he asks them whom they play for, each responds with the name of his college or university. In an attempt to eliminate this excessive individualism and make his players into a cohesive team, Brooks makes them skate "suicide" drills repeatedly until they are physically exhausted. Throughout the intense ordeal, the coach emphasizes to the players, "When you pull on that jersey, you represent yourself and your teammates. And the name on the front is a helluva lot more important than the one on the back! Get that through your head!" Finally, just as it seems that Brooks will never let them leave the ice, team member Mike Eruzione (Patrick O'Brien Demsey) suddenly shouts: "Mike Eruzione. Winthrop, Massachusetts." Brooks turns to him and pointedly asks, "Who do you play for?" Eruzione responds: "I play for the United States of America!" Coach Brooks says, "That's all, gentlemen."

Discussion Questions

1. Explain Coach Brooks's plan for winning a gold medal. What does he hope to train his team to do differently than previous U.S. Olympic hockey teams?

2. What does Brooks mean when he says, "The name on the front of the jersey is more important than the name on the back"?

3. In what ways can too much individualism be detrimental to a hockey team?

4. Why is Mike Eruzione's statement an important turning point for the team?

5. Do you think Coach Brooks and his players are able to find the right balance between the "me" and the "we"?

In today's increasingly common team-based environments, having a group of people who are capable of self-leadership is necessary, but not sufficient, to guarantee the success of a team. The next generation of leadership will need to be fully engaged in shared leadership such that all team members are capable self-leaders, capable of leading others, and capable of being led. A team of self-leaders who step forward to lead when they are most needed and step back and let others with greater expertise lead when necessary can accomplish great things.[13]

GROUPTHINK VERSUS TEAMTHINK

To reiterate, too much "we-ness" can lead to a situation in which members act like caterpillars and blindly follow the team as a whole. When this happens, the team is trapped in the vicious circle, neither progressing nor performing well. This type of situation, in which group members engage in groupthink, is a common pitfall to team success. The phenomenon of groupthink leads groups to become overly conforming and ineffective in their decision making.[14]

Consider an example of too much "we-ness" (groupthink) in a team. Have you ever been in a team situation in which members were discussing a particular problem, and in the course of that discussion you had an important thought that went against the predominant view of most of the team? Did you remain silent or speak up? If you remained silent, you were helping your team experience groupthink—or too much "we-ness." You were not maintaining your individuality; you were not expressing your personal viewpoints. The outcome of your inaction, especially if other members also were suppressing their divergent views, was likely defective decision making and consequently poor team performance.

An effective team member in a scenario such as this one would not remain silent. Teams that practice team self-leadership exhibit "teamthink" behaviors as opposed to groupthink behaviors. When team members engage in teamthink, they strike a balance between themselves (the "me") and the team (the "we").[15] This balance involves members working together as a cohesive unit but at the same time constructively disagreeing when it is necessary to do so. This type of scenario can create synergy, as discussed above—that is, a situation in which the team's total results are greater than the sum of what each member could accomplish individually. Additionally, a team that employs teamthink encourages each member to express *all* of his or her views and ideas so that the team can determine the optimal manner of performing a task or handling a problem. In short, the most effective self-leadership teams are those that demonstrate teamthink behaviors. Table 6.1 contrasts the characteristics, or symptoms, of teams experiencing groupthink with those of teams engaging in teamthink.

Before we conclude this chapter, we want to share one final word about how working in teams is evolving in today's organizations and about the importance of self-leadership in these new team contexts. Many people in organizations across the globe now work in virtual teams.[16] Members working in a virtual team rarely, if ever, interact face-to-face. Instead, they accomplish their work from remote locations and communicate through electronic media such as e-mail, video conferencing, instant messaging, and Skype. Virtual teams provide substantial cost savings to organizations, eliminating travel costs and enhancing long-distance information sharing, while allowing greater flexibility for team members through their ability to accomplish team tasks from any location, including their homes. Although to date little research has examined the role of self-leadership in virtual teams,[17] self-leadership processes would appear to be especially important in a virtual context, where team members are expected to work more autonomously and with less direct supervision and social support than in traditional face-to-face teams.

Table 6.1 Groupthink Versus Teamthink	
Groupthink	**Teamthink**
Direct social pressure against divergent views	Encouragement of divergent views
Self-censorship of concerns	Open expression of concerns/ideas
Illusion of invulnerability to failure	Awareness of limitations/threats
Illusion of unanimity	Recognition of members' uniqueness
Self-appointed mind guards that screen out external information	Recognition of views outside the group
Collective efforts to rationalize	Discussion of collective doubts
Stereotyped views of enemy leaders	Utilization of nonstereotypical views
Illusion of morality	Recognition of ethical and moral consequences of decisions

In summary, we have attempted to show in this chapter that self-leadership and teams are not conflicting concepts. Self-leadership is not only an integral dimension of individual performance but also a key element of team success.

REAL-WORLD SELF-LEADERSHIP CASE

Tragedy on Mount Everest

On May 10, 1996, four expeditions of climbers set out to summit Mount Everest, the highest mountain in the world at more than 29,000 feet above sea level and the grandest objective in all of mountaineering. Hours later, eight of the climbers would be dead and several more injured in what would become one of the most disastrous days in the mountain's history. Climbing Everest is an inherently dangerous undertaking, and hundreds of climbers have perished attempting to reach the summit. Summiting involves careful planning, tight controls, and close coordination. Climbers often leave the highest base camp, Camp IV, at midnight carrying canisters of oxygen that will last 16 to 17 hours. The objective is to summit early in the day, followed by a quick descent in advance of the relatively common afternoon snowstorms and full oxygen depletion, which occurs around 4:00 to 5:00 p.m. A turnaround time of noon is considered conservative, while a return time of 2:00 p.m. is viewed as risky.

By 1996, the Everest experience had been commercialized to the point that four groups of climbers were attempting to summit the relatively overcrowded mountain that day. Of note were two commercial expeditions, the first led by Rob Hall of Adventure Consultants and the second by Scott Fischer of Mountain Madness. Both were skilled and knowledgeable climbers who had experience summiting Everest. Hall's team was composed of fifteen climbers including clients and professional guides Mike Groom and Andy Harris, while Fischer's team had twelve members, including clients and guides Neal Beidleman and Anatoli Boukreev. Both teams included local Sherpa guides, whose mountaineering skill and experience are critical to successful Everest expeditions.

As they planned for the final push to the top, Hall and Fischer decided that they would pool their resources and work together. One Sherpa from each team would be dispatched ahead of the main groups to set the fixed ropes necessary to climb a technical area known as "The Balcony." However, one of the Sherpas, Lopsang Jangbu, was busy assisting a client and did not ascend in advance of the team to assist the second Sherpa, Anj Dorje, in setting the ropes. Dorje refused to work alone and consequently the ropes weren't set. When the main group of climbers reached The Balcony, a bottleneck ensued that substantially slowed down all the climbers while Anatoli Boukreev and Neal Beidleman worked on getting the ropes in place.

With a nasty storm forming beneath them, the delays and resulting slow climbing made it apparent that the teams would not be able to reach the summit by 2:00 p.m. However, instead of turning their clients around and heading back down the mountain, guides from both teams decided to keep going and attempt to summit. As was his habit, Boukreev climbed ahead of the main groups and reached the summit by himself. Although his boss, Fischer, disagreed with this practice, Boukreev believed that guides should not be responsible for babysitting clients and that anyone attempting to climb the mountain should be able to watch out for themselves. Consequently, Boukreev climbed entirely alone that day and did not help any climbers up or down the mountain, which could have resulted in a faster descent for all ahead of the fierce storm that would soon break.

Around 4:00 p.m., Rob Hall assisted client Doug Hansen in reaching the summit. Moments later as they began their descent, Hansen collapsed with his oxygen supplies exhausted. Hall refused to abandon him there. Meanwhile, Fischer and Jangbu were in serious trouble a few hundred feet lower, while the rest of the climbers, scattered at other locations on the mountain, were being enveloped by the thickening snow storm. In the end, Hansen, Hall, and Fischer would all die, along with five other members of the expeditions. The death toll could have been even worse if Boukreev (who later claimed he descended quickly in order to be fresh if called upon to assist in rescuing other descending climbers) and Beidleman had not literally dragged several of the remaining struggling climbers back to the safety of Camp IV. The 1996 Everest disaster remains one of the darkest chapters in the history of the lonely mountain.

Questions for Class Discussion

1. Do you think that better self-leadership among the members of the 1996 Everest expedition teams could have led to better decisions? How?

2. In what ways might groupthink have played a role in this disaster, and how could a teamthink approach have been beneficial in this situation?

3. In what way might the outcome have been different if members of the expeditions had more effectively balanced the "me" with the "we" in this case?

4. What would you have done if you had been a member of one of the 1996 expedition teams?

Sources/Additional Readings

Burnette, Jeni L., Jeffrey M. Pollack, and Donelson R. Forsyth. 2011. "Leadership in Extreme Contexts: A Groupthink Analysis of the May 1996 Mount Everest Disaster." *Journal of Leadership Studies* 4, no. 4 (Winter): 29–40.

Leger, C. J. 2016. "The 1996 Everest Disaster—The Whole Story." *Base Camp Magazine*, December 31, 2016. https://basecampmagazine.com/2016/12/31/the-1996-everest-disaster-the-whole-story/.

SELF-LEADERSHIP, HEALTH, AND WELL-BEING

Maintaining Physical and Emotional Fitness on the Journey

Physical fitness is the basis for all other forms of excellence.

—John F. Kennedy

U.S. Senator Arlen Specter once said, "There's nothing more important than our good health—that's our principal capital asset."[1] We agree with the senator that health and well-being, including both physical and emotional fitness, are an essential part of leading a productive and satisfying life. In this chapter, we will examine the relationships between self-leadership and physical fitness, emotional well-being, and stress management and coping.

SELF-LEADERSHIP AND FITNESS

Our author team truly believes that our physical fitness levels play an important role in determining our effectiveness in all aspects of our lives and that self-leadership strategies can help us obtain the fitness levels we desire.[2] For example, Christopher Neck has run twelve marathons and runs almost every day. He has completed a run of more than forty miles, and he follows a strict diet. Charles Manz also does aerobic exercise daily, as well as strength training; in addition, he watches what he eats and practices meditation and Tai Chi. Jeff Houghton has run a couple of marathons, rides mountain bikes, plays racquetball, and skis (downhill and cross-country), while following

Learning Objectives

After studying this chapter, you should be able to do the following:

1. Recognize the importance of fitness for overall physical and mental health and job performance.

2. Employ the self-leadership strategies presented in this book in the context of fitness.

3. Explain the concept of emotional self-leadership.

4. Contrast emotional intelligence with self-leadership.

5. Describe the process through which self-leadership can help to facilitate stress coping.

6. Recognize the relationships among optimism, explanatory style, and self-leadership.

7. Describe the relationships among happiness, flow, and self-leadership.

a healthy and nutritious diet. We all rely on a variety of self-leadership strategies (self-goal-setting, self-reward, cueing strategies, self-talk, mental imagery) to help us maintain our fitness activities. In fact, we have found that self-leadership contributes to good fitness habits, and good fitness enables us to be more personally effective in our work and lives. It is important to note that the focus of this chapter is on executives, but the lessons apply to all individuals, especially those who live hectic lives with busy schedules—which probably describes most people.

WHAT EXECUTIVES SAY ABOUT THE IMPORTANCE OF FITNESS

There's no question that people who are fit are more productive; they enjoy their work more and accomplish more.

—Dr. Jerome Zuckerman, exercise physiologist

The job of the executive has become more intense over the past decade. Executives are confronted with a profusion of demands—including physical ones. The global economic thrust of many businesses today has increased the amount of traveling CEOs must do to develop and maintain international presences for their companies. Another major physical demand is created by the stress related to being responsible for many people, their welfare, and the success of a company. Endless meetings and extremely long working hours are par for the course for executives. Executives who enjoy optimal fitness—that is, the ability to accomplish life's activities without undue fatigue—are able to handle these demands more constructively than their less fit counterparts and thus perform better in their daily tasks.

Data from personal interviews and related research provide evidence for this relationship between fitness and performance. For example, Rob Donat, founder and CEO of GPS Insight, states,

> Working out and staying fit is helpful to keep my overall stress down. It's great to go for a run or workout and think through issues or sometimes just clear my head of them until I can focus on them more clearly afterward.[3]

Eric R. Goldberg, M.D., clinical assistant professor of medicine at NYU Langone Medical Center, holds a similar perspective:

> Exercise and a healthy diet make me a better doctor—I am more focused and have more energy when I'm healthy. It also allows me to lead by example.[4]

Likewise, Tom Hatten, founder and CEO of Mountainside Fitness Centers, says,

> Staying fit gives me the competitive edge as an entrepreneur. Some may ask, how do you find time for exercise? My comment is how do I not find time for exercise? Getting adequate exercise and eating right actually gives me more time each day. I have more energy and think much clearer, plus, the more fit I am the better I can deal with the stressors that entrepreneurs have to confront each day.[5]

Matt Benedick, founder and CEO of What Could Be Better?, LLC, also believes that fitness can enhance performance in all areas of a person's life:

> I strive, daily, to keep my body and mind optimally fit through sound exercise, nutrition, and stress management principles, and have found that seeking and living by these greatly improves performance in all activities. Optimizing fitness, quite simply, optimizes effectiveness in all aspects of one's life.[6]

THE IMPACT OF FITNESS ON JOB PERFORMANCE

Various studies have shown that fitness promotes job performance. For instance, researchers have found that firefighters with higher levels of physical fitness perform better on the job. But the relationship between fitness and job performance is not limited to people with physically demanding jobs. Another study found a relationship between physical fitness and the academic performance of medical students. Similarly, a study found that commercial real estate brokers who participated in an aerobics training program (walking and/or running once a day, three times a week, for twelve weeks) earned larger sales commissions during and subsequent to the training program than did brokers who did not participate in the exercise program. Also, workers from a hospital equipment firm who participated in a similar aerobics training program (walking, running, swimming, and/or bicycling once a day, four times a week, for twenty-four weeks) enjoyed greater productivity and job satisfaction than did nonparticipating workers.[7]

In addition, the findings of a variety of studies support the relationship between fitness and mental performance, especially for individuals within the age range of many executives. For example, one study of fifty-six college professors revealed that in comparison with physically inactive people, active people process data faster and experience a slower decline in information-processing speed as they age.[8] Similarly, a study of postal workers ages eighteen to sixty-two found that older (forty-three to sixty-two years of age), less fit individuals consistently performed less well than older, more fit people and younger individuals (eighteen to thirty years old) on mental tasks involving information processing.[9] Another recent study reports similar results. Study participants engaged in an exercise test evaluating cardiorespiratory fitness assessed as peak VO_2 (maximum rate of oxygen consumption) followed by cognitive assessments using neuropsychological testing. Study findings suggest a relationship between peak VO_2 and cognitive function in older adults, but not in younger adults.[10]

An abundance of other benefits also are related to being fit. Individuals who are fit are less likely to become obese and more likely to have higher levels of energy and enjoy enhanced feelings of well-being.[11] Studies have shown that fit individuals (those who participate in aerobic activity) tend to enjoy various positive psychological outcomes as well, including a reduction in anxiety, depression, tension, and stress.[12] For example, Ken Reese, former executive vice president at Tenneco, utilized exercise to help him cope with the pressures of being a top executive:

> [There's] no question my exercise program has helped me cope with stress. If it starts to build up, I just go out and run like hell. I'm a morning runner, and that sets the tone for the whole day. By the time I get to the office, I'm relaxed.[13]

Physiological benefits have also been documented in individuals engaged in fitness programs. One study revealed improvements in cardiovascular function and strength, as well as reductions in body fat and weight, for sixty-six men engaged in a two-year exercise program located at their company's headquarters. A study led by Dr. Dean Ornish showed that lifestyle changes that included improved diet and exercise habits could reverse the atherosclerotic changes of coronary heart disease and unblock arteries enough so that subjects could avoid surgery. Finally, it has been estimated that 35 percent of cancers, the second leading cause of death in the United States, are related to diet.[14] In fact, a growing body of epidemiological evidence correlates diet with the incidence of cancer, particularly cancers of the esophagus, breast, prostate, and colon.[15]

Additionally, solid evidence shows that physically fit people live longer. In 1999, the *New England Journal of Medicine* published a study of more than 1 million adults over a fourteen-year period that confirmed that being overweight shortens a person's life. Additionally, several landmark studies at the Cooper Institute for Aerobics Research in Dallas have investigated the association between fitness and death. One of these seminal research projects investigated the relationship between fitness level and the risk of dying in more than ten thousand men and three thousand women. The study revealed that men and women with low levels of physical fitness had more than twice the mortality rate of persons with even a moderate level of physical fitness. Fitness in this case helped individuals overcome all causes of mortality, including diabetes, cancer, and heart disease.[16]

The major finding from this study and others—that physical fitness can prolong one's life—has tremendous significance for organizations and executives. Companies need to consider the fitness level of their executives in relation to potential company success. A top executive's illness or death can have far-reaching consequences for an organization. Dr. Jerrold Post, coauthor of *When Illness Strikes the Leader*, states,

> In a company where you have an entrepreneurial leader who is so identified with the company, that kind of event [death or serious illness of a key executive] will strike at the core of its corporate identity.[17]

To put it briefly, executive fitness is important not only to executives themselves but also to all the constituents of executives' organizations. The economic costs of cardiovascular disease (which research shows can be related to poor fitness habits) amounted to an estimated $320.1 billion in 2015.[18] Such losses affect both employers and employees in terms of lost workdays, lost wages, lost productivity, increased health care costs, and decreased morale.[19] The importance of employee and executive fitness is increasingly being recognized by CEOs such as Ryan Holmes of Hootsuite, who sees the value of fitness to his company:

> In my office—we're a tech company with around 600 employees focused on social media—exercise before, during and after working hours is encouraged. When we moved into a new headquarters several years ago, we installed a small gym and yoga room, as well as showers and changing rooms.

> . . . Yoga classes are packed before work, at lunch and after work. In the gym, volunteers from our company lead sweaty bootcamps and cross-training classes. Groups set out from our office for lunchtime runs and evening hikes. We have a hockey team and a road biking team and even a Quidditch team that does battle on broomsticks in the park.[20]

EXECUTIVE FITNESS BEHAVIORS AT A GLANCE

In light of the information above, the question arises: If fitness is so important, how many executives are doing something to optimize their fitness levels? According to various accounts, many executives indeed place a priority on their physical fitness. A survey of executives conducted by TheLadders.com, a privately held company offering online job search services to recruiters and job seekers in the high-end employment market, found that 75 percent of respondents agreed that good physical fitness is "critical for career success at the executive level," and 75 percent said that being overweight is a "serious career impediment." In addition, 73 percent of the executives surveyed felt that employers should provide on-site workout facilities or pay for gym memberships for employees.[21]

Despite these statistics suggesting that executives are prioritizing fitness in their lives, room for improvement still exists. A primary concern is that executives who are dedicated to fitness might be basing their exercise and diet routines on obsolete or incomplete data—that is, they may be following the fitness fad of the month or relying on outdated training methods and nutritional folklore.[22]

EXERCISE AND DIET: THE KEYS TO FITNESS

In their *Academy of Management Executive* article "The Fit Executive: Exercise and Diet Guidelines for Enhancing Performance," Christopher Neck and Kenneth Cooper attempt to correct misinformation on fitness as they outline exercise- and diet-related prescriptions that can help executives achieve the optimal levels of fitness necessary for superior performance.[23] They argue, in short, that endurance, strength, and flexibility are the focal points of an effective exercise program. Further, they state that adults should complete thirty minutes of moderate exercise per day, a recommendation supported by the American Heart Association's 2015 guidelines for optimal exercise.

What exactly is moderate exercise? Moderate exercise can be labeled as lower-intensity exercise. It involves exercising at one's target heart rate, which is the scientifically established higher-than-normal but less-than-maximum rate that allows an individual to improve his or her endurance. To determine your personal target heart rate, subtract your age from 220 to get your predicted maximal heart rate. Then calculate 65 percent and 80 percent of that figure to obtain your target heart rate range. For example, a forty-year-old would have a predicted maximal heart rate of 220 minus 40, or 180. Multiplying that figure by 0.65 and by 0.80 produces a target heart rate range for endurance exercise of 117 to 144 heartbeats per minute.

In regard to diet, Neck and Cooper suggest that for optimal fitness an adult should follow these guidelines:

- No more than 20 to 25 percent of daily calories should come from fat. Most of this fat intake should consist of monounsaturated and polyunsaturated fats; saturated fats should be avoided.

- About 50 to 70 percent of daily calories should come from complex carbohydrates, such as fruits, vegetables, legumes, and whole-grain products.

- About 10 to 20 percent of daily calories should come from protein sources such as fish, poultry, and lean meats.

Did You Know?

The following is a list of the calorie counts of some of the foods found at popular restaurants. Note that the average person needs about 2,000 to 2,500 calories per day.

Food	Calories
Cheese fries with ranch dressing	3,010
Fried whole onion with dipping sauce	2,130
Orange beef	1,770
Movie theater popcorn (large) with butter	1,640
Kung pao chicken	1,620
Sweet-and-sour pork	1,610
General Tso's chicken	1,600

Carrot Cake (The Cheesecake Factory)	1,560
Fettuccine Alfredo	1,500
House fried rice	1,480

Source: Center for Science in the Public Interest.

SELF-LEADERSHIP, FITNESS, AND PERSONAL EFFECTIVENESS

For most of us, health will depend not on who we are, but on how we live. The body you have at 20 depends on your genes, but the body you have at 40, 60, or 80 is the body you deserve, the body that reflects your behavior.

—Harvey B. Simon, M.D.

It is tough to motivate ourselves to exercise. Given our jobs, families, and other obligations, it is not difficult to talk ourselves out of going for that run or heading to the gym. It is much easier to grab fast food than to plan a healthy meal. The question is, How can you motivate yourself to stay fit, to exercise most days of the week, and to watch what you eat? The answer to this question lies in the concept of self-leadership. Next, we will discuss briefly how some of the self-leadership strategies outlined in the previous chapters can help you become more fit and thus more healthy and productive.

Self-Observation and Evaluation

Recall that self-observation and evaluation involve determining when, why, and under what conditions you exhibit certain behaviors. For example, if you feel you are not accomplishing enough each day (e.g., getting your workouts done) because you are wasting time, you can study the distractions you experience. If you discover that the TV sucks you in when you might otherwise be exercising, then you can remove the TV, or you could put a treadmill in the TV room so you can exercise while you watch. Are you failing to stick to an optimal diet? Perhaps by observing yourself you will notice that you eat inappropriately primarily when you are dining out. If that is the case, perhaps you can better achieve your fitness goals by limiting the number of times you go to restaurants during the week.

Removing Negative Cues

One strategy we can use to eliminate our fitness-related behaviors that we don't like is to eliminate cues that lead to these behaviors. For example, if we want to cut down on our consumption of sweets, we can remove the candy dish from the coffee table. Similarly, the TV may be serving as a negative cue. If we are disturbed about excessive time spent watching television (and the effect it is having on our exercise activity) and we don't want to remove the TV completely, we can move it to another room where we spend less time.

We are surrounded by physical cues that tend to encourage certain behaviors. If we can identify the things that encourage our undesired behaviors, we can either remove or alter them. In addition, we can remove ourselves from their presence. For example, if we want to eat a diet that follows the guidelines specified above, we might make that easier by eliminating cookies from the pantry and high-fat ice cream from the freezer. In fact, we can plan the furnishings and other features of the rooms in our homes with healthy, constructive living in mind. Similarly, we can design our work spaces to eliminate cues to destructive, unproductive behavior.

Increasing Positive Cues

We can also employ cues as a positive part of our self-leadership practices. For example, we can use physical objects to remind us of, or to focus our attention on, things we need to do. George W. Bush relies on this self-leadership strategy when he travels by making sure exercise equipment is located in his hotel room. For the former president, having the equipment in his room serves as a reminder and focuses his attention on his need to exercise when he travels. Other examples might include displaying a sign on the refrigerator that reminds us to eat a healthy, well-balanced diet, or placing an inspiring picture on the wall, such as one depicting an athlete performing well in a physical sport in which we engage.

Self-Goal-Setting

One especially effective way we can lead ourselves to perform challenging behaviors (e.g., exercising and eating right) is by setting personal goals. For example, we could set a goal of running a 10K race or a marathon, or taking a substantial hike. Such longer-term goals help create the context for setting shorter-term goals that can help us maintain fitness on a daily basis.

Self-set goals need to address both long-range targets and short-run objectives along the way. If we decide on a long-range goal of losing fifty pounds, we need to accomplish many shorter-range goals, such as exercising for thirty minutes five days a week. Meeting the shorter-range goals allows us to feel a sense of accomplishment on a smaller scale on the way to achieving the long-range goal. This process takes effort, and although our goals are likely to change over time, it is important that we have current goals for our immediate efforts.

Finding Natural Rewards

We need to find natural rewards in the tasks that we do to motivate ourselves to exercise and eat properly. An important part of self-leadership relies on the natural motivation derived from activities that we find rewarding because they make us feel more competent and self-controlling. Thus, an important lesson for becoming and staying fit is this: the fitness activities you choose should be those you like to do and are reasonably good at doing.

Purpose Development

In order to motivate yourself to exercise and eat appropriately on a daily basis, you have to decide that it is important to you. If it is, then you need to make exercise a priority in your life and pursue it with a sense of purpose. For instance, when he was the president of the United States, George W. Bush practiced this self-leadership strategy of "purpose development" by insisting that time for exercise be set aside each day (preferably at lunchtime) at the best time for his busy schedule. The importance that the president placed on fitness was reflected in the fact that he scheduled exercise into his workday. As Bush explained,

> A reporter who had looked at my calendar noticed that I had about an hour and a half off per day. I said, that is because I exercise every day. They asked if this was an indication that I do not work very hard. I said, no, it is an indication that I prioritize exercise. I told them [reporters] that I have given some of the greatest speeches of my life while running. . . . Running is therapy, running is a chance to be alone, a chance to think. . . . Running is an opportunity to be outdoors in fresh air. Running is a wholesome and important experience for me.[24]

Mental Imagery

Your mind can have a big impact on whether or not you achieve your goals—including your fitness goals. In short, if you think you can become fit, you can. Conversely, if you think you are too old, too busy, or too tired to maintain a fitness program, then you are!

Assume that you and a colleague have read the material in this book and have agreed to begin a fitness program in order to make you more fit individuals and thus more personally effective in your work and life. Suppose you picture in your mind becoming frustrated with your workout program because you keep finding excuses to skip your workout and not eat correctly, and eventually giving up on the program. You feel humiliated. This imagined experience could lead to lack of confidence and thus poor performance when you do begin your fitness program. Suppose your colleague imagines a positive experience (losing weight, feeling more energized) that results in enormous praise from coworkers and clients. This executive would likely possess a higher level of self-confidence before starting the fitness program and probably will enjoy the kind of success imagined. Mental imagery can help or deter you from becoming fit. It depends on which picture you choose to create in your mind.

Self-Talk

If you are having problems getting to the gym and eating the right types of foods, your difficulty could be related to what you are saying to yourself. For example, think for a moment. Have you ever told yourself any of the following?

- I don't have the talent.

- I don't feel like working out today.

- I hate to exercise.

- I don't have enough time to go running today.

- I've eaten two cookies so I might as well eat the whole bag.

- Running on a treadmill is boring.

- If I don't order dessert like everyone else, I'm going to look like a wimp.

If you are like most of us, you have told yourself negative things similar to these examples. These negative types of self-talk reduce your energy, your self-confidence, and your happiness; they also prevent you from achieving your fitness goals and feeling good about yourself. If you tell yourself you won't have a good day, you won't. If you tell yourself you can't lose weight, you won't. If you tell yourself that you don't enjoy working out, you won't. It is that simple. On the other hand, if you purposely choose positive self-statements (e.g., "This may be challenging, but I can do it and I will be healthier, feel better, and be more confident as a result"), you can improve your self-leadership of your fitness activities significantly.

Beliefs

Recall the categories of dysfunctional thinking outlined in Chapter 5 (extreme thinking, mind reading, and so on). Imagine that an executive attempts to eat in a more healthy manner but ends up gaining weight after two weeks of this new nutritional program (due to too much late-night snacking). The executive thinks, "I am a failure. I'll never be able to get fit."

This scenario presents an example of dysfunctional thinking based on the distorted belief of extreme thinking, which, as stated earlier, involves the tendency to evaluate a personal situation in extreme terms, seeing it as black or white. Rather than recognizing that some of the most fit people have failed in their early attempts to start fitness programs, the executive takes the extreme view that she has failed.

To alter this destructive belief, the executive must identify the dysfunction and then change the underlying thoughts so that they are more rational and constructive. She can challenge her private thoughts of being a complete failure and revise those beliefs by thinking, "Some of the most healthy and fit people have failed in attempts to lose weight and exercise more. I shall learn from this mistake. It's not the end of the world; I will do better next time."

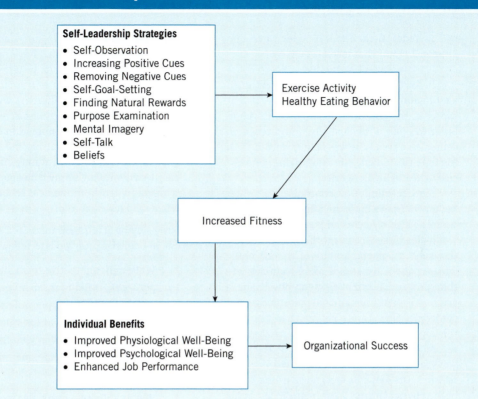

Figure 7.1 Self-Leadership/Fitness Framework Model

Self-Leadership Strategies
- Self-Observation
- Increasing Positive Cues
- Removing Negative Cues
- Self-Goal-Setting
- Finding Natural Rewards
- Purpose Examination
- Mental Imagery
- Self-Talk
- Beliefs

Exercise Activity
Healthy Eating Behavior

Increased Fitness

Individual Benefits
- Improved Physiological Well-Being
- Improved Psychological Well-Being
- Enhanced Job Performance

Organizational Success

To summarize this discussion of fitness and how self-leadership strategies can help you achieve optimal fitness levels (and the related benefits), Figure 7.1 depicts the "self-leadership/fitness" framework. As the figure illustrates, self-leadership can help you increase your fitness, which in turn will result in a plethora of benefits to you as well as to your organization.

CHOOSING HOW YOU FEEL: EMOTIONAL SELF-LEADERSHIP

Although the self-leadership of physical fitness is extremely important, we have another particularly powerful perspective to share that concerns the direct self-leadership of emotion, or *emotional self-leadership*. First, consider the meaning of the concept of *emotion*. Researchers Salovey and Mayer have defined emotions as "organized responses, crossing the boundaries of . . . physiological, cognitive, motivational, and experiential

Dr. Kenneth H. Cooper

by T. L. (Tedd) Mitchell, M.D., Cooper Clinic, and Emmet C. (Tom) Thompson II, DSL, MS

In 1970, Dr. Kenneth H. Cooper resigned as a lieutenant colonel from a thirteen-year career in the U.S. Air Force Medical Corps in order to open a medical clinic and research center. As a result, he was able to devote all of his time to studying the relationship of exercise to health and longevity.

Since that time, the Cooper Aerobics Center has grown from a one-man office in a shopping center to a thirty-acre campus that includes a world-class fitness center with more than three thousand members, a state-of-the-art clinic with a patient register of more than seventy thousand and a staff of eighteen physicians, a sixty-two-room colonial-style guest lodge and conference center, and a research institute with the largest computerized exercise database on record (containing approximately 350,000 person years of data). Because of his writings and research, Dr. Cooper is recognized as the father of the physical fitness movement. Today, in his eighties, he still helps to lead the Aerobics Center as its founder and chairman.

Information obtained in an interview with Dr. Cooper clearly indicates that self-leadership is a key to his career success. For example, self-goal-setting and purpose examination are important self-leadership tactics he has practiced to achieve personal, fitness, and career success. When Dr. Cooper was asked how he had achieved so much, he was quick to point out that maintaining a daily routine was his first goal. If this initial goal is achieved, Dr. Cooper reasons, all other goals are achievable. The following outlines a typical day in the life of the "father of fitness":

I start my day with prayer and Bible study. My staff knows that that is my quiet time, and I do not want interruptions. In addition, I have my prayer list that I refer to daily. When I finish my day, I exercise. If I cannot exercise before I go home, I will walk approximately two miles at ten o'clock at night. That combination of spiritual and physical discipline is one reason I am still functioning efficiently when many of my colleagues who graduated from medical school when I did have expired.

Obviously, staying fit is important to Dr. Cooper's success. His exercise program is as follows:

- **Walking/jogging:** five to six days per week; walking three miles at thirteen minutes per mile or jogging three miles at ten minutes per mile or walking/jogging three miles at eleven minutes per mile (averages)

- **Weights:** Twice a week; five exercises at 65 percent capacity; twelve to fifteen repetitions for approximately twenty minutes' duration total

- **Stretching:** Twice a week for three to five minutes

Having a purpose is fundamental to self-leadership. Indeed, having a purpose is a catalyst for achieving happiness and productivity and for organizing life. Dr. Cooper's purpose has been to provide a medical practice that is built on his own personal core values. This internalization of values has provided Dr. Cooper with passion for his purpose. By combining purpose with a passion, he has created a force that has helped him achieve his goals.

systems."[25] This definition suggests that emotions are experienced both mentally and physically. In other words, emotions might be thought of as reflections of ongoing thought activity in the body. Any given emotion involves not only thoughts but also physical sensations, such as pain or discomfort felt in particular parts of the body as a result of negative thoughts or pleasant sensations as a result of positive thoughts. Being able to choose what emotions we experience could have a profound impact on how we feel and thereby influence how we behave and perform.

Research completed under the general label of "emotion regulation" has focused specifically on the potential for self-regulation of emotion. According to James Gross, a leading researcher in this area, emotions can be misleading, and when individuals experience emotions that do not match their situations well, they may attempt to regulate their emotional responses to help them reach their goals.[26] Gross defines emotion regulation as "the processes by which we influence which emotions we have, when we have them, and how we experience and express them."[27]

More recently, researchers have introduced the concept of *emotional self-leadership*, which involves the self-leadership of one's emotional experiences.[28] We can apply emotional self-leadership strategies to regulate our emotions more effectively when we are dealing with difficult emotional situations, increasing positive emotions while reducing both negative emotional experiences and dysfunctional behaviors.[29] Emotional self-leadership offers the potential to reduce negative effects such as those connected with "emotional labor"—the stress and strain associated with being pressured to display artificial emotions in many service jobs, such as acting like a courteous and cheerful wait staff member or salesperson even when upset about a sick child at home or a rude customer. The keys to emotional self-leadership appear to be that it is exercised with awareness and authenticity, and that it fosters positive emotion.

The strategy of emotional self-leadership seems especially promising because evidence suggests that the experience of positive, as opposed to negative, emotion can enhance both our effectiveness and our health. For example, University of North Carolina researcher Barbara Fredrickson's studies suggest that positive emotions such as joy, interest, contentment, gratitude, and love can provide many valuable benefits. Research on her "broaden and build" theory indicates that positive emotions expand our options for thought and action and thereby open up the possibilities for creativity, exploration, integration, and engagement in a variety of activities that increase our mental, behavioral, and social resources.[30] Positive emotions have been connected with beneficial states such as increased attention and improved information processing as well as a variety of significant cardiovascular, immune response, and other health benefits.[31] In contrast, negative emotions, such as fear and anger, tend to reduce our potential options to limited choices such as escape or attack.[32]

Emotional self-leadership is all the more significant given that emotions expressed in the workplace and other life settings have demonstrated a capacity to be contagious. For example, emotional self-leadership efforts that result in positive emotions can lead to similar emotional experiences for others, and this can consequently foster increased constructive behaviors within organizations, such as helpfulness toward customers.[33]

Emotional Self-Leadership Strategies

There are many strategies for influencing emotions.[34] Some are applied before emotion arises. For example, we can choose pleasant activities or redesign a work process in order to make it more enjoyable, or simply focus on the positive aspects of a work situation. We can also reinterpret a difficult situation—for example, we can view a disagreement with a coworker as a useful problem-solving session rather than as a frustrating argument. Other strategies are applied after emotion has already been triggered, such as purposely suppressing an emotional reaction (by taking a deep, relaxing breath or counting to ten) to avoid a destructive argument that might create longer-term work relationship problems. We might also choose to view an upsetting situation as an opportunity to further develop healthy coping skills.

Many other strategies for emotion regulation are available. For example, we can use strategies that appeal to our primary senses. Some colors can foster positive, motivating, and more secure feelings about ourselves and our current life contexts.[35] Also, some music and other sounds can promote positive feelings such as relaxation; we might expose ourselves to these when we are feeling stressed or when we are seeking emotional inspiration before making a speech.[36] Even fragrances can trigger moods and reduce stress.[37] A multitude of strategies can be used in unique ways that fit well with particular individuals or specific circumstances, such as strategic use of physical exercise, meditation breaks, and reflective thought techniques. The possibilities are nearly endless.

EMOTIONAL INTELLIGENCE AND SELF-LEADERSHIP

Emotional self-leadership and emotion regulation processes have some similarities with the popular concept of *emotional intelligence* (EI).[38] In fact, emotion regulation is usually included as one of the four primary components of emotional intelligence, along with emotion perception, emotion assimilation, and emotion understanding.[39] EI involves the ability to perceive, understand, and regulate our own or another person's emotions.[40] It may be further defined as a subset of social intelligence involving "the ability to carry out accurate reasoning about emotions and the ability to use emotions and emotional knowledge to enhance thought."[41] An emotionally intelligent person can be described as having the capability to "recognize and use his or her own and others' emotional states to solve problems and regulate behavior."[42] However, even if we have confidence in our capabilities to perform our work tasks, if an upsetting situation arises and causes us to feel emotionally disturbed, and if we have little confidence in our capacity to cope effectively with these feelings, we can end up feeling powerless. Thus, having confidence in our ability to self-lead our emotions can be a critical part of our effectiveness.

Although some people may view emotion regulation as simply one component of emotional intelligence, the two concepts can be distinguished at a more basic level.

EI is often conceptualized as either (1) a capacity or an ability demonstrated by certain people, known as *ability* EI, or (2) a constellation of personality traits and self-perceived abilities, known as *mixed* EI.[43] Both types of EI represent *abilities* or *characteristics* on which individuals can draw in their efforts to cope with and respond to emotion-provoking situations and events. Emotion regulation and emotional self-leadership, in contrast, involve *actual processes* of influencing emotions, including specific choices and actions designed to shape emotions both before and after they arise.[44] Thus, it appears that EI and self-leadership, especially emotional self-leadership, may be complementary concepts that work together to help people manage their emotions and increase their personal effectiveness.

COPING WITH STRESS: SELF-LEADERSHIP AND STRESS MANAGEMENT

Being in control of your life and having realistic expectations about your day-to-day challenges are the keys to stress management, which is perhaps the most important ingredient to living a happy, healthy and rewarding life.

—Marilu Henner

A substantial amount of research has examined the negative impacts of stress on people in the workplace in general and on students in educational contexts specifically.[45] It has been estimated that the annual cost of stress in the workplace in the United States is approximately $300 billion.[46] Stress may be defined as "a relationship between the person and the environment that is appraised by the person as relevant to his or her well-being and in which the person's resources are taxed or exceeded."[47] Research further suggests that there are three types of psychological stress: threat, challenge, and harm/loss. When a person evaluates a situation and arrives at a threat assessment, he or she perceives the likelihood of harm that will create a loss. When a challenge assessment is made, an individual perceives the situation more as an opportunity for growth or achievement. In contrast, a harm/loss appraisal occurs when an individual perceives that an injury or loss has already occurred.[48]

Stress is often studied in the context of emotions.[49] As discussed above, emotion is often experienced both physically and mentally. Consequently, researchers have suggested that "the ability to generate alternative explanations for emotional events, and keeping these alternative appraisals in mind for the duration of the eliciting stimulus, is required for effective reframing of the emotional stimulus."[50] Effective emotional, behavioral, and cognitive self-leadership strategies may be capable of providing the means for the "alternative appraisals" needed for the "effective reframing" of emotions. More precisely, self-leadership strategies such as positive self-talk, visualizing successful outcomes, and challenging dysfunctional beliefs and assumptions may help us to reframe threat assessments as challenge assessments, resulting in more positive emotions and a greater ability to cope with stress. Positive emotions are one of several key predictable outcomes of self-leadership strategies, and a growing body of research evidence provides support for this relationship.[51]

Self-leadership research and theory suggest that a major objective of self-leadership strategies is the enhancement of individuals' perceptions of self-efficacy (see Chapter 2).[52] For instance, a study of self-leadership training showed a significant difference in self-efficacy levels between a training group and a no-training control group, and another study reported significant relationships between self-leadership strategies and self-efficacy perceptions, as well as between those strategies and task performance.[53] In addition, stress researchers have identified positive emotions as a key factor in individuals' ability to appraise and cope with stressful situations effectively.[54] For example, two longitudinal studies involving caregivers for persons with AIDS showed that three kinds of effective stress coping resulted from positive emotions: positive reappraisal; goal-directed, problem-focused coping; and infusion of ordinary events with positive meaning.[55] Research also has suggested a relationship between self-efficacy perceptions and effective stress coping.[56] For example, a recent study involving athletes reported a significant relationship between self-efficacy for coping with stressful situations and actual coping effectiveness, while another study found that in stressful job situations people with high self-efficacy tend to behave more proactively and use problem-centered coping more often than do people with low self-efficacy.[57]

SELF-LEADERSHIP RESEARCH

Self-Leadership, Coping, and Stress in College Students

In this chapter, we suggest that self-leadership is related to effective stress coping. Recently, two studies examined self-leadership relative to coping and stress in college students. The first study, involving 575 students at two Chinese universities, found a direct relationship between self-leadership and active stress coping by students.[1] However, this study did not examine actual student stress. In an effort to delve deeper into the role of self-leadership as a potential stress management tool for students, a second study of 634 students at a university in the United States found that self-leadership was negatively related to actual student stress levels and that the relationship was moderated by the level of students' coping skills.[2] Taken together, these studies suggest that self-leadership, especially when combined with active coping, may be an effective tool for reducing stress levels, especially among college students.

Notes

1. Yefei Wang, Guangrong Xie, and Xilong Cui, "Effects of Emotional Intelligence and Self-Leadership on Students' Coping With Stress," *Social Behavior and Personality* 44, no. 5 (2016): 853–64.

2. Sherry A. Maykrantz and Jeffery D. Houghton, "Self-Leadership and Stress Among College Students: Examining the Moderating Role of Coping Skills," *Journal of American College Health* (Forthcoming).

Figure 7.2   A Model of Self-Leadership and Stress Coping

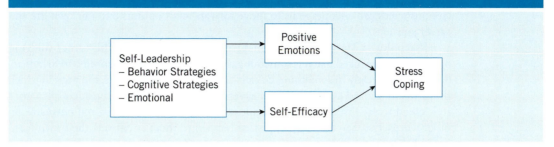

Source: Adapted from Jeffery D. Houghton, Jinpei Wu, Jeffrey L. Godwin, Christopher P. Neck, and Charles C. Manz, "Effective Stress Management: A Model of Emotional Intelligence, Self-Leadership, and Student Stress Coping," *Journal of Management Education* 36, no. 2 (April 2012): 220–38.

The model presented in Figure 7.2 serves to summarize this discussion of the relationship between self-leadership and stress coping. This model suggests that self-leadership strategies, especially emotional self-leadership strategies, result in more positive emotions and higher self-efficacy for coping with stressful situations. More positive emotions and higher self-efficacy levels in turn lead to more effective stress coping.

In Chapter 2, we introduced some ideas from the field of positive psychology. In the following sections we expand on the roles of three key concepts from positive psychology—optimism, happiness, and flow—as they relate to self-leadership and personal well-being.

OPTIMISM AND SELF-LEADERSHIP

In his book *Man's Search for Meaning*, Austrian psychiatrist Viktor E. Frankl describes his experiences as a prisoner in Nazi concentration camps and shares the life lessons he learned from his own and others' responses to terrible circumstances.[58] Utilizing his medical education and professional experiences as a psychiatrist, Frankl taught himself to view the world and the human condition optimistically in the midst of his being subjected to horrific conditions. He developed what he called "tragic optimism" as he learned to exert intentional control over his own internal life and thus control how he personally made sense of and responded to external events. His idea is illustrated in the following example:

> We who lived in concentration camps can remember the men who walked through the huts comforting others, giving away their last piece of bread. They may have been few in number, but they offer sufficient proof that everything can be taken from a man but one thing: the last of the human freedoms—to choose one's attitude in any given set of circumstances, to choose one's own way.[59]

Fortunately, most of us will never have to experience the life-and-death circumstances of a concentration camp. But Frankl's ability to choose optimism in the midst of such circumstances can encourage us to move forward with optimism in our own life and career journeys.

Psychologist Martin E. P. Seligman, who has spent much of his career studying optimism, is convinced that it is something that can be learned.[60] According to Seligman, people differ greatly in something he calls explanatory style—that is, the ways in which they explain the bad events that they experience. People with pessimistic explanatory styles tend to see problems and difficulties as personal, permanent, and pervasive. In other words, they see the bad things that happen to them as entirely their own fault, as unlikely ever to get better, and as having impacts on every aspect of their lives. This type of explanatory style is very similar to obstacle thinking, as discussed in Chapter 6. In contrast, people with optimistic explanatory styles tend to see bad events in their lives as impersonal, temporary, and specific. That is, they see these bad things as unrelated to them personally or at least not entirely their fault, as things that can be overcome, and as relating only to particular aspects of their lives. The optimistic explanatory style is comparable to opportunity thinking. In addition, Seligman has found in his research that people who express gratitude on a daily basis and enjoy their daily experiences tend to be more satisfied with their lives.

Many studies have shown that individual differences in explanatory style can have a direct bearing on success in life areas such as work, school, and sports.[61] For example, one study found that people with optimistic explanatory styles were more successful in selling life insurance than people with pessimistic explanatory styles.[62] The reason for the difference is simple. Insurance salespeople are told no many times a day, often several times in a row. Optimists are not easily discouraged by these types of setbacks and tend to keep trying no matter how many times they are told no. In contrast, pessimistic salespeople tend to become discouraged by their failures. They do not persist in the face of such difficulties—they are more likely to give up and stop trying. Another group of studies suggests that professional sports teams and individual athletes with optimistic explanatory styles tend to outperform teams and athletes with comparable talent levels but more pessimistic outlooks.[63] Explanatory styles may even help to determine who wins political elections! In 1988, researchers were able to predict George H. W. Bush's election victory over Michael Dukakis based on Bush's higher levels of optimism in his campaign speeches. In fact, an analysis of campaign speeches of presidential candidates from 1900 to 1984 found that the more optimistic candidate won in eighteen out of twenty-two elections.[64]

Fortunately, as we have mentioned, optimism can be learned, and self-leadership skills can help. Although we know that some people naturally tend to think more pessimistically than others, with a little effort we all can learn to make our explanatory style more optimistic.

Many of the self-leadership strategies discussed in Chapter 5 can have direct influence on our thought patterns, making our thinking increasingly optimistic or opportunistic. We can improve our explanatory style by identifying and subsequently disputing negative self-talk that explains disappointing outcomes as personal ("It's all my fault"), permanent ("It will never get better"), and pervasive ("It relates to every aspect of my life"). We can build a more successful explanatory style with positive and functional self-dialogue that views setbacks as impersonal, temporary, and specific. Furthermore, through the process of confronting, challenging, and replacing our dysfunctional beliefs with more rational, realistic, and functional ones, we can lead ourselves to a more optimistic outlook. Finally, we can increase our optimism by engaging in mental practice in which we visualize successful performance of a task before actual performance.

HAPPINESS, FLOW, AND SELF-LEADERSHIP

Happiness depends upon ourselves.

—Aristotle

Some people appear to be happy and content all the time, whereas others appear to be generally depressed and discontent. The differences in people's outlooks undoubtedly relate in part to the circumstances in which individuals find themselves, but as Frankl and others who have experienced difficult and even tragic circumstances have shown, happiness is possible even under the most trying of conditions. Many people feel that happiness and depression are emotions over which they have little or no control, but recent advances in the field of psychology suggest that happiness may have more to do with the way we interact with the world around us than with the actual circumstances in which we find ourselves.

In addition to his work on optimism, Seligman has carefully studied human happiness, and he suggests several ways in which we can change our approach to the world around us to increase our individual happiness.[65] Specifically, Seligman recommends that people identify their "signature strengths." These are strengths that they already possess to varying degrees and include things such as creativity, persistence, and humor. Seligman identifies twenty-four specific strengths organized into six categories. The key is to identify your own set of signature strengths and then practice these strengths on a regular basis. By routinely utilizing your signature strengths, you will learn to interact more positively with the world around you. You will also be better equipped to deal with, and appropriately react to, the negative things that happen to you; this in turn will reduce your experiences of negative emotions and increase your happiness.

If you are interested in identifying and learning more about your signature strengths and your general levels of happiness and optimism, we encourage you to visit Seligman's Authentic Happiness website (www.authentichappiness.sas.upenn.edu). The site provides eighteen self-assessment questionnaires that will help you to identify your signature strengths and your general levels of happiness and optimism. Site usage is free with required registration, which involves providing some nonidentifying demographic data (e.g., sex, age, occupation).

Beasts of the Southern Wild (2012)

The opening scene from the movie *Beasts of the Southern Wild* helps to illustrate the relationship between self-leadership, optimism, happiness, and stress management. A six-year-old girl named Hushpuppy (Quvenzhané Wallis) lives with her father, Wink, in "The Bathtub," an isolated offshore bayou community near New Orleans that recently has been cut off from the world by a new levee system built in the aftermath of Hurricane Katrina. Hushpuppy provides a narration at the beginning of the movie that describes how her father tells her that "The Dry Side" (i.e., the industrialized, first-world city areas) doesn't have anything that The Bathtub doesn't have. As Hushpuppy explains, "They think we all gonna drown down here. But we ain't goin' nowhere. The Bathtub has more holidays than the whole rest of the world!" The residents of The Bathtub are aware of what life is like on The Dry Side, but they make it clear that there is nowhere else they would rather live.

Discussion Questions

1. Do the people living in The Bathtub take an optimistic or pessimistic view of their situation, and how does this affect the "reality" of their world?

2. Mihaly Csikszentmihalyi has said, "People who learn to control inner experience will be able to determine the quality of their lives, which is as close as any of us can come to being happy." Why are the people living in The Bathtub happy, despite their poverty and difficult living conditions?

3. What self-leadership strategies do you think the people living in The Bathtub could use to further reduce their stress and increase their happiness?

Psychologist Mihaly Csikszentmihalyi (pronounced CHICK-sent-me-high-ee), one of the primary founders of the positive psychology movement, has developed a concept that he calls "psychological flow." This concept has parallels to the idea of majestic moments that we presented in Chapter 4. Csikszentmihalyi describes his concept of psychological flow in terms of the joy and creativity that come from the process of total involvement with life.[66] His insightful ideas about flow, published over the past twenty-five years, provide a general framework for developing a theory of life enjoyment as well as practical methods that can help you achieve happiness within your personal life and career.

Csikszentmihalyi states that we must be the creator and protector of our own personal happiness:

Happiness, in fact, is a condition that must be prepared for, cultivated, and defended privately by each person. People who learn to control inner experience will be able to determine the quality of their lives, which is as close as any of us can come to being happy.[67]

Thinking about controlling our inner experiences introduces the concept of human consciousness, which Csikszentmihalyi defines as "intentionally ordered information" regarding our relationships with the external physical and social world. Csikszentmihalyi suggests that "the most important step in emancipating oneself from social controls is the ability to find rewards in the events of each moment."[68] Essentially, he is saying that to discover happiness, we need to focus on the moment and the journey rather than on following social norms or expecting the perceived rewards for our efforts.

Flow tends to occur when goals are clear and provide immediate feedback and when the challenge of an activity is roughly equivalent to the individual's capacity to perform the activity. Flow experiences are generally characterized by an intense concentration that allows the person to become completely absorbed by the activity while being distracted from any unpleasant aspects of life. Flow creates feelings of control and an absence of worry about losing control of one's situation. Interestingly, the experience of time itself can seem to be suspended, and the individual can sometimes lose all awareness of the self. When the flow experience ends and awareness of the self returns, it is often a new and improved self that has been enriched by the enhanced skills and achievements that have resulted from the flow experience.

The comments of a rock climber who experiences flow while climbing may serve as an illustration: "You are so involved in what you are doing [that] you aren't thinking of yourself as separate from the immediate activity. . . . You don't see yourself as separate from what you are doing."[69] Likewise, a dancer explains the feeling accompanying a dance performance: "Your concentration is very complete. Your mind isn't wandering, you are not thinking of something else; you are totally involved in what you are doing. . . . Your energy is flowing very smoothly. You feel relaxed, comfortable, and energetic."[70] Similarly, a chess player speaks of the concentration required in a chess tournament: "The concentration is like breathing—you never think of it. The roof could fall in and, if it missed you, you would be unaware of it."[71] And finally, a young athlete describes the sense of flow that comes from participating in his sport: "Kids my age, they think about a lot . . . but when you are playing basketball, that's all there is on your mind—just basketball. . . . Everything else seems to follow right along."[72]

People tend to describe their flow experiences in very similar terms regardless of their gender, age, cultural background, education, occupation, or chosen sport or personal interests. And flow experiences are not limited to affluent people living in industrialized countries. Flow experiences have been described in similar ways by inner-city teenagers, assembly-line workers, welders, elderly women in Korea, Navajo shepherds, and Italian alpine farmers.[73]

Happiness, then, far from being a fleeting and uncontrollable emotion, is to a large extent something over which we have direct control. By using our signature strengths (Seligman) and cultivating our personal flow experiences (Csikszentmihalyi), we can have significant influence on our overall levels of happiness. Furthermore, our self-leadership skills can play an important role in these processes. For example, through self-observation of our behaviors (Chapter 3) and analysis of our thinking patterns, we can become more aware of how we might better utilize our signature strengths on a regular basis. Likewise, we can use self-goal-setting (Chapter 3) to create clear goals with immediate feedback—the kinds of goals that are integral to experiencing flow. The goals we set for ourselves should allow us to use our signature strengths and should be challenging enough to require intense concentration and cause us to utilize our fullest capacities in performing the tasks. Self-leadership strategies would also suggest that we should focus much of our effort on pursuing goals involving activities that we find naturally rewarding. Natural rewards (Chapter 4) can help us to enjoy the moment as well as the journey, finding happiness in both. Finally, engaging in positive self-talk, identifying and replacing irrational and dysfunctional beliefs, and mental practice can all lead to more optimistic and opportunistic thinking patterns, which in turn can put us in a healthier frame of mind that will better enable us to utilize our signature strengths and experience psychological flow. As Leo Rosten once said, "Happiness comes only when we push our brains and hearts to the farthest reaches of which we are capable."[74] Self-leadership can help us to apply our signature strengths effectively, so that we can find those farthest reaches of our capabilities and experience psychological flow, personal satisfaction, and, ultimately, happiness.

In this chapter we have examined the key role that self-leadership can play in helping us to maintain our health and well-being. Self-leadership strategies can be especially useful in facilitating physical fitness, and emotional self-leadership strategies can help us to experience more positive emotions and enhance our overall emotional well-being. Self-leadership strategies may offer very useful tools for coping with stressful situations, resulting in lower levels of stress and fewer stress-related illnesses. Finally, self-leadership strategies may play a key role in increasing optimism, happiness, and the experience of flow. We hope that the information in this chapter will help you in your personal journey toward physical and emotional fitness and well-being.

REAL-WORLD SELF-LEADERSHIP CASE

U.S. Olympic Athletes, Mental Imagery, and Performance Stress

Olympic athletes face tremendous pressure and scrutiny as they compete for medals, often resulting in high levels of stress and anxiety. Two-time Olympic gold medalist alpine skier Mikaela Shiffrin is not immune to battling nerves and has been known to become physically ill before her races. This is why Shiffrin and other Olympic athletes are spending increasing amounts of time on mental preparation. "I think it's

something that's undervalued," Shiffrin explains. "I've experienced a lot more mental stress these last two years than I ever had. I don't know what it was about last season, but I . . . felt a lot more anxiety."

One of the primary self-leadership strategies that has become increasingly popular among world-class athletes is mental practice (see Chapter 5), sometimes referred to as "visualization" or "imagery." Imagery is preferred by some because of the multisensory nature of the technique. "Visualization, for me, doesn't take in all the senses," said former Olympic skiing aerialist Emily Cook. "You have to smell it. You have to hear it. You have to feel it, everything." Cook first began using mental imagery while working with sport psychologist Nicole Detling of the University of Utah after breaking bones in both her feet during a crash. While recovering, she couldn't physically practice, so she mentally practiced using imagery strategies involving writing and making recordings of detailed scripts that explained every minute component of the competition process. "I would say into the recorder: 'I'm standing on the top of the hill. I can feel the wind on the back of my neck. I can hear the crowd,'" Cook said. "Kind of going through all those different senses and then actually going through what I wanted to do for the perfect jump. I turn down the in-run. I stand up. I engage my core. I look at the top of the jump. I was going through every little step of how I wanted that jump to turn out." She would then play back the recording while she closed her eyes and focused on the feeling of her muscles firing as she imagined the jump. If fear or negative thoughts invaded her imagery, she would instantly switch to imagining a red balloon being popped with a pin. "That sound and that immediate switch would kind of snap me out of it," she explained. "The last couple years, I've definitely gotten to a point where when I'm on the hill, it's very quick for me to switch from a negative thought to a positive one." Detling stresses the importance of positive imagery: "It's absolutely crucial that you don't fail. You are training those muscles, and if you are training those muscles to fail, that is not really where you want to be. So one of the things

I'll do is if they fail in an image, we stop, rewind and we replay again and again and again."

Shiffrin uses imagery and visualization techniques too. Prior to a race, she usually visualizes the course once after her inspection and again just before the start of her run when she can often be seen with her hands thrust forward, moving back and forth, as she simulates the race course in her mind. "Sometimes eyes closed, sometimes eyes open, but I'm always kind of zoned out," Shiffrin notes. Although some elite athletes warn that too much visualization can lead to "paralysis by analysis," most Olympic athletes find mental imagery techniques to be both helpful and reassuring. "I don't think I could possibly do a jump, or especially a new trick, without having this imagery process," Cook stated near the end of her successful Olympic career. "For me, this is so very key to the athlete I have become."

Questions for Class Discussion

1. In what ways can Olympic athletes benefit from self-leadership strategies in their sports?

2. Give some specific examples of how an athlete could use the strategy of mental imagery to overcome stress and improve performance.

3. Could people in pressure performance situations other than those in sports benefit in similar ways from applying these strategies? Give some specific examples.

Sources/Additional Reading

Clarey, Christopher. 2014. "Olympians Use Imagery as Mental Training." *New York Times*, February 22, 2014. https://www.nytimes.com/2014/02/23/sports/olympics/olympians-use-imagery-as-mental-training.html.

Peters, Josh. 2018. "Olympic Ski Star Mikaela Shiffrin Felt Like She'd Throw Up Before Races." *USA Today*, February 11, 2018. https://www.usatoday.com/story/sports/winter-olympics-2018/2018/02/11/olympic-ski-star-mikaela-shiffrin-felt-like-she-throw-up-before-races/327120002/.

8

INDIVIDUAL DIFFERENCES, DIVERSITY, AND PRACTICAL APPLICATIONS

Multiple Paths to Uniqueness

What lies behind us and what lies before us are tiny matters compared to what lies within us.

—Ralph Waldo Emerson

No two people are exactly alike. The term *individual differences* is sometimes used to refer to the characteristics that make people different from one another. Individual differences include things such as personality traits, gender, age, cultural background, education, and work experience. Your innate or learned self-leadership abilities and skills can help you to both shape and respond to the characteristics and tendencies that make you who you are. A first purpose of this chapter, therefore, is to examine how self-leadership interacts with individuals' own distinct attributes. By gaining an understanding of these interactions, you may become better prepared to discover and follow the path to your own uniqueness.[1]

A second purpose of this chapter is to provide some real-life examples and applications in support of our argument that self-leadership techniques and strategies offer many potential benefits when they are practiced effectively and systematically. The discussion will touch on three categories of self-leadership application: personal problems, athletics, and organizational/work problems. We will address applications to personal problems and athletics briefly before turning to organizational/work challenges, which are the primary focus of this book. By presenting these different types of applications, we hope to demonstrate the wide applicability and potential of self-leadership strategies.

Learning Objectives

After studying this chapter, you should be able to do the following:

1. Explain the concept of individual differences.

2. Compare the relationships between various personality concepts and self-leadership.

3. Discuss the relationships among age, gender, cultural differences, and self-leadership.

4. Identify the concepts of the protean career and work–life balance.

5. Provide examples of the ways in which self-leadership strategies can be applied to personal problems.

6. Describe some of the ways in which self-leadership strategies can be applied to athletics.

7. Recognize the ways in which self-leadership strategies can be applied to work/organizational positions, including uniquely autonomous jobs, organizational management jobs, and nonmanagement jobs.

PERSONALITY AND SELF-LEADERSHIP

Personality is one of the most fundamental ways in which people differ from one another. Personality may be described as the relatively stable pattern of traits and characteristics that help to shape a person's behavior and make the person unique. Unlike optimism and happiness, which can be changed and shaped by our self-leadership, personality characteristics remain fairly stable and constant over time. Nevertheless, psychological research suggests that personality is related to self-leadership in important and interesting ways.[2] Our personality characteristics play a large role in determining whether we are predisposed to be natural self-leaders or will have to learn, practice, and work a little harder to develop our self-leadership skills. Below, we provide a brief overview of the relationships between self-leadership and several key personality characteristics.

The Myers-Briggs Type Indicator

The Myers-Briggs Type Indicator (MBTI) is one of the most popular and widely used means of assessing and understanding personality differences.[3] Based on the personality theories of Swiss psychiatrist Carl Jung, the MBTI was created by the mother–daughter team of Katherine Briggs and Isabel Briggs-Myers; it is used to assess the ways in which individuals perceive their environments, make decisions, and process information. The MBTI determines a person's orientation on four sets of preference dyads: extraversion–introversion, sensing–intuition, thinking–feeling, and judging–perceiving.

Extraverts are energized by the external world of people and things, while introverts are energized by the internal world of ideas and images. Consequently, extraverts tend to be outgoing, talkative, and sociable, whereas introverts tend to be reserved. While introverts may also engage in outgoing, talkative, and sociable activities, they are energized or recharged internally, in contrast to extraverts, who are charged up through social interactions. People with a preference for sensing gather information with their five senses. In contrast, intuitive people look for patterns and possibilities as they interpret the world around them. Thinkers tend to make decisions with rationality, facts, and objective principles, while feelers tend to decide things with a greater concern for people and values. Finally, people with a judging or closure orientation prefer an ordered, structured, and resolved situation, whereas perceiving types tend to be more flexible, adaptable, and open-ended when approaching the world around them.

These four sets of preference dyads create sixteen different MBTI combinations or types of distinct personalities, such as ESTJ (extraversion, sensing, thinking, judging) or INFP (introversion, intuition [abbreviated as N], feeling, perceiving). Knowing your own MBTI type can help you to understand your distinct personality and how it both differs from and is similar to the personalities of others.

Certain aspects of self-leadership seem to be related to the various MBTI dimensions. Specifically, the world-altering and self-imposed self-leadership strategies discussed in Chapter 3 can be seen as related to the MBTI judging–perceiving dimension. People with a strong judging orientation prefer structure, order, direction, and control in their lives and are more likely than people who prefer less structure to engage naturally in self-leadership behavioral strategies such as making to-do lists and setting goals. Research findings provide some evidence to support this relationship. In one study, all eight judging MBTI types scored higher on a measure of the self-leadership strategies discussed in Chapter 3 than all eight of the perceiving MBTI types.[4] The ESTJ type scored highest, while the INTP type scored lowest. Although all personality types could benefit from applying self-leadership strategies, it appears that people with a perceiving preference, especially the INTP type, stand to benefit the most from utilizing the self-leadership techniques discussed in this book.

The Big Five Model

The Big Five model is another way of thinking about personality differences and characteristics. It is based on the lexical hypothesis, which states that all meaningful differences in personality are encoded in language.[5] In other words, if there is an important difference between two people's personalities, we probably have a word to describe that difference. Many decades ago, personality experts began extracting trait descriptors from dictionaries, compiling lists of thousands of words. Over time, and with the use of some sophisticated statistical techniques, investigators discovered that these trait descriptors could be reduced to five primary categories: extraversion, agreeableness, conscientiousness, neuroticism, and openness to experience. Extraverts tend to be outgoing, talkative, and assertive. People high in agreeableness are courteous, good-natured, and caring. Conscientiousness involves being well ordered, planful, and self-disciplined. Neuroticism is characterized by anxiousness, depression, and insecurity. At the opposite end of the spectrum from neuroticism, this trait is sometimes positively called emotional stability and refers to people who are well-adjusted, stable, and secure. Finally, openness to experience incorporates imagination, curiosity, and originality.

Research has shown that conscientiousness, extraversion, and emotional stability are related to self-leadership.[6] Conscientiousness appears to have a particularly strong relationship to the use of the world-altering and self-imposed self-leadership strategies discussed in Chapter 3. Studies suggest that people low in conscientiousness, extraversion, and emotional stability are less likely than people high in these characteristics to engage in self-leadership effectively. Again, although everyone can benefit from using the self-leadership strategies presented in this book, people low in these traits are not natural self-leaders and could therefore gain the most from using these strategies.

Locus of Control

Other personality characteristics beyond those contained within the two broad views of personality just discussed may also be related to self-leadership. One of these is locus of control, or the extent to which people believe they can control the events and outcomes they experience in their lives. People with an internal locus of control believe that they have direct control over their personal outcomes and that this control comes from within. People with an external locus of control, in contrast, believe that they have little control over their outcomes and that control comes primarily from factors in their external environment. Not surprisingly, research has shown that self-leadership is related to an internal locus of control.[7] As we discussed in Chapter 2, our behavior and the world around us are closely related and influence one another in significant ways. To the extent that we believe that our choices and behaviors can influence the world around us, we are more likely to practice self-leadership. On the other hand, if we feel that our choices and behaviors are largely shaped and limited by our external world, we will be less likely to engage naturally in self-leadership. Thus, people with an external locus of control are likely to benefit more from learning to use the self-leadership concepts presented here than are people with an internal locus of control, who may already be effectively leading themselves.

Self-Monitoring

Yet another personality characteristic that may be related to self-leadership is self-monitoring, which involves assessing a given social situation and the behaviors of others within that situation before adjusting one's own behaviors so that they will be appropriate to the situation. High self-monitors closely control the self-image they present in social situations, while low self-monitors follow the beat of their own drummer and are more concerned with just "being themselves" regardless of the situation. High self-monitors are likely to be natural self-leaders because they see self-leadership strategies as effective ways to manage their self-presentation.[8] In contrast, low self-monitors are likely to engage in self-leadership only if it helps them to align their personal values with their behaviors. For example, people who value achievement or who are high in conscientiousness will see self-leadership as useful in helping them to behave in ways consistent with their values and characteristics. Thus, while high self-monitors are natural self-leaders, low self-monitors are also likely to benefit from applying self-leadership strategies, particularly if these strategies help them to maintain congruence among values, characteristics, and actions.

The Need for Autonomy

The need for autonomy is the concluding personality characteristic we will examine that may have important connections with self-leadership. The need for autonomy is the extent to which a person needs or is eager to express individual initiative in performing a job. One study suggests that people with a high need for autonomy are more likely than those low in this characteristic to engage in self-leadership.[9] In addition, the same study found that when leaders empowered their followers and encouraged them to lead themselves, those followers high in need for autonomy were more likely to actually engage in self-leadership. Another study demonstrated that people scoring low in self-leadership were more satisfied in highly structured job environments with little autonomy, whereas people scoring high in self-leadership were more satisfied in unstructured, autonomous work environments that provided opportunities for individual initiative.[10] Taken together, these findings suggest that not all people may be interested in leading themselves. Some may be happier taking direction from others and working in highly structured environments. Nevertheless, in today's world, the ability to lead oneself is

Logan Lucky (2017)

Two scenes from the movie *Logan Lucky* help to demonstrate the relationship between high internal locus of control and effective self-leadership. After being fired from his job, Jimmy Logan (Channing Tatum) tries to convince his brother Clyde Logan (Adam Driver) to help him pull off a heist at the Charlotte Motor Speedway during a NASCAR race. But Clyde believes there is a "Logan Family Curse" that controls the family's destiny.

In the first scene, which takes place in a bar where Clyde is bartending, Clyde tries to explain the curse to his brother. "Did you know Aunt Maggie, in 1983, won the lotto but then lost the ticket?" Jimmy interrupts, "Folktales and backwoods gossip." Clyde continues, "Well, you gotta admit this kind of stuff don't happen to normal folk." "Not tonight, Clyde," Jimmy interjects. Clyde goes on, "But there's a pattern. Pappaw's diamond, Uncle Stickley's electrocution, Mommy gets sick after Daddy's settlement, the roof collapse. You blow your knee out. And a roadside mine takes my arm as I was transpo-ing out. I was almost at the airport!"

In the second scene, Jimmy is explaining his plans for the speedway heist, when Clyde interrupts him: "Do you hear the words comin' out your mouth? 'They have their own police force.'" Jimmy responds, "I'm midway through my presentation, so you can just not interrupt me and let me get it out. How many times have I listened to that 'Logan Family Curse' thing of yours? Thank you. Now, as you very well know, speedway's got a big problem on its hands right now. Forty-year-old pipe bursts and since the whole thing is built on landfill, it's turnin' to mush, which is causin' all these sinkholes in the infield. Now, they wanted to fix this thing up right. So what'd they do? They called a bunch of us that used to work down in them mines. 'Cause we know the work.'" "And you do good work," says Clyde. "We do good work," Jimmy agrees. "But you were just fired," Clyde points out. "I was let go for liability reasons involving insurance," Jimmy explains. "Can you just get to the part of why you think you can do this?" Clyde asks. Jimmy says, "I know how they move the money!"

SELF-LEADERSHIP IN THE MOVIES

As their plans develop, the brothers realize that they will need assistance from safecracker Joe Bang (Daniel Craig) to open the speedway's vault. Unfortunately, Joe is currently serving a jail sentence. But Jimmy remains confident and undaunted. In order to successfully pull off the heist, he says, they only need to break Joe out of jail, blow open the safe at the speedway, escape with the money, get Joe safely back in jail, all before making sure that Jimmy arrives in time to see his daughter's beauty pageant!

Discussion Questions

1. Which Logan brother appears to have a high internal locus of control and which brother appears to have a high external locus of control? Explain.

2. Which Logan brother is more likely to be a natural self-leader? Why?

3. Could someone like Clyde increase his self-leadership? If so, how?

becoming increasingly important in many different situations. Even people who are low in the need for autonomy and who may not naturally be interested in leading themselves will benefit from learning and utilizing self-leadership strategies.

To summarize, personality appears to be related to self-leadership in numerous important ways. Experts suggest that our personality traits play an important role in shaping our behaviors. People who are high in the personality traits of judging, extraversion, conscientiousness, emotional stability, internal locus of control, self-monitoring, and need for autonomy are more likely than those who are low in these traits to engage naturally in self-leading behaviors. This should not be taken to suggest that people who are low in these traits cannot be effective self-leaders. Self-leadership strategies can be learned and used effectively by anyone, even people who are not natural self-leaders. In fact, people low in personality traits such as conscientiousness may stand to gain the most from learning to use the self-leadership strategies discussed in this book. For example, one study of employees at a resort found that those who scored low in conscientiousness showed much greater improvement in self-leadership behaviors following self-leadership training than did their counterparts who scored high in conscientiousness.[11]

DIVERSITY AND SELF-LEADERSHIP

In addition to the individual differences we have already discussed, self-leadership may interact with a number of other personal factors, including age, gender, and cultural background. For example, research suggests that age is negatively related to self-leadership.[12] In other words, younger people may tend to engage in self-leadership more than older people. One reason for this could be that younger people, who are still in the process of creating identities for themselves in their careers and personal lives, are generally more goal oriented than older, more established, and more stable people, who may have already achieved many of their important career and personal goals. On the other hand, generational differences may help account for lower self-leadership in older people. Older generations, including matures or traditionalists (those born before World War II) and baby boomers (born in the post–World War II baby boom, 1946–64), tend to respect rules, policies, and formal authority systems. They are often dedicated to their jobs and have a sense of duty. These statements tend to be truer for traditionalists than for baby boomers who grew up during the 1960s. During the formative years of these generations, most work and social organizations had traditional hierarchical command-and-control bureaucratic structures that allowed little room for individual initiative. People of these generations may therefore rely more on organizational structures, systems, and processes for motivational and behavioral guidance than on self-leadership. (Note that these statements about generational categories are all broad generalizations; the many individuals in any given generation can differ widely in their beliefs and behaviors.)

In contrast with their elders, younger people, including those who are part of Generation X (born 1965–80) and the millennial generation (born 1981 to approximately 1996), tend to be more pragmatic and self-reliant. They are achievement oriented but also value versatility and are much more likely to be following a protean career path. Seeing their elders experience plant closings and organizational restructuring has taught them to be less loyal and dependent on their work organizations. During their formative years, people of these generations were exposed to organizations with structures that were becoming more flexible and less rigid and that were demanding greater individual initiative from employees. This is not to suggest, however, that self-leadership is unimportant for older people. Quite to the contrary, older people can benefit greatly from self-leadership. Self-leadership strategies can help more mature individuals to develop and pursue additional life goals and purposes, increase flow and happiness, avoid depression, and maintain an independent lifestyle well into their golden years.[13]

Gender is another factor that may have some bearing on a person's self-leadership, although studies have generally found no relationship between gender and self-leadership.[14] That is, overall, women appear to be no more or less effective than men in leading themselves, and vice versa. Nevertheless, gender may have a subtle effect on various aspects of the practice of self-leadership. For instance, some studies suggest that women are more likely than men to engage in rumination or negative, obstacle-type thinking in response to negative emotions.[15] One study found that women tended to choose easier performance tasks than did men, but it did not demonstrate lower performance for women compared to men because points were awarded based on the level of task difficulty; thus, choosing a task that was too difficult or too easy was detrimental to performance. The same study also found an interaction among culture, gender, and self-regulation. For example, Singaporean women seemed to prefer tasks that were too easy, whereas Israeli men chose tasks that were too difficult.[16]

As these findings imply, cultural differences represent another important factor that may affect self-leadership. People in the various cultures around the world can be very different from one another in terms of their behavior and thinking processes. These differences are often discussed in terms of the five cultural dimensions Geert Hofstede developed after many years of extensive cross-cultural research.[17] These dimensions are power distance (the degree of equality or inequality between people in a country's society); individualism (the extent to which a society values individual or collective achievement); masculinity (the degree to which a society reinforces traditional masculine roles, including male achievement, control, and power); uncertainty avoidance (the level of tolerance for uncertainty and ambiguity in a society); and long-term orientation (the extent to which a society embraces long-term devotion to traditional or forward-thinking values). People's experiences of these cultural dimensions are quite likely to influence how and to what extent they are able to lead themselves.[18] Specifically, people in cultures with high power distance are likely to engage in a restricted form of self-leadership that is contingent on social hierarchies, whereas people in low power distance cultures are likely to engage in a more individually unique and autonomous type of self-leadership. Likewise, people in high uncertainty avoidance cultures are more likely to lead themselves in the context of formal plans and rules, whereas people in low uncertainty avoidance cultures may be more innovative and flexible in their self-leadership. Self-leadership in collectivist cultures is likely to be guided by group, communal, or shared principles. In contrast, self-leadership in individualist cultures may be guided more by personal interests, material rewards, and short-term objectives. In addition, it seems that self-leadership in masculine cultures is motivated by material and economic outcomes, whereas self-leadership in feminine cultures tends to be directed more toward enhancing relationships. Finally, people in cultures with long-term orientations tend to focus on leading themselves toward longer-term objectives while deferring immediate gratifications, whereas people in short-term cultures tend to focus on more immediate personal or organizational self-leadership objectives.

Self-Leadership Applied to Personal Problems

Probably the most extensive application of systematic self-regulatory strategies has occurred in the field of psychology.[19] More specifically, major strides have been made in developing the ability of individuals to deal effectively with their own problems. The many different kinds of difficulties that have been addressed are too numerous to discuss fully here; instead, we offer brief comments on a sampling of self-leadership applications to personal problems. These examples are useful because much of the idea development that is included in this book ultimately can be traced to psychology-based applications to personal problems.

Consider the challenge of controlling eating behavior when confronted with a weight problem. Various strategies have been applied to this difficulty, many with impressive success. One approach, for example, involves various cueing strategies. The logic employed is that many dysfunctional eating behaviors stem from personal exposure to dysfunctional cues in our environment. Because cues such as watching television, reading, and socializing often become associated with eating, one way of controlling eating is to control these cues. Thus, numerous individuals have benefited (lost substantial weight) from restricting their eating to only a limited number of infrequent situations (e.g., dinnertime) and purposefully not eating in other situations that potentially could become cues to future eating (watching television).

Taylor Swift

Taylor Swift isn't just one of the most popular singer-songwriters in the world—she is also an extraordinary self-leader. Raised in Wyomissing, Pennsylvania, Swift moved to Nashville, Tennessee, with her family when she was fourteen years old so that she could pursue a career in country music. Her self-titled debut album, released in 2006, made her a country music star, and her single "Our Song" made her the youngest person ever to write and perform a song that was ranked number one on Billboard magazine's "Hot Country Songs" chart. Swift has never looked back, and her accomplishments now include ten Grammy Awards, twenty-two Billboard Music Awards, eleven Country Music Association Awards, and eight Academy of Country Music Awards. She has become one of the best-selling artists of all time, having sold more than 40 million albums.

Perhaps best known for her introspective lyrics based on her personal experiences, Swift has reflected many self-leading principles in her actions, her comments, and her song lyrics. For example, in her song "Shake It Off," Swift reminds us that we create our own psychological worlds (Chapter 5) and that we have the power to dismiss the negativity of others. In a recent interview she stated, "It's human instinct to try and defend yourself when people have the wrong impression of you, but you have to let go of that and just get rid of it because it's not yours anymore." Similarly, Swift advocates being aware of and comfortable with who you are, reflecting the self-leadership concepts of self-observation and purpose (Chapter 3). She puts it this way: "You have to be happy with who you are and the choices you make. If you don't like yourself, you'll never be truly happy. It's important to be self-aware about what people are saying about you, but even more so, be very aware of who you actually are, and to have that be the main priority."

Swift also embraces the self-leadership concepts of hard work and leading oneself to do necessary but unattractive tasks (Chapter 3): "My parents raised me to never feel like I was entitled to success. That you have to work for it. You have to work so hard for it. The world doesn't owe you anything. You have to work for everything you get and you have to appreciate every bit of success the world gives you." Finally, Swift seems to understand the ideas of happiness and flow (Chapter 5): "Happiness isn't a constant. You get fleeting glimpses. You have to fight for those moments, but they make it all worth it." Taylor Swift's success is no accident—she is an extremely talented songwriter and singer, but she has also been very effective at leading herself into a satisfying and successful career.

Sources/Additional Readings

DiPirro, Dani. "13 Inspiring Life Lessons from Taylor Swift." PositivelyPresent.com, November 3, 2014. http://www.positivelypresent.com/2014/11/taylor-swift.html.

"Taylor Swift Biography," Biography.com, accessed September 2, 2018, http://www.biography.com/people/taylor-swift-369608.

Similar techniques have been applied to smoking behavior, with significant success (in reducing smoking) in many cases. One particularly interesting example involves the use of a specially designated smoking chair that is located in unpleasant surroundings (e.g., the garage). With smoking limited only to this chair, many other potential cues for smoking behavior (e.g., watching television, drinking a cup of coffee at the dinner table) are eliminated.

Many other self-regulatory strategies have been applied to dysfunctional habitual behaviors. For instance, many individuals have achieved beneficial results in weight loss by altering self-statements regarding their efforts (e.g., from "I've been torturing myself with starvation and I'm just not losing much weight" to "I'm making progress; I'm losing pounds slowly but surely"). Similarly, self-reinforcement for improving eating habits has been of significant help to those who are trying to lose weight. A nice dinner out (nutritionally balanced, of course) as a reward for achieving a weight-loss goal (e.g., losing ten pounds) can provide incentive for future weight loss. Various forms of imagery (e.g., imagining negative results such as excessive weight problems or cancer) also have been used in the treatment of eating and smoking problems.

One particularly interesting application of imagined experience has been to alter a type of interpersonal behavior—assertiveness.[20] Specifically, individuals were instructed to imagine scenes that called for them to be assertive and to imagine positive results from their assertive behavior. They might imagine themselves in a restaurant, for example, receiving a steak cooked medium well when they had ordered it medium rare. They would then imagine themselves sending the steak back and asking to receive another one cooked as ordered (medium rare). Finally, they would imagine receiving an excellent steak just as they wanted, as well as other positive results stemming from their assertiveness (such as the restaurant manager reducing the amount of their check because of the inconvenience). Such systematic use of imagery over a period of time was found to benefit many individuals by helping them increase their subsequent assertiveness significantly.

APPLICATIONS IN ATHLETICS

Many self-leadership techniques have been applied, in various forms, to athletics.[21] A comprehensive review of the extensive applications of self-leadership strategies to athletic activity is beyond the scope of this book. Indeed, a growing area known as *sport psychology* has provided much knowledge on the subject.[22] It is instructive, however, to review some particularly interesting examples. The use of self-set goals is one strategy that is especially relevant to athletics. Whether the goal involves improving the field goal percentage for a basketball player, completing the mile in a specific time for a runner, or achieving a specified score for eighteen holes of golf, self-goal-setting can provide athletes with direction for their efforts. Some athletes set goals that are too high, however, making achievement of those goals impossible. For goals to be effective, it is important that they be challenging but achievable.

For athletes, this frequently means that the focus needs to be on process-related goals—such as effort, form, and strategy—rather than on the outcomes of particular contests. In young soccer players, for example, evidence shows that stress, which can undermine the natural enjoyment of a recreational activity, results from individual perceptions of an inability to meet performance demands and may predict injury frequency.[23] Because competition usually means that someone or some team has to lose (and usually that means 50 percent of those participating), goals focusing on winning might not be particularly effective. In many cases, athletes might do their best but simply not possess the ability to beat outstanding opponents.

An especially intriguing area of self-leadership's application to athletics is that of the creative use of imagery to facilitate desired performance. A review of sixty different sports studies across a wide range of activities and ages of performers found a consistent positive relationship between constructive mental imagery and performance.[24] For example, as Maxwell Maltz relates, both a highly successful golf instructor and a well-known professional golfer strongly advocated that players should picture the ideal golf swing in their minds to improve their game.[25] The logic employed is that if players can imagine themselves smoothly and cleanly performing a golf shot that accomplishes what they desire (and they do this before swinging), the result is likely to be a more natural and effective shot.

Athletes in other sports often use similar processes. According to reports, many Olympic gymnasts, for example, employ imagery as an aid to performance.[26] One gymnast said that before an event, she imagines what she will see when she performs. Another explained that she feels the motion in her muscles as though she is performing. Likewise, at least one world-class high jumper has employed imagery—if he could mentally picture himself slowly floating over the bar, he knew he could make the jump. A highly successful swimming team at a major state university employs imagined experience as part of its preparation for competition. Swimmers are encouraged to imagine the race, including the feeling of the water on their bodies, their strokes, breathing, and so forth, before the race begins.

The overall pattern of thinking that an athlete brings to a sport appears to be especially important. Expressions that are frequently used in reference to preparing for competitions, such as getting "psyched up" or being "psyched out," reflect the importance many place on this critical role. Recall our earlier story about Olympic gold medalist Dan O'Brien. His change in thinking was a catalyst for his winning effort in the Olympic decathlon. Athletes' belief in their ability to perform and their engagement in facilitative rather than destructive thoughts might be as important as physical practice and preparation in many cases. The idea of "psychological barriers" to performance in athletics is an interesting example.[27] The four-minute mile, the seven-foot high jump, and the eighteen-foot pole vault are examples of obstacles to athletic achievement that are as much psychologically based as they are physical. Interestingly, some evidence suggests that if weight lifters are deceived into believing that they are lifting less weight than they actually are, they are able to lift significantly more weight than they could otherwise.[28] Recall from Chapter 5 our discussion of the Russian Olympic weight lifter Vasily Alexeev, whose achievement provides an example of this psychological phenomenon.

The need for athletes to focus on the positive aspects of an event and to engage in constructive rather than destructive self-statements (e.g., "I've practiced hard and I can do well" rather than "I hope I don't blow it; I'm just not sure I can do it") has been emphasized.[29] Remember that after Roger Bannister became the first man to run the mile in less than four minutes, runners finally came to *believe* that it could be done, and many have now surpassed Bannister's record.

APPLICATIONS IN WORK/ORGANIZATIONAL SITUATIONS

Systematic attempts to apply self-leadership methods to work organizations are still at a relatively early stage of development. Nonetheless, a number of innovative applications indicate a great deal of promise across a wide range of organizational positions, including uniquely autonomous jobs that are particularly suited for and in need of self-leadership (e.g., salesperson, dentist, medical doctor, auditor, college professor, high school teacher); management jobs; and nonmanagement jobs. We discuss some of these applications briefly below to demonstrate the progress that has been made, as well as the vast potential for the future.

Uniquely Autonomous Jobs

Uniquely autonomous jobs in organizations are of special interest for self-leadership study. Certainly salespersons who spend a great deal of time traveling by themselves and calling on customers find that to a large degree they must be their own managers. Training in sales techniques and the expression of confidence in their abilities by the home office are often not enough to enable many to handle this challenge successfully. In the short run, for example, treating herself to an expensive dinner for closing a big sale might be the only material reward a salesperson receives until she returns home from a trip in the field. Salespersons need to play a critical role in their own development, motivation, and systematic self-leadership. Setting personal goals, rehearsing sales presentations, administering self-rewards, and seeking the natural rewards in their jobs could mean the difference between success and failure.

Indeed, many other jobs present similar challenges—from the loosely supervised machine operator on a midnight shift to the chief executive officer of a large corporation who has ultimate authority for the direction of the business. Our own lines of work, as college professors and consultants, demand a high level of self-leadership. Yet our experience has revealed numerous cases in which individuals (including ourselves) have had personal and professional setbacks because of ineffective self-leadership practices. Many of these setbacks resulted from the individuals' setting unrealistic goals, being overly self-critical, and engaging in dysfunctional thought patterns (e.g., inaccurate and debilitating imagined experiences relating to immediate behavior choices).

Entrepreneurship

To explore more fully the role of self-leadership for individuals who are in highly autonomous positions, we single out one especially challenging type of job—that of the entrepreneur. For our purposes, an entrepreneur can be described as an owner-manager of a firm who sets its course and largely determines its fate: success or failure. Entrepreneurs are in a difficult position, because they must, largely on their own, beat the staggering odds against new business ventures. (It has been estimated that as few as one out of one hundred new businesses survives three years.) A growing body of research has linked self-leadership strategies with entrepreneurial success.[30] For example, Charles Snyder and Charles Manz conducted a series of personal interviews with several successful entrepreneurs (i.e., their businesses had survived, against all odds, longer than three years and were currently doing well) operating a wide range of businesses.[31] They found that although these entrepreneurs might downplay the use of any systematic management strategies on their part, they displayed several common threads of a systematic self-leadership fabric in their behavior. Descriptions of a few of the self-leadership applications they revealed follow.

Consider Mr. Air (the name is changed to protect confidentiality), the majority stock owner and manager of a commuter airline in the southern United States. Mr. Air uses the strategy of self-observation, for example, by keeping a daily log (a detailed record) of how he spends his time. He also keeps records of what he says to others over the phone regarding business matters to help him be consistent in his future dealings with these people. Mr. Air has adopted various cueing strategies to help manage himself. He uses a chalkboard directly in front of his desk, for example, to record notes that serve as reminders and guides for his work efforts. He also makes use of self-applied and natural rewards. He enjoys reviewing his performance and feeling good about (mentally rewarding himself for) his achievements, and, in general, he just seems to get a kick out of (experiences the natural rewards of) what he is doing. (He even continues to exercise his pilot's prerogative by occasionally flying some of the airline's routes.)

Perhaps the most striking feature of Mr. Air's approach to his work is his eye for opportunities. Many of his competitors have gone out of business, yet he is determined to expand to take advantage of new opportunities rather than reduce services. In fact, shortly before his interview, Mr. Air had worked out a creative financial plan to buy a larger airplane, despite low funds. He was exuberant, and rightly so, as he spoke of this accomplishment. He didn't need others to tell him that this was quite an achievement—it was apparent from the satisfied expression on his face and the energetic tone of his voice that he had already taken care of that himself. As he put it, "Self-gratification—that's what it's all about."

Mr. Air is just one of many successful entrepreneurs who, although seemingly unaware that they are doing so, reveal obvious signs of systematic self-leadership practice. Consider Mr. Notes, the owner-manager of a successful company in the Midwest that distributes synopses of college textbooks. He relies heavily on self-set goals to help him direct his own behavior and facilitate the success of his business. Particularly in the early days of his business, he found goals to be invaluable in directing his efforts toward the development of his company; they also serve as a basis for his exercise of another self-leadership strategy—self-reward. More specifically, Mr. Notes has found that providing himself with monetary bonuses contingent on his achieving sales goals is an effective strategy for facilitating his performance.

Mr. Restaurant, the owner of a small family restaurant, has found posting checklists (a cueing strategy) to be a useful method of ensuring that he and his employees consistently follow established procedures and maintain acceptable levels of performance. In addition, when they meet important performance goals, Mr. Restaurant and his employees close up and throw a party for themselves.

Mr. Sport, the owner-manager of a sporting goods store, combines the strategies of self-goal-setting and self-observation to manage himself. He sets two-year goals and records them on a checklist (a self-observation strategy), which enables him to make additions and deletions and keep track of delays in goal attainment. He is always searching for new goals and frequently breaks down longer-term goals into more immediate targets for his daily efforts. Mr. Sport also reported an especially powerful self-reward process that helps him maintain his motivation: as he accomplishes goals and reviews his own performance favorably, he feels a "rush of adrenaline" and experiences a "terrific high." Indeed, Mr. Sport appears to be urged onward by a combination of internal self-praise and the natural rewards of succeeding on the job.

Boundaryless Career Paths

The concept of the career has changed dramatically over the past two decades. As a result of the tumultuous downsizing and restructuring of the 1980s and 1990s, today's organizations are lean, flexible, and adaptable. No longer do organizations provide good employees with "cradle-to-grave" job security and a long, but steady, climb up the corporate ladder. Today the more authentic career contract is not between the worker and the organization but between the worker and her- or himself. In short, the "path to the top" has been displaced by what some have called the "path with a heart."[32] This phrase refers to the process of building a career based on one's uniqueness and individual values. No longer will success be narrowly defined in terms of a vertical ascent to the summit of the corporate landscape and the accumulation of large sums of money; rather, success will be defined in terms of psychological factors such as the feelings of pride and accomplishment that come from achieving important life goals of all types.[33]

This new type of career path is known as a "boundaryless" career or a "protean" career.[34] The word *protean* comes from the name of the Greek god Proteus, who was able to alter his shape.[35] The protean career path is self-directed rather than organization-directed and requires occasional reshaping and reformulation as changing situations dictate. The protean career is becoming increasingly common and more valued. A study that followed MBA graduates over a thirteen-year period found that only one-third of them were following traditional organizational career paths; the majority were following more protean career paths.[36]

Although some people find the autonomy of the protean career exciting and invigorating, others find the lack of traditional organizational support structures and safety nets to be frightening. An individual needs particular skill sets to take advantage of the opportunities afforded by the protean career. Career expert Douglas T. Hall suggests that in order "to realize the potential of the new career, the individual must develop new competencies related to the management of self and career. Since the new career will be increasingly a continuous learning process, the person must learn how to develop self-knowledge and adaptability."[37] According to Hall, career growth is a process of continuous learning facilitated by work experiences and challenges and by relationships with others in formal and informal networks. In the future, these learning structures will largely replace traditional organizational development structures, such as formal organizational educational and training programs.[38]

The need for self-leadership in the context of managing a protean career path is obvious. The self-imposed strategies discussed in Chapter 3 can provide the means by which an individual can develop the self-awareness and self-discipline necessary to take on the responsibility of managing his or her own career development. Likewise, the various mental strategies outlined in Chapter 5 could prove extremely valuable to individuals attempting to navigate the psychological worlds surrounding the protean career path. Through effective self-leadership, you can take charge of your own career while finding yourself a "path with a heart."

Self-Leadership and Social Responsibility at Work

In recent years it has become painfully apparent that some businesses have lost their way. Companies like Enron, WorldCom, and Tyco have received so much attention concerning their infamous business scandals that they have all but become clichés. Add to these other monumental ethical failings worthy of membership in a virtual Hall of Shame, such as the major abuses in the mortgage industry that caused a housing market collapse and Bernie Madoff's infamous Ponzi scheme, and it is clear that all is not well in many of today's work settings.

In the cases of Enron and other firms, bankruptcy ultimately followed. More important, thousands of workers lost their life's savings as a result. For these firms, perhaps it was significant competitive and financial pressures, along with long-accepted management norms, that fostered an overemphasis on traditional business values such as profitability, efficiency, and control at the expense of more virtuous and ethical standards. In many organizations, less traditional business concerns, such as caring, compassion, integrity, and justice, have often been largely ignored in favor of achieving ends related to the bottom line, such as high return on investment and competitive advantage.[39]

Mental images of greedy managers operating out of lavish executive suites, misusing power to manipulate organizations (and the people who work for and depend on them) for personal gain, can be discouraging. Yet each of us has a choice in terms of our own self-leadership stance concerning social responsibility. And it is heartening that increasing attention has recently been devoted, both in the management literature and in practice, to more hopeful contemporary management concerns such as corporate social responsibility, social entrepreneurship, and sustainability.[40] Ultimately we are confronted with an array of self-leadership choices regarding the organizations we choose to work for, the ethical stands we are willing to take in our careers, and the personal outcomes we choose to pursue (ranging from making the highest salary possible at any cost to sincerely serving others and trying to make the world a better place as a result of our efforts).

Organizational Management Positions

Managers are well suited for systematic self-leadership practice. Organizational research, as well as personal experience and observation, has made us acutely aware of the difficult challenges that require managers to be especially good self-managers.

SELF-LEADERSHIP RESEARCH

Individual Differences, Diversity, and Empowerment: Key Antecedents of Self-Leadership

As noted in Chapter 1, a substantial body of research supports the role of self-leadership for enhancing a variety of outcomes including job satisfaction, creativity, and job performance. Although less research attention has been focused on what causes people to engage in self-leadership, findings to date suggest that individual differences and empowerment may be two key antecedents of self-leadership. One study of 341 supervisor–subordinate dyads found that conscientiousness and internal locus of control were both significant predictors of self-leadership, which mediated the relationship between these two personality variables and the outcomes of job satisfaction and job performance.[1] However, the study found that gender did not moderate (i.e., strengthen or weaken) this mediated relationship, suggesting that this diversity factor may not be an antecedent of self-leadership.

Another set of studies found that self-leadership and psychological empowerment, which occurs when people experience feelings of meaning, competence, self-determination, and impact, both mediated the effects of empowering leadership, a leadership approach that involves power sharing and the promotion of self-reliance and autonomy, on the outcomes of job satisfaction, creativity, and work effort.[2] These findings suggest that empowering leadership may be another key antecedent of self-leadership, especially in an organizational context. More research is needed to identify what other factors beyond personality and empowering leadership may help to shape individual self-leadership processes.

1. Jessie Ho and Paul L. Nesbit, "Personality and Work Outcomes: A Moderated Mediation Model of Self-Leadership and Gender," *International Journal of Management Excellence* 10, no. 2 (February 2018): 1292–1304.
2. Stein Amundsen and Øyvind L. Martinsen, "Linking Empowering Leadership to Job Satisfaction, Work Effort, and Creativity: The Role of Self-Leadership and Psychological Empowerment," *Journal of Leadership & Organizational Studies* 22, no. 3 (August 2015): 304–23.

If they are not, they can easily become poor managers of others and of organizational resources. For many, the fast-paced, multifaceted demands of a management position can become overwhelming. As phones ring off the hook, subordinates wait for their attention, multiple deadlines loom, a seemingly endless onslaught of meetings compete for their time, and they are snowed under by mountains of information and "urgent" demands, managers face enormous potential for ineffectiveness and inefficiency. Peter Drucker has described effectiveness as "doing the right thing" and efficiency as "doing things right."[41] In essence, managers—despite typically working in sizable organizations that impose guidelines and constraints and offer various incentives—must largely choose among the vast demands made on them, deciding what to spend time on and how to expend effort on the tasks chosen. For managers, self-leadership practices can be instrumental in determining whether they are doing the right things and doing them correctly.

Some interesting applications of self-leadership strategies that managers have employed successfully have been reported in the research.[42] These applications have involved managers in a variety of jobs in retailing, manufacturing, public service, and advertising, including line and staff positions. In the various cases reported, specific behaviors were identified (e.g., time spent on the phone, timely completion of expense forms, informing others when leaving the office) for improvement, appropriate to the individual manager.

The advertising manager of a newspaper, for example, was able to deal effectively with several behaviors he identified as needing improvement. One problem targeted was his tendency to leave the office without telling anyone where he was going and when he would be back that day (if at all). The manager used a simple cueing strategy to solve the problem: he placed a "checkout" board on the office door, which he could not miss seeing when leaving. By moving magnetic disks on the board, he could easily indicate if he was out of the building, if he would return, and when.

Similarly, this manager eliminated the problem he had in getting himself to fill out expense forms in a timely manner (a chore he neglected sometimes for several months) by having a secretary place the appropriate form on his desk at the same time each day (in the evening, just before he went home). He always tried to be back in his office just before leaving for home and usually did not have many demands placed on him at this time. Thus, he could complete this task easily when cued by the form on his desk to do so. In addition, he posted a wall chart in his office for the purposes of self-observation. Soon the manager was filling out the expense form every day, and the wall chart, which indicated this performance improvement, provided the occasion for self-reinforcement. Also, by properly filling out the expense forms, the manager received the added benefit of not incurring personal financial loss (from not being reimbursed for his expenses in a timely manner) and was able to get a more accurate picture of expenses in his department.

In another case, an assistant retail store manager identified a behavior she wanted to improve: frequent visits to her boss, resulting in excessive dependence (her boss agreed that the visits were detracting from the assistant manager's effectiveness). To deal with the problem, she used a simple self-observation strategy—she carried an index card on which she recorded the time of each visit, the type of information she was seeking from her boss, and what happened when she handled the problem herself rather than consulting her boss. Subsequently, the frequency of her visits was reduced drastically, and she and her boss were pleased with her performance.

In addition to the case studies described above, we have conducted considerable research on this topic with individuals in more traditional work environments and more contemporary participative and team-based environments.[43] We also have observed numerous instances that provide insight regarding self-management of managers. We have witnessed, as you probably have, many instances when managers have developed their own tailor-made self-leadership strategies to deal with behaviors that need improvement. We have seen countless managers use checklists to guide their daily behaviors. We have seen managers take coffee breaks after successfully completing important tasks or switch their attention to more enjoyable activities to reward themselves for their accomplishment. We have seen managers turn routine tasks into a kind of game or competition to make their work more naturally rewarding. We also are familiar with managers who visualize the potential rewards of successfully handling current challenges (recognition, promotion, or the achievement of some of the dreams they have regarding their work).

Unfortunately, we also have seen managers mentally and physically beaten by the way they approached their work. One manager, for example, reported extreme worry associated with his work. His thoughts seemed always to be occupied by images of impending disaster on the job—failure, reprimand from his boss, humiliation resulting from poor performance, even dismissal. The pressures associated with his job (most of which were greatly exacerbated in his mind, he admitted) made him irritable at work and at home and dissatisfied with his job and brought him significant physical problems. He reported difficulty in sleeping and exhibited excessive tension that was sometimes debilitating to the point of making him physically ill. The pattern of his physical and mental behavior may well have been leading him to other more serious problems, such as ulcers or perhaps worse: One of his associates had recently had his second heart attack, apparently brought on by "overpressing" at work.

We are also familiar with another manager who worked in the same organization. He, in contrast, was enthusiastic about his work and seemed to be well-adjusted. He practiced several self-leadership strategies (he was especially sold on "time management" techniques) and was well organized, relying heavily on systematic analysis of business information. In particular, he had a strong sense of task completion. Until he achieved immediate goals, he was persistent in his work efforts. In many ways, he seemed like the model contemporary manager.

Unfortunately, this individual's strong sense of self-leadership did not extend to his impact on his environment or, more specifically, his immediate subordinates. His systematic approach to management was, frankly, not palatable to his subordinates. They preferred to operate using a "sense of the business" or intuition based on experience rather than to gather data and fill out reports systematically. Ultimately, the friction between the manager and his subordinates became problematic, and the manager was squeezed out of the organization—despite his solid performance record.

The case of this manager illustrates once again the complexity of self-leadership. Indeed, we must recognize the importance of the indirect impacts of our actions on our external world (e.g., the work environment) at the same time we are managing our own behavior and thoughts. Unfortunately, work environments are often difficult to manage. We have observed the frustration of many managers as they attempt to maintain a consistent level of performance and motivation in the face of seemingly irrational organizational roadblocks. We remember an instance when a customer in a large furniture store wanted an odd table leaf owned by the store, and the store wanted to get rid of the leaf, which was taking up space. Unfortunately, the computer ticket that reported the leaf's style number, manufacturer, and other information for inventory purposes had become detached and lost. There was the customer, and there was the table leaf, but the manager in charge of the selling area could not for the life of him—despite numerous inquiries regarding appropriate procedures—figure out how to sell the leaf to the customer without violating company policy regarding inventory control.

We also remember a manager who was assigned, essentially, one and one-half jobs: his usual tasks in addition to the bulk of what another individual had previously worked on full-time. A few months after he took on the other person's work, computer reports revealed that business was up 70 percent over the previous year. Despite the improved figures, the manager received little, if any, positive feedback from his superiors. In fact, a short time later when some inventory was temporarily misplaced (by persons working for advertising and display without his knowledge and permission), he was vigorously chewed out by a vice president. Similarly, the manager's superiors expressed concern when financial indicators showed performance had dropped temporarily to a mere 40 percent, rather than 70 percent, ahead of the previous year. Fortunately, the manager was able to maintain his performance level and reasonably good morale by recognizing and reinforcing himself in the absence of external recognition.

Consider also the case of the manager whose peers saw her as somewhat ridiculous and sometimes openly chided her because she refused to distort certain financial figures to make performance look better on paper than it was. This was a commonly accepted practice in the organization, despite the fact that to an outsider it would appear unethical. This manager's sense of ethics (her own personal standards) conflicted directly with those of her peers. To maintain the personal stand she believed in, she had to exercise self-leadership influence in excess of the external forces she faced.

Managers face difficult challenges. With significant pressures and often inhospitable external work environments (not to mention the difficulty involved in trying to manage oneself effectively), achieving personal effectiveness can be difficult. Although special problems such as managing time and controlling stress have received specific research attention, managing one's day-to-day behavior has been largely neglected. This book is intended to be a significant first step in providing managers, and others, with practical tools for self-leadership that are useful for dealing with challenges such as those discussed in this chapter.

Nonmanagement Jobs

Lower-level, hourly jobs—seemingly the most unlikely focus for self-leadership application—have received perhaps the greatest research attention. Recent growth in the adoption of self-managed or autonomous work teams in production/manufacturing plants and various other types of work settings (e.g., coal mines; warehouses; paper mills; and service organizations in insurance, finance, and even psychiatric care) is the most striking example of this emphasis.

The primary method we will use here to illustrate the potential of self-leadership methods for hourly workers is to draw on examples from our personal experience and research. We have completed research projects in many self-managed team work systems across a wide variety of industries (manufacturing and service) and work settings. In particular, we will place special emphasis on nonmanagement jobs by contrasting the experiences of workers in these settings with the personal experiences of Charles Manz (CM), a coauthor of this book, as a machine operator in a "traditionally managed" manufacturing plant some years ago, when he was a college student. More recently, CM took part in a research project conducted in a manufacturing plant that uses a self-managed team work system. That plant and the one where he worked as a machine operator were similar in numerous ways: both used assembly-line technology and employed blue-collar workers with relatively low levels of education, and both were even owned by the same corporation. A primary difference existed, however, in the ways people were managed in the two plants.

A common impression of blue-collar jobs in production/manufacturing plants is that they are monotonous, boring, and dehumanizing. CM's experience did not contradict this impression. The extent to which people in such work settings typically have been underutilized is especially striking. CM witnessed an interesting illustration of this tendency while working as a machine operator on a midnight shift. He had been operating a lathe, as had several other workers around him, for several nights. On this particular evening, CM was approached by the foreman, who expressed in some heated words that CM was not producing enough output. Up to this time, CM had been attempting to work at about the same pace as the other workers, being sensitive to productivity norms that assured workers would not make each other look bad. The foreman's comments, however, apparently hit a raw nerve concerning CM's need for achievement, and he began working "like crazy." Soon CM's output had increased noticeably on the conveyer line that wound its way through his part of the plant. A short time later, the foreman approached CM again, this time grinning. "Wow, you're really going now. Good job," he remarked.

Meanwhile, another worker nearby had been observing all this. He was a man in his mid-thirties. He had always struck CM as a particularly bright individual (though not well educated) but not motivated. In fact, CM had learned recently that this coworker would press the production counter lever on his lathe to make it appear that his production was higher than it was (CM later found out this was a common practice in the plant). The man moved slowly and looked lazy. On this occasion, however, he suddenly came to life. CM was awed by the controlled speed and smoothness of his motions. The coworker started producing "like hell," although with apparent lack of effort or fatigue. His face had come to life as well, with determination and even pride. He apparently was trying to show the college punk a thing or two—and he did. CM felt rather awkward and inadequate in comparison.

The funny thing about the episode is that soon it seemed as if it had never happened. A couple of days later, CM had fallen back to a more restricted level of production, encouraged by various subtle pressures from other workers. Meanwhile, the "super" lathe operator returned to his normal behavior, and he recaptured the dull, bored look on his face. During the remainder of CM's tenure in the plant, he never again produced the way he had that night.

Workers suffering from a severe lack of motivation are not found only in manufacturing plants; unfortunately, they are everywhere. Often the motivation that these workers possess is much more oriented to avoiding work than to doing it. For example, CM was familiar with one individual working in a warehouse who displayed an amazing aptitude in this regard. The creativity and effort he expended on avoiding work often exceeded that required to just go ahead and do the work. He enjoyed avoiding his work much more than doing it, so that's what he did.

Individuals such as this are not just lazy people without ambition. In fact, we have encountered many "work avoiders" who have displayed obvious enthusiasm when talking about their dreams of what they would *really* like to do. One factory worker CM knew related to him with excitement the dream he planned to fulfill someday: opening a Disneyland type of park for African Americans. As he talked about it, the detail that he had worked out for his plan impressed CM—the idea sounded like it could work! A warehouse worker reported his ambition to own and operate his own ice cream parlor. The energy and enthusiasm he displayed as he talked about his dream were in sharp contrast to the dull lack of motivation he displayed on his current job. Indeed, people such as these have a burning desire inside to put themselves into something they believe in. Unfortunately, when CM knew them they lacked the confidence and self-leadership capabilities to find a reasonable fit between their interests and their immediate and longer-term career efforts. They were wasted on their jobs.

One striking example of this sad state of affairs occurred on CM's last day of work on the midnight shift. CM had become good friends with most people on the shift, and many wished him a warm and hearty good-bye. One of the workers (we'll call him Ed), however, was being conspicuously aloof. Because CM had developed a particularly close tie with Ed and another worker on the shift, CM was surprised at his behavior. Ed seemed rather depressed and perhaps a bit angry for some reason. CM finally asked his other friend what the problem was. He explained that Ed was feeling down because CM was going back to college and he was stuck in a job he did not like. It seems that years earlier, Ed had chosen to work at the plant because the money was good, but he had always planned to get into some other more rewarding type of work. Now he was finally realizing that it was, perhaps, too late. He had become dependent on the money, and his youth had been largely spent; he had led himself into what he now saw as the trap of many unmotivated, demoralized American workers. This reality was dealing him a painful blow that evening. CM never saw Ed again after he left, but he'll never forget the cold reality of the psychological defeat that showed on Ed's face that night.

It is little wonder to us that the United States has severe productivity problems when we see workers such as these. They derive no enjoyment from their work. Fortunately, it does not have to be that way. In fact, CM observed a situation in another manufacturing plant, this time as a researcher conducting a joint project with his colleague Henry Sims Jr., that supports this premise. What he saw was a sharp contrast to the examples related thus far. This was a plant that was organized on a self-managed team basis.[44] That is, production workers were provided with the autonomy and even the responsibility to do many things handled by managers in traditionally organized plants (e.g., assigning group members to tasks, solving quality problems, and handling interpersonal problems between group members). Self-managed groups might be described as a step beyond the quality circles that have received so much attention because of their widespread use in Japan and extensive adoption in the United States. The important point for this discussion is that this plant, in contrast to the one CM had worked in, allowed and even encouraged blue-collar workers to exercise self-leadership.

Perhaps a few examples will serve to illustrate the point. In one case, a worker was observed asking his coordinator (in this plant, supervisors were referred to as *coordinators* because of the unique aspects of the work system) how he should go about repairing a guardrail on a loading ramp. The coordinator's response was essentially a question: "How do you think you should do it?" The worker responded by stating what he thought the appropriate solution was and then, consistent with the nature of the work system, proceeded to act on his solution. He also went about the work with conviction and commitment that probably wouldn't have been there if he had been complying with an order. This case is not especially remarkable in itself, but multiply it many times and you have a situation that can only be described as amazing in comparison to the usual atmosphere found in most production plants today.

Some of the actions that CM and Sims observed were much more striking. They witnessed one instance, for example, in which a worker apparently saved the plant a great deal of money.[45] He left his workstation to test some production materials that he suspected were defective. He proceeded to a laboratory area, where he performed a test that proved he was right. After quite a bit of commotion in the plant, corrections were made that possibly saved the plant a day or more of production and thousands of dollars. This same worker stayed after his shift without pay to help make the necessary corrections.

Having both worked in settings with climates more consistent with typical impressions of production plants—where employees are placed in monotonous jobs that turn people into unmotivated "machines" who don't care about productivity or quality—Sims and CM were particularly amazed by instances such as these. They saw workers solve difficult technical and personal problems, saw them volunteer to help complete difficult tasks without being told to do so, heard them praise one another for work well done and provide negative feedback to fellow workers for not pulling their weight, heard them refer to their work team's task responsibilities as "our business," and saw them talk with members of plant management (including the plant manager) as though they were equals. Most of all, they saw one of the best plants (and in many cases the best) in its product classification on many performance indicators, including productivity, quality, safety, morale, turnover, and absenteeism.

The employees at the plant did not have the benefit of familiarity with the research and knowledge available regarding the systematic self-leadership strategies outlined in this book. Manz and Sims found, however, that they already were using many of these strategies without realizing they were doing so. The advantage these workers did have over workers in more traditional plants stemmed from their work environment, which provided them with the opportunity to use their innate abilities to lead themselves. This plant, we believe, represents just the tip of the iceberg in terms of what is possible. The primary stand of this book is that self-leadership can be used to improve one's personal effectiveness. It also can be used, however, to help others become more effective. The manager who is wise enough to provide an environment for workers where they can exercise their self-leadership potential, for example, could reap substantial benefits on several bottom-line performance measures. In addition, by helping workers master self-leadership skills (such as those outlined in this book), a manager can create significant benefits for both the workers and the manager. All this calls for a new, contemporary style of leadership—leadership that centers on the power of self-leadership.[46]

The tremendous potential of human beings to lead themselves to personal effectiveness is an expansive frontier just waiting to be explored. The examples related in this chapter offer but a glimpse of a few grains of the vast sands of self-leadership possibilities waiting to be tapped. Indeed, the ultimate journey is not the exploration of new lands or the outer regions of the cosmos; instead, it is the expedition to discover the tremendous unexplored regions of the human potential (the miracles) locked inside each one of us.

REAL-WORLD SELF-LEADERSHIP CASE

John Johnson and *Ebony* Magazine

John H. Johnson was born in 1918 in Arkansas City, Arkansas. Because there were no high schools in Arkansas that African Americans were allowed to attend, in 1933 Johnson's widowed mother moved the family to Chicago, where Johnson enrolled in DuSable High School. He was an outstanding student, becoming president of his class and editor of the school paper. He eventually won a scholarship to the University of Chicago.

After college he worked at Supreme Liberty Life Insurance Company.

At that time, mainstream news publications provided very little coverage of African Americans, so at the request of the insurance company's president, Harry Pace, Johnson began compiling an in-house "digest" of events and happenings in the African American community. When he discussed his digest with friends, they often commented that it sounded very interesting, and many asked him where they could get copies of what he was talking about.

This gave Johnson an idea. He went to his mother and announced that he intended to start a magazine. His mother said, "What are you going to start it with? You don't have any money. How are you going to start a magazine?" Johnson replied, "Well, I don't know, but that's my idea." Mrs. Johnson mortgaged her furniture for five hundred dollars and gave the money to her son, which allowed him to start Negro Digest in 1942.

Early on, Johnson was unable to attract advertisers, and the magazine nearly failed. "I lived with failure, but I never accepted it," Johnson later stated. "In fact, I discharged one of our early employees because he kept telling me that I wasn't going to make it. I said, 'Gee, I'm not secure enough myself to have anyone around me saying I can't make it.' There were many times when I doubted it. But I would go into a room and, as a teacher very often kept kids after school repeating things, I would repeat to myself, 'I will not fail, I will not fail, I will not fail!'"

In 1945, Johnson published his first edition of Ebony magazine, which showcased the successes of African Americans around the country. Ebony was a fast success, with readership climbing from 25,000 to more than 200,000 in a single year. Six years later, Johnson founded Jet, a magazine devoted to covering African Americans in politics, entertainment, business, and sports. The Johnson media empire has expanded to include book publishing, Fashion Fair Cosmetics, and radio and cable TV stations. Johnson was the first African American to be included in Forbes magazine's listing of the "400 Richest Americans."

Questions for Class Discussion

1. How would you compare the psychological world that John Johnson created for himself to the "reality" of the world around him in the 1940s?

2. In what ways did positive thinking affect Johnson's life?

3. What specific self-leadership strategies did Johnson use to help him achieve his objectives?

4. How does Johnson's life reflect the saying, "You can't control the wind, but you can certainly adjust the sails"?

Source/Additional Reading

Johnson, John H. 1993. Succeeding Against the Odds. New York: Amistad.

9

REACHING THE DESTINATION

But the Journey Continues . . .

What we call the beginning is often the end. And to make our end is to make a beginning. The end is where we start from.

—T. S. Eliot

He set out on the journey with the best of intentions and true determination. He would discover the place of peace, contentment, and fulfillment. That wonderful land was out there—he would find it and then return to his hopeful, hardworking people and lead them to it. Then all would at last be released from their toil-laden and imperfect existence.

He traveled long and hard; he crossed vast deserts and the highest of snowcapped mountains; he fought with wild beasts and defended himself against strange and hostile peoples. Still he could not find the wonderful land for which he searched.

At last, one day many years after he began his journey, he wearily entered a land that seemed somehow peaceful. It was pleasant to look upon, and, yes, the people were quite friendly. Somehow the land seemed new yet comfortably familiar. He enjoyed himself there for several days while he recovered from his long travels and regained his clarity of perspective.

Then one morning, having significantly recovered his faculties, he experienced the strangest of sensations. He realized that this land had seemed familiar because it was the home he had left

Learning Objectives

After studying this chapter, you should be able to do the following:

1. Synthesize the full array of self-leadership strategies into a comprehensive self-leadership framework.

2. Apply the comprehensive self-leadership framework to real-world situations and cases.

3. Describe the concept of personal effectiveness and explain how it is influenced by self-leadership strategies.

4. Recognize the importance of the

concept of self-efficacy in the context of self-leadership.

5. Explain the concept of SuperLeadership.

6. Examine the future development of self-leadership, especially in relation to the untapped power of the mind.

behind so many years before. The people had not recognized him because of his greatly increased age and weather-worn features. Once they realized who he was, they were in a state of excitement and curiosity to know of the wonderful land of peace, contentment, and fulfillment that he must surely have discovered after so many years. They had eagerly waited for his return so that they too might go there. Slowly he responded to their questions. "Yes," he said, "there is a wonderful land and I have discovered it. It is not as I thought, though. You see, to go there is to be *here*—we were there all along but did not see."

"Well then, you have wasted many years, and our hopes have been in vain!" the people cried. "And look at you—you are but a shell of the fine physical specimen you were when you left."

"It is true," he said. "I have traded many years of my life and a large portion of my physical strength for the realization that the wonderful land I sought for so long was mine all along. But I say to you, it is the best exchange I have ever made. You too can enjoy the contentment that I now know if you will but travel, not foolishly as I did, but with your mind into your heart so that you might know your soul."

We have now completed our journey together, and we hope you have found it worthwhile. It has been a long journey, but the destination and a beginning are at hand. Before you lay this book aside, however, we would like you to consider a few more ideas. In this chapter, we offer an illustrative case that is designed to exemplify how the various self-leadership elements discussed thus far might be combined into a comprehensive self-leadership framework that can help you to develop a new, more effective way of working and living in our complex and often troublesome world. We also discuss the concept of personal effectiveness—what it is and where it comes from. Finally, we consider briefly how each of us can go about improving our world by contributing to the self-leadership of others and offer some thoughts concerning self-leadership possibilities for the future.

A SELF-LEADERSHIP FRAMEWORK

To promote a fuller understanding of self-leadership and the various factors involved, we need to describe an integrative framework. In essence, we have thus far been focusing on and examining the details of the various pieces of a larger self-leadership puzzle. At this point, we will examine how these pieces fit together to form the complete picture.

Figure 9.1 presents a diagram that combines the key elements of self-leadership discussed in the previous chapters. The four major parts of the diagram correspond with the topics in Chapters 3, 4, 5, and 6: strategies used primarily to alter our immediate physical world and to help us exercise control over ourselves, strategies for tapping the power of natural rewards, techniques for redesigning our psychological worlds, and tools to lead ourselves within team settings. Note that consistent with Chapter 5, beliefs, imagined experiences, and self-talk are depicted as interacting factors that lead to the thought patterns that establish a unique psychological world for each of us. The diagram also illustrates that each of the four key dimensions to self-leadership influences and complements the others in forming a comprehensive framework.

The center of the diagram, labeled "Mind and Body," represents the ultimate focus of self-leadership—the primary concerns of self-leadership are our behaviors, thoughts,

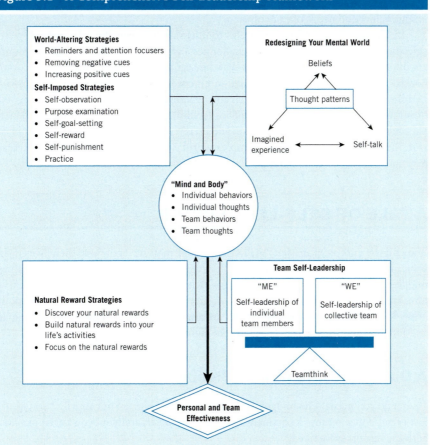

Figure 9.1   A Comprehensive Self-Leadership Framework

World-Altering Strategies
- Reminders and attention focusers
- Removing negative cues
- Increasing positive cues

Self-Imposed Strategies
- Self-observation
- Purpose examination
- Self-goal-setting
- Self-reward
- Self-punishment
- Practice

Redesigning Your Mental World

Beliefs

Thought patterns

Imagined experience ⟷ Self-talk

"Mind and Body"
- Individual behaviors
- Individual thoughts
- Team behaviors
- Team thoughts

Natural Reward Strategies
- Discover your natural rewards
- Build natural rewards into your life's activities
- Focus on the natural rewards

Team Self-Leadership

"ME"
Self-leadership of individual team members

"WE"
Self-leadership of collective team

Teamthink

Personal and Team Effectiveness

and emotions, and how these affect our personal effectiveness (our success in achieving our goals as well as our satisfaction with our work, ourselves, and our lives) and our effectiveness as members of teams. The diagram points out that each of the four parts of self-leadership has an impact on our behaviors and thoughts, and ultimately on our personal and team effectiveness. The model also shows the reciprocal influences (as depicted by the double arrow) of a person's psychological world and his or her corresponding thoughts and behaviors.

Figure 9.1 allows us to view the comprehensive systematic approach to self-leadership in its totality. A complex system of multiple variables is suggested, indicating that we have several points of departure in our undertaking to improve our self-leadership. Applying principles suggested by the various strategies that have been outlined also should contribute to improvements in the other approaches. For example, by effectively applying self-leadership techniques such as self-goal-setting and self-reward, we also foster indirect benefits like increased enjoyment of our work (natural rewards) and improved, more beneficial patterns of thought. Ultimately, beneficial application of the various techniques should contribute to a changed, more effective and rewarding lifestyle and outlook. Ideally, this new pattern of self-leadership will be tailored to the unique values and needs of each of us.

In Chapter 8, we offered examples to illustrate how specific self-leadership strategies have been applied to various challenges and problems. Although such examples are informative, their shortcoming is that they cannot adequately illustrate the comprehensive self-leadership system outlined in Figure 9.1. Consequently, we now provide a fictitious case, inspired by our research and experience with self-leadership, designed to illustrate how a number of specific self-leadership strategies might combine to benefit a particular individual: one who, like you and us, is trying to cope effectively and enjoyably with the many challenges of our complex world. We hope that you find this excursion instructive as well as entertaining.

A TALE OF SELF-LEADERSHIP

Tom Bigsby and Jennifer (Jen) Wilks have never met; nevertheless, their lives display some amazing parallels. They both work for regionally based, medium-size companies in middle-management positions. Each has a loving spouse and a son and a daughter, ages nine and eleven, respectively. Both live in nice suburban homes in large metropolitan areas. In countless ways, their situations are amazingly similar. The ways in which Tom and Jen live their lives, however, differ like night and day.

A Day in the Life of Tom Bigsby

"What do you mean 'The budget is out of line'?" Tom blurted out angrily. "You guys are just great! You want my department to achieve miracles, and you won't even provide us with the resources we need."

Don Greenlaw, the vice president of financial control, scowled back at Tom. "We don't want excuses here—we want performance; and as for your budget, it is just plain too extravagant."

"If we didn't clamp down on unreasonable budget requests like this one, we would have everyone feeding at the troughs too long," chimed in Bob Harris, the division manager, with an obvious tone of superiority in his voice.

Tom felt the veins bulging in his neck. It was obvious to him that the members of the budget committee had their minds made up before the meeting even started and were basing their judgments on a narrow-minded, conservative stance, as they always did. He had had it this time. He rose to his feet to vent his rage and . . .

"Honey, I wish you wouldn't gulp your food that way. You know the doctor said you need to learn to take things easier and relax."

"Never mind, Helen. I've got things on my mind," Tom snapped back. He leaned back stiffly into his chair a bit and let out a sigh. "This is going to be some day," he thought to himself miserably.

"Damn snow," Tom muttered as he scraped the ice from his car's windshield. As he climbed in and started the engine, he felt symptoms of a nagging case of heartburn, apparently resulting from his hurried breakfast. Soon he was out on the expressway, on his way to work with the radio tuned to the news, as usual. He occasionally commented sarcastically about "those incompetents in Washington" and complained about other news issues as he wove in and out of traffic in an attempt to get to work more quickly. He did not notice the sunshine gleaming on the new-fallen snow that blanketed the trees, or the smiling snowman with hand raised in a gesture of friendly greeting next to a home visible from the road. Tom was deep in thought, recounting the problems he had faced the previous day and visualizing distasteful results of the budget meeting he was to have that afternoon.

After parking his car, Tom quickly entered the tall office building in the beautifully landscaped complex in which he worked, occasionally muttering a hurried hello through a forced smile when he encountered someone he recognized. Tom felt that many of the people working for his company seemed friendly, but he did not spend much time interacting with them on a personal basis. He felt the purpose of his job was clear—and that was to work. Personal conversation or interaction was not important, including that which occurred over lunch, which he frequently skipped.

Tom threw a quick hello at his secretary and a nearby colleague as he entered his office, where he promptly removed his coat and hat. He heard, but hardly noticed, the rather stiff, proper responses to his greeting as he passed by. Tom sighed as he looked around his office. He did not like this room because it was here that he faced and suffered through the burden of troublesome problems. Soon he was shuffling through a pile of paper on his desk, scarcely noticing that his secretary had brought him his usual cup of black coffee.

The next two hours were mostly a blur to Tom as he repeatedly shifted his focus from one task to another. He was frequently interrupted by phone calls and employees with problems—mostly minor ones. Several stacks of reports and files had been pushed to the far side of his desk—some had been there for several days—while he worked on the immediate problems before him. It seemed he never had time to think about or plan his actions.

Meanwhile, snow started falling again, and the view of the white-blanketed countryside from Tom's twelfth-story window was breathtaking. A shimmering frozen lake was in the foreground, and farther away lay thick forests and rolling hills. Tom rarely looked up from his work, however, even when conversing on the phone. When he did have occasion to glance out the window, his thoughts were directed to potential problems with road conditions for his return trip home. "Damn winter," he muttered to himself.

At about 11:30 an employee in obvious distress entered Tom's office. "Mr. Bigsby, we're out of materials again," he complained, "and Supplies says there are none in stock."

"Damn!" said Tom to no one in particular. "I haven't had time to look at the supplies situation. I'll try to arrange for a rush order, although I haven't had much luck in the past trying to push things through. Maybe I can use possible cancellations in the future as leverage if they don't come through for us," said Tom, turning to the employee. "In the meantime, do what you can."

The employee left, frowning and obviously dissatisfied. At that moment, Tom's phone rang again. "Hello," Tom said as he picked up the receiver.

"Tom, I'm in a jam," said the voice on the line. "Your estimated sales report is long overdue, and the production folks say they can't wait any longer—they need the information today. Have you been working on it, Tom?"

"Uh, yes," Tom responded, a bit anxiously, as he reached for one of the piles at the edge of his desk.

"I've got to have it today, Tom. I wish you would try to plan ahead a little more," said the voice.

"Okay!" Tom replied in an angry tone and a bit too loudly.

Tom worked through his lunch hour, as usual. He did not like working through lunch, but he felt the best way to get ahead in the company was to push hard. His intention this day was to complete the overdue sales projection report and the rush order on materials. He was distracted by several minor problems, however, and found he had made little headway by 2:00 P.M., when he had to stop to throw some materials together for the budget meeting that was scheduled for 2:15.

Tom entered the meeting room in an uneasy, defensive frame of mind. He felt sure the budget committee intended to provide him with minimal support, and his short, terse greetings to the individuals present reflected this belief. The members of the committee responded in kind, and soon the atmosphere in the room was uncomfortably strained.

Tom's presentation to the committee took about an hour and fifteen minutes. Several times as he was speaking he noted inconsistencies in what he said. Also, the committee members raised several issues that he had not anticipated. His already strained manner of presenting his case became even more strained as time passed. Each time he encountered an issue for which he was not adequately prepared, he tried to compensate by expressing his opinions especially emphatically, despite the obvious lack of substantive support for these views. In desperation, he tried to push his budget proposal through by sheer aggressiveness. Meanwhile, he found that he was continually prodding himself with negative internal thoughts such as "Why did you say that? Now you really opened a can of worms, you dummy!"

By the end of the presentation, Tom was noticeably exhausted and frazzled. The committee members seemed to realize this, and they were even a little gentle in the delivery of their negative feedback to Tom. In short, they told Tom he had not adequately thought through and documented his needs. They explained that they could not approve the budget in its current form, and they recommended that he revise it, either substantially reducing it or providing much better documentation, and resubmit it in a week.

At this point, Tom was no longer hearing all that was being said. He had, in essence, joined what he saw as his opposition by lambasting himself on the inside with negative internal self-statements: "I blew it again. . . . I never get anything right. . . ."

"You don't seem to have a sense of direction in your department—no specific goals that you're working toward . . . ," the budget committee continued.

"Maybe I'm not cut out to be a manager," Tom thought. "I just don't know what's wrong with me."

The meeting was over. Tom felt deflated, and the committee members seemed sorry and disturbed about what had transpired. One committee member with obvious good intentions spoke to Tom privately as the others departed. "Tom, I've been in your shoes before. I know what you're feeling. I've found that going over my presentations ahead of time helps a lot. It can help in detecting problems and making adjustments before you do it for keeps. Also, you need to do a little thinking about the direction of your department. You need to spend some time planning."

"I don't have time to waste that way," Tom snapped back.

"Frankly, Tom, having to redo the budget is not going to save you much time either," the committee member responded with a smile that he intended to be friendly and reassuring. Despite this individual's good intentions, Tom was irritated. He left the meeting room in a huff.

After spending a couple more disorganized, hurried hours back in his office, Tom left the building, his briefcase full of troublesome problems that needed his attention. It had been another difficult day that had gone just as badly as he had expected. A light snow had continued to blanket the landscape, which was now sparkling under the bright-orange setting sun. A small group of employees laughed as they playfully threw snowballs at one another in the parking lot. Tom didn't hear their laughter. "Damn snow," he muttered, sweeping the windshield of his car.

A Day in the Life of Jennifer Wilks

Jen's presentation to the budget committee had gone extremely well. "I appreciate your input," Jen told the committee members, "and your responsiveness to new ideas." She felt good about the strong support she had been given as a result of her effective budget proposal presentation. She had done a good job in providing convincing documentation and a well-thought-out, logical proposal for her requests.

Jen felt a sense of satisfaction surge through her. She was impressed with the integrity and sincerity with which the meeting had been conducted. This was the kind of meeting Jen enjoyed—challenging her to refine her ideas, yet with an atmosphere of openness and flexibility.

Feeling exuberant, Jen rose to her feet to express her appreciation and . . .

"Would you like some more coffee, dear?" asked Chris, Jen's husband.

"Uh, yes. Would you pour it into my thermos, please?" she answered.

"You really seem to be deep in thought this morning. What's on your mind?" Chris asked as he poured the coffee.

"It's this budget committee meeting today. I think it's really going to provide me with an opportunity to state my case for the department to those who can make a difference. I expect it to be challenging, but I'm ready. I'm looking forward to it," Jen told him.

Jen settled back in her chair. "This is going to be some day," she thought enthusiastically.

After clearing the snow from her car's windshield, Jen paused to toss a couple of snowballs at a nearby tree before climbing in and starting the engine. "This weekend will be a good time to take the kids sledding," she thought to herself. She imagined the kids laughing as they whooshed down a snow-covered hill.

She turned on the radio as she pulled onto the expressway. A newscast was on, so she changed the station, choosing one that was playing some quiet music. She liked to start the day with music rather than with the news, which was often bad—she sometimes found that listening to distressing news reports had a negative effect on her thinking early in the day. She would catch up on important events with the newspaper and evening newscasts later on. After driving a few minutes through the scenic, snow-covered landscape, Jen decided to get a little work done. She turned off the radio and proceeded to dictate a couple of memos into a tape recorder she had conveniently located next to her on the passenger seat. She drove at a leisurely pace, sipping her coffee and enjoying the view.

When Jen reached her office complex, she felt relaxed and ready for the day. She strolled into the building, once again enjoying the snow-covered setting around her as she took some deep breaths of the clean, fresh air. She paused to deliver hearty greetings to fellow employees she passed. She enjoyed the people she worked with and found personal interactions to be a good source of information and ideas. Jen also realized that they helped establish important relationships that fostered cooperation when she needed assistance from others to get things done.

Jen stopped for a friendly chat with her assistant and a small group of colleagues who were conversing outside her office. After a short but pleasant and relaxed conversation, Jen entered her office. She smiled as she looked around the room that she had decorated (within a limited budget) to her personal tastes. Jen liked her office because it was here that she faced many stimulating challenges. She made a determined effort to keep her job enjoyable by working to mold it to her liking. She found that there were many things to enjoy in her work if she looked for them—and she did.

Before she began to work on specific tasks, Jen picked up a notepad and pen, eased back in her chair, and just thought for a bit while she savored a cup of coffee. She then made a list of the more important activities that needed her attention during the day—"preparation for the budget meeting," she wrote on the pad, adding a star next to her notation for emphasis. Jen spent the next couple of hours working on the items on her list, using a good portion of that time to review the presentation she had planned for the budget meeting. She even spent some time quietly rehearsing the most important points she would make while also picturing a positive response and a desirable outcome from the meeting.

As usual, Jen's assistant held her calls, allowing only the most important ones to go through to her. Jen had worked out a routine some months back where she would spend the better part of her mornings working on her more important activities, including planning. She designated a two-hour period after lunch as her "communication/troubleshooting" time. She would spend this time discussing problems directly with employees and following up on phone calls. Employees understood that only emergencies were to be brought to Jen's attention outside the two-hour period after lunch. At first, they had resisted this limited open-door policy a little, feeling a bit shut out. But soon they came to look at it as an expression of confidence in their abilities. It was amazing how many problems they were able to solve on their own when they knew they had only limited access to Jen. On the other hand, they knew Jen's door was always open in the early afternoon.

While working, Jen paused every so often to look at some of the pictures on her walls (photos of many beautiful, resort-type settings that she had either visited or wished to visit someday) or to gaze out the window. The snow was still falling outside, and the view of icy ponds and snow-covered trees from her tenth-story window looked to her like the most beautiful of Christmas cards come to life. She sometimes let her thoughts drift, picturing herself enjoying a cup of hot chocolate in front of her blazing fireplace with one of her kids in her lap or some other pleasurable scene. She found that short breaks such as these helped keep her relaxed and refreshed.

A small plaque Jen had placed on her wall caught her attention. It read, "There is nothing so powerful as the human mind well maintained and purposefully set into motion." As though answering, she thought, "I need to do some more developmental reading."

A determined smile came over Jen's face as she gazed far off somewhere into the realm of possibility. Suddenly her attention snapped back to the present as she was struck by a powerful idea. She had been struggling for days to come up with a more efficient way to process the work going through her department. At this moment a new, innovative approach was clear in her mind. She quickly reached for a notepad (as she often did when a new idea came to mind). "This will save us time and money," she thought enthusiastically. (The idea would later prove to reap these desirable results for the department and would play an instrumental role in Jen's next promotion.)

About 11:30 an employee in obvious distress entered Jen's office. "Jen, the last shipment of materials we received is defective. We can't get any work done without materials."

"Call Frank Smith in Supplies," Jen responded in a concerned but controlled voice. "We have a couple days' worth of emergency materials in stock. In the meantime, I'll call

Fred Harris and have him rush us an order. We have a good working relationship, and I know he'll come through for me. Also, Dave, would you and the others take some time to think through a strategy for dealing with this kind of problem in the future? Maybe some kind of sample inspection could be made when the materials first arrive to help us detect problems *before* we're under the gun. Or maybe some other precautionary measure could be taken. Let me know what you think is best."

As Dave left Jen's office, he looked less concerned, and there was a sense of responsibility in his stride. Things hadn't always worked out perfectly since Jen had become department manager, but the employees always knew where they stood and felt that they were a part of things. Jen certainly did not try to do everything herself or be involved in all decisions concerning the department. The look of confidence and determination frequently seen on her employees' faces reflected the sense of responsibility they had come to feel under Jen's guidance.

The remainder of Jen's morning went well. Just before lunch, she looked at her list of the things she wanted to work on during the day and noted with a sense of satisfaction that she had already finished most of them. She then left the office and had a leisurely lunch with two of the employees in her department. She tries to arrange to go out with a couple of members of the department twice a week, rotating whom she goes with so that she spends roughly equal time with all. Jen finds that the generally relaxed conversations over lunch, away from the office, are invaluable in keeping her abreast of the concerns of her workers and new developments in the organization. The lunches also foster good working relationships among Jen and members of the department.

After lunch, Jen handled employee concerns and returned phone calls during her open office hours. This time is often rather hectic, but Jen tries hard to handle one matter at a time and to keep calm. She had arranged to shorten her office hours a little this day so that she would have a chance to collect her thoughts and briefly review her budget proposal one more time before the meeting. She made a list of pending matters and calls she had not been able to make and planned to address them during her office hours the following day. She usually found two hours a day to be more than adequate for these tasks, so she felt confident she would catch up within a few days.

After brief reviewing her budget proposal, Jen went to the meeting room early, feeling a little nervous but mostly confident and prepared. She delivered a friendly greeting to each budget committee member individually. Jen was pleased to have the opportunity to make the planned direction and resource needs of her department known to those individuals who held the purse strings in her company. She wanted to make the most of the time she had with them.

Jen's presentation lasted approximately an hour. It went smoothly, as planned—and Jen knew it. Even the issues raised by the committee posed no problems. "I understand your concern about the increase in materials costs I've requested, and that's why I've prepared these charts," Jen explained toward the end of the session. "As you can see, the expansion we've made in our product lines *as well as* increased materials costs make the request only a slight increase over last year."

"Yes, I see," responded Stan Jones, the vice president of financial control. "In that light, the request does seem very much in line."

"It appears you've done your homework, Jen—I like the innovative changes you're establishing in your department," added Harry Willis, the division manager, who obviously was pleased.

Jen's budget was approved as proposed, and, perhaps even more important, Jen was able to improve her professional relationships with instrumental persons in her organization. She felt good about the support she had been given. Her most important approval, though, came from Jen herself. She was liberal in her self-praise. The meeting was significant; Jen had done well, and she let herself know it. "This is just the beginning," she thought. "I'm going to make things happen. I'm going to make a difference around here—I know I can do it."

After receiving some compliments from individual committee members, Jen returned to her office feeling good. She spent a couple more hours working and made progress on some pending tasks, although she was a bit distracted in her elation. She left the office that day with no work remaining to be done. She is usually able to finish what needs to be done (those matters that cannot be delegated) at the office, so she rarely does much work at home—although she often comes up with creative ideas for her department during her leisure hours, which she writes down on pads she has located conveniently in her home. Many of these ideas have saved Jen a great deal of effort over the long run.

She was ready to celebrate this evening. She found herself singing a couple of times while she reviewed her successes of the day, and once again she stopped to enjoy the snow-covered landscape. She thought to herself, "I really love this job. I believe this job utilizes my strengths, and it allows me to make a difference in the lives of my colleagues and the organization. What a day," she thought, "what a day."

THE TALE IN PERSPECTIVE

The case you have just read represents an attempt to illustrate two divergent patterns of self-leadership under essentially identical conditions. Both individuals are trying hard. Their general patterns of living, however, are leading to different results. Simply put, Jen is exercising effective self-leadership à la this book—Tom is not. Jen is applying many of the strategies and techniques that have been suggested, and she is doing so in a way that is consistent with her own situation and personal makeup. She is controlling cues (having phone calls held and limiting office hours), for example. She also is monitoring her progress (self-observation) by using a list of pending tasks as a guide. Items on the list represent her goals for the day. Also, rehearsing her presentation apparently contributed significantly to her success at the budget meeting—the major challenge of her day.

A primary strength in Jen's approach is her overall constructive and positive orientation to thinking and behaving. For example, she is liberal in her use of self-rewards at the physical level (enjoying a good lunch after a hard morning of work, taking occasional rest breaks while gazing at the pleasant pictures on her walls and the view out her window, planning to celebrate the day's success when she gets home) and at the mental level (making positive self-statements, imagining desirable experiences in the future). Perhaps even more important, Jen tries to build in, focus on, and otherwise experience the natural rewards of her work itself (surrounding herself with pleasant pictures on her office walls; she works in a steady and controlled, rather than frantic and haphazard, style; and she purposefully seeks out the enjoyable aspects of her job). Also, it seems that Jen from time to time performs a mental examination of her purpose in life (thinking about why she loves her job and the contribution she is making as a result of her job).

Finally, and perhaps most important of all, Jen has adopted a desirable pattern of thinking. She has developed the ability to see through the often obstacle-laden exterior of challenges and to be especially responsive to the opportunities within. Her orientation is to strive to achieve further advances and progress rather than to flounder and give in to formidable problems. Jen's actions are controlled and well thought out, reflecting her recognition of the obstacles that do exist. Rather than retreating from those obstacles, Jen advances toward existing opportunities. Jen has indeed established a positive world, psychologically and physically (e.g., through her actions toward others, she has won their support when she needs it), in the way she lives her life.

Tom's mode of living reflects to a large degree an opposite pattern of self-leadership. Tom does not manage his behavior through the use of self-leadership strategies. Instead, he works in a disorganized, haphazard manner; in addition, he takes a basically negative, destructive stance toward his work. He focuses on the distasteful aspects of his job and keys his efforts primarily on the immediate obstacles he faces. Tom expects his work experiences and outcomes to be unpleasant—and so they are. What little time he *does* spend thinking about positive aspects of his job is devoted to thoughts centering on future promotions or pay raises and not on what he does. He has created a negative world for himself through his thoughts and actions (e.g., he does not behave in a manner that helps ensure that he will have the support of others when he needs it). Tom has a self-leadership problem that will likely preclude his achieving personal and professional effectiveness unless he makes some major changes.

Do either of these two fictitious characters remind you of yourself? Perhaps you see a little of both Tom and Jen in you when you gaze into the mirror. The point is, you *do* have choices. These include the way you choose to think about things and the way you choose to behave. This book offers a framework to help you choose intelligently and act on your choices wisely and efficiently.

We could present yet another type of fictitious character—one who does not try at all or, in essence, one who does not care about personal effectiveness. We assume, however, that those who would read a book on self-leadership *do* care and *do* want to succeed (according to their own standards). Consequently, the framework we have presented is designed to help you gain insight into the choices you have concerning how you lead yourself to get more out of the effort you exert and the types of overall self-leadership patterns you can choose to establish for your life. If you are going to spend the effort to work and live, why not spend it wisely? Greater awareness of and competence in applying the varied tools of self-leadership can be powerful sources of personal effectiveness. How are you spending your life? Are you moving ahead to benefit from the abundant opportunities that lie before you, or are you forever surrendering to obstacles along the way? The pursuit of self-leadership may well be the ultimate journey into yourself and your life. The destination is within your reach if you choose to seek it.

PERSONAL EFFECTIVENESS

"Tell me, oh great one, why are you so triumphant and able in your every endeavor?" asked the admirer.

"It is because I believe that I am so," he responded in a powerful and confident tone of voice.

"But then tell me, great one, why do you believe you are so triumphant and able?"

"Because I *am*," he responded confidently.

At this the admirer scratched his head and thought for a while. Then he asked, "Are you triumphant and able because you *believe* you are so, or just because you *are*?"

At this question he turned to the admirer with a faint trace of a smile on his face and a gleam in his eye that said the admirer had asked well. Then he answered, "Yes, I have already told you so."

Some key self-leadership ideas have been presented in this book. It should be clear that to be effective self-leaders, we need to recognize our interdependent relationship with the world in which we live, as well as the way we influence ourselves directly. Indeed, we largely create our own personal world through our actions, and our world acts on us in countless ways. We also need to recognize the importance of our mental behavior as well as our physical behavior. The observable actions we take to deal with problems and challenges are important, but our thoughts about these challenges (mental behavior) are just as important. Ultimately, understanding all this should help us become effective self-leaders and achieve personal effectiveness.

What is personal effectiveness? It varies from person to person, but some basic aspects of personal effectiveness can be distinguished for most situations. We would describe individuals as being personally effective, for example, if they are able to reasonably accomplish what they set out to do with their lives, if they develop a healthy belief in their capabilities and value as persons, and if they develop a fundamental and fairly stable satisfaction with life. To be personally effective is to believe we can deal with life's many challenges and enjoy the successful handling of them.

One insightful view of the ingredients of personal effectiveness is encompassed in the concept of self-efficacy, which we discussed in detail in Chapter 2. Recall that self-efficacy is, in essence, our level of effectiveness in dealing with our world, or our perception of our own ability to overcome the situations and challenges we face in life. Also recall that one of the most important sources of self-efficacy perceptions is our own performance history. When we experience successes in difficult situations, our perceptions of our self-efficacy tend to be improved, and when we experience failure, they tend to be undermined.

This bit of information provides us with the basis for a valuable insight—that personal effectiveness leads to personal effectiveness. If we can master self-leadership skills such as those suggested in this book and consequently take control of our lives and our situations, we can enhance our current and future performance—our current performance through more intelligent, purposeful, and motivated immediate thought and behavior, and our future performance through enhanced self-perceptions of our personal efficacy or, in essence, our own effectiveness. Thus, if we believe we are personally effective, we are likely to become even more so. The best way to develop a positive belief in our own effectiveness is by handling the challenges we face in life successfully. Mastery of systematic self-leadership skills can help us achieve personal excellence.

These ideas are illustrated in Figure 9.2. Self-leadership skills are an instrumental part of our level of personal effectiveness. They have a direct impact on our performance capability by helping to motivate and guide us in our immediate performances, and they influence our future performances through their effect on our self-efficacy perceptions.

Self-Leadership, Self-Efficacy, and Personal Effectiveness

In Chapter 2 and again in this chapter, we have suggested that self-efficacy may be an important mechanism through which self-leadership strategies affect individual performance outcomes and personal effectiveness. As shown in Figure 9.2, self-leadership theory suggests that the effective use of self-leadership strategies will result in more intelligent, purposeful, and motivated behavior and thinking, which will in turn result in positive perceptions of self-efficacy and ultimately successful performances and personal effectiveness. Empirical research has tended to support this conceptual model of self-leadership, self-efficacy, and performance. For example, in a study of 151 participants, researchers found significant relationships between the use of self-leadership strategies and self-efficacy evaluations, and between self-efficacy evaluations and performance, suggesting that self-leadership influenced performance by first increasing self-efficacy perceptions.[1] More recent studies have provided additional evidence in support of the mediating role of self-efficacy in the self-leadership to performance relationship across a variety of different contexts. For example, a study of 130 soldiers in the Austrian army found that those in a self-leadership training intervention group experienced higher levels of self-efficacy, lower levels of strain, and higher levels of objective performance outcomes on both physical and educational tests.[2] Findings such as these point to an important role for self-efficacy perceptions as a key cognitive mechanism through which self-leadership strategies affect performance outcomes.

Notes

1. Gregory E. Prussia, Joe S. Anderson, and Charles C. Manz, "Self-Leadership and Performance Outcomes: The Mediating Influence of Self-Efficacy," *Journal of Organizational Behavior* 19, no. 5 (September 1998): 523–38.

2. Gerhard A. Lucke and Marco R. Furtner, "Soldiers Lead Themselves to More Success: A Self-Leadership Intervention Study," *Military Psychology* 27, no. 5 (September 2015): 311–24.

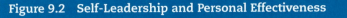

Figure 9.2 Self-Leadership and Personal Effectiveness

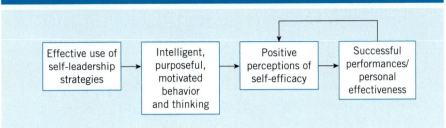

SOME ADDITIONAL THOUGHTS

Before we conclude this book, we want to offer some tips on developing the self-leadership skills of others. We will then close with some thoughts on future issues in self-leadership.

Throughout our discussion, we have emphasized the importance of the interrelationship between ourselves and our world. In addition, in Chapters 3 and 4 we suggested that for an individual to enjoy an activity naturally, the activity must provide the person with a sense of purpose, which in many cases is encompassed in the notion of altruism. Here we would like to suggest a powerful method for improving our personal world and achieving a sense of altruistic purpose at the same time: the practice of Twisted Leadership.

In their book *Twisted Leadership*, Charles C. Manz and Craig L. Pearce argue that the outdated centralized, top-down, and hierarchical style of leadership, involving "petty dictators" who dominate their subordinates, is no less than a disease that results in wasted human talent, corruption, and abuse.[1] The book prescribes a cure for the disease: to "twist" it out of the organization using the "Four 'Ss' of Twisted Leadership"—Self-Leadership, SuperLeadership, Shared Leadership and Socially Responsible Leadership. These four strands of leadership are interwoven into a strong cord with self-leadership at its core. In harmony with concepts we introduced in Chapter 1, Twisted Leadership maintains that we must effectively lead ourselves before we can effectively lead others.

SuperLeadership, the second S of Twisted Leadership, can be described as the process of helping others develop and practice systematic effective self-leadership. It involves bringing out and stimulating the development of personal effectiveness in the people with whom we associate. SuperLeadership consists of three primary components: setting a good example, guidance, and reinforcement of self-leadership. The first step is to display self-leadership skills in your own behavior. It has been said that "actions speak louder than words," and in this case that old adage is especially true. By displaying systematic self-leadership practices in your behavior (setting goals for yourself, purposefully making your work naturally enjoyable, seeking out opportunities rather than shrinking in the face of obstacles, and so on), you are serving as an effective, concrete model and stimulus for others to do the same.

Black Panther (2018) and Spiderman: Homecoming (2017)

Scenes from two recent Marvel superhero movies help to demonstrate empowering others to take responsibility for leading themselves. In *Black Panther*, T'Challa (Chadwick Boseman) has become the new king but he's very reluctant to take action until he is challenged by Killmonger (Michael B. Jordan). T'Challa first takes responsibility for leading himself and thus becomes the true leader of his nation.

In *Spiderman: Homecoming*, Tony Stark (Robert Downey, Jr.) decides to take Peter Parker's (Tom Holland) Spiderman suit: "OK, it's not working out, I'm gonna need the suit back." Peter responds by saying, "You don't understand, I'm nothing without this suit." Stark says, "If you are nothing without this suit, you shouldn't have it" and then challenges Peter to develop his own self-leadership.

Discussion Questions

1. In what ways are both Killmonger and Tony Stark functioning as SuperLeaders?

2. Specifically, what causes both T'Challa and Peter Parker to realize the necessity of "leading themselves"?

3. How would you have reacted to these challenges?

Providing an example for others, however, is not enough. They also will likely need a considerable amount of specific guidance. Here encouragement and instruction in self-leadership skills are important. The goal is to get the target of your efforts thinking and behaving in a self-leading manner appropriate to that person. One useful approach to accomplishing this end is to ask appropriate questions: Do you have any goals for your efforts? How well do you think you did, and how do you feel about that? What aspects of your work do you enjoy? How could you make your work more enjoyable? What kinds of opportunities are you pursuing right now? Are you looking for new ones?

When the individual does start putting self-leadership techniques into practice, suggestions and feedback are important. In particular, positive reinforcement of self-leadership effort is crucial (e.g., "I'm glad to see you setting goals for yourself. This should help you better accomplish what you set out to do"; "Your outlook has really improved. I can tell that opportunities, rather than obstacles, are your primary motivators now"). It's important to remember, however, that your aim is to shift the leadership function to the other person. SuperLeadership ultimately means assisting others to become their own primary sources of goals, rewards, work enjoyment, opportunities, and so forth in the ways that are best suited to them.

The third S of Twisted Leadership is Shared Leadership. Shared leadership involves engaging the knowledge, skills, and abilities of multiple individuals in leadership processes and roles within groups and teams. Team members share expertise and information, stepping forward as needed with specific skills and aptitudes, taking the lead and providing influence while engaging in collaborative planning, work, and decision making.

The final Twisted Leadership S is Socially Responsible Leadership, which entails taking a long-term perspective based on higher-level values and ideals rather than focusing on selfish short-term gains. Socially responsible leaders focus on the triple bottom-line (social, environmental, and financial) while emphasizing specific "virtuous" workplace values as being foundational for the other three Ss, thereby resulting in a greater sense of purpose and meaning for all organizational members.

He looked carefully into the eyes of the very intelligent being from another world. Then he asked, "Do you think we on earth are primitive?"

"No," the being answered, "at least not in all ways."

"Then you do think we are primitive in *some* ways," he continued, intending the statement as a question. But the being did not respond. "I mean," he went on, "we have explored the universe, and we have harnessed the power of the atom. We have made great advances in the control of disease, and we have even mastered the art of manipulating genes for improving our race in future generations. Given all this, how can you think we are primitive in some way? In what way?" he asked now in an irritated voice.

"Yes, you have explored much," the being responded. "In some ways you have even surpassed the beings of my planet in your mastery of the physical world, though not many." The human nodded his head in acknowledgment. "But also you have neglected much."

"What do you mean? What have we neglected?" the human asked.

"Your focus has been outward. You have neglected what is within. It's as though you have tried to master living but have forgotten to explore life."

"What do you mean? We have made great advances in biology and medicine. We are closer to controlling life itself than we have ever been!" he responded a bit too emphatically.

"I'm not talking about your physical bodies," continued the being. "I'm talking about the core of life, the mind and the spirit."

"But we've made great advances in psychology and psychiatry, and tremendous discoveries regarding the functioning of the brain!" exclaimed the human.

"The brain is but a part of the physical body—a sort of computer to be used in dealing with the world. Life is more. You have spent so much time trying to control the world that you have forgotten the mastery of yourselves."

"But science indicates that we are ultimately what the world makes us through evolution, socialization, and so forth. It is the world that makes us what we are, isn't it?" the human asked, now thoughtfully—unsure, as though he was beginning to understand. "Isn't that the true order of things and why we must focus our major efforts on the world?"

"Only if you choose it to be," the being answered simply. "We of my planet have chosen to focus our primary efforts inward instead of outward. We have discovered that the world is largely what we make it. But we must first make something of ourselves before we can make the world. Yes, you have surpassed us in some things: weaponry to

Nelson Mandela: Twisted Leader Extraordinaire

The late Nelson Mandela, South Africa's iconic leader who helped to bring an end to apartheid (a system of racial segregation and economic-political discrimination controlled by the country's white minority government from the 1940s to the early 1990s), provides an excellent example of the four "Ss" of Twisted Leadership. In the 1960s, a young Mandela took a stand against the centralized, top-down, hierarchical apartheid government that reflected the "leadership disease" found in many organizations today. Mandela was arrested in late 1963 and charged with sabotage and conspiracy to violently overthrow the government. Toward the end of his trial, Mandela gave his famous "Speech from the Dock," which ended with the following words:

> During my lifetime I have dedicated my life to this struggle of the African people. I have fought against white domination, and I have fought against black domination. I have cherished the ideal of a democratic and free society in which all persons will live together in harmony and with equal opportunities. It is an ideal for which I hope to live for and to see realized. But, My Lord, if it needs be, it is an ideal for which I am prepared to die.

Mandela's attorneys urged him to leave out the final sentence because they feared it might provoke the judge into ordering his execution, but Mandela reasoned that he likely would be executed anyhow and decided to leave the statement in the speech, although he qualified it with "if it needs be." Mandela was convicted and sentenced to life in prison. It was in prison that Mandela began winding together the twisted strands that would make him one of the most remarkable leaders in world history.

Mandela was sent to a prison on Robben Island near Capetown. Just two miles long and one mile wide, the island was brutally cold in the winter and scorching hot in the summer. Mandela's cell was 9 x 7 feet. Here he would spend the next 18 years of his life. With no entertainment and few distractions, Mandela had plenty of time to think, reflect, and really get to know himself. Mandela had come to appreciate the power of the mind during an earlier prison term in 1956 when he observed a fellow prisoner staring into the distance and obviously thinking. Mandela turned to a friend and said, "Do you see that man? That is the mark of a great man. A man who can think and consider things . . . a man who stares into the horizon, thinking and so on." It was during his time in prison that Mandela began to carefully develop his **Self-Leadership** capacity, his ability to regulate his behaviors and cognitive processes, proactively choosing not only *what* he would do and *how* he would do it, but also spending time thinking about *why* he would do it. In a letter to his wife, Mandela wrote,

> You may find that the cell is an ideal place to learn to know yourself, to search realistically and regularly the processes of your own mind and feelings. In judging our progress as individuals we tend to concentrate on external factors such as one's social position, influence and popularity, wealth and standard of education . . . but internal factors may be even more crucial in assessing one's development as a human being: honesty, sincerity, simplicity, humility, purity, generosity, absence of vanity, readiness to serve your fellow men—qualities within the reach of every soul—are the foundation of one's spiritual life. If for nothing

else, the cell gives you the opportunity to look daily into your entire conduct to overcome the bad and develop whatever is good in you.

Mandela was finally released in 1990 after 27 years in prison. An incident that occurred on the day he was released demonstrated the mental and emotional self-leadership capabilities he had developed. As the crowds and television cameras pressed closer, Mandela's face flashed for a moment with rage and hatred. Then, as quickly as it appeared, Mandela's anger seemed to dissipate. Later, Mandela explained, "When I was in prison the son of a guard started a Bible study and I attended. That day when I stepped out of prison and looked at the people observing, a flush of anger hit me with the thought that they had robbed me of 27 years. Then the Spirit of Jesus said to me, 'Nelson, while you were in prison you were free, now that you are free don't become a prisoner.'"

After his release from prison, Mandela helped facilitate negotiations that would ultimately end apartheid. But he did so not as a top-down, inflexible, hierarchical leader enamored with his own power and influence, but rather as a **SuperLeader** focused on enabling and empowering others. Mandela often enjoyed remembering the time he spent during his boyhood herding cattle: "You know, you can only lead them from behind." He was also profoundly influenced by the tribal king, Jongintaba, who raised him. According to Mandela, when the king's court met, Jongintaba would wait until everyone had spoken before he began to speak. The focus was not on telling people what to do, but on building a consensus. Mandela used a similar empowering leadership style, allowing everyone at a meeting to speak before he carefully summarized everyone's perspectives and delicately shaped the direction of the outcome without imposing it. "It is wise," he said, "to persuade people to do things and make them think it was their own idea."

In 1994, Mandela was elected as the first black president in South Africa's history. After his election, Mandela surprised many people by embracing collaboration and **Shared Leadership** in his new government. Mandela created what some have called a "power-sharing" cabinet comprised of members of his own African National Congress as well as members of the National Party and Inkatha Freedom Party. He even included his Zulu rival, Chief Mangosuthu G. Buthelezi. Finally, throughout his life and career, Mandela reflected **Socially Responsible Leadership** by focusing on the higher-level values and ideals of tolerance, inclusion, reconciliation, equality, and freedom. "What counts in life is not the mere fact that we have lived," Mandela once said. "It is what difference we have made to the lives of others that will determine the significance of the life we lead."

Sources/Additional Reading

Eberl, Nik. 2017. "Three Secrets of Personal Leadership From Nelson Mandela." *LinkedIn*, December 7, 2017. https://www.linkedin.com/pulse/three-secrets-personal-leadership-from-nelson-mandela-dr-nik/.

Freiberg, Kevin and Jackie. 2018. "Madiba Leadership: 5 Lessons Nelson Mandela Taught the World About Change." *Forbes*, July 19, 2018. https://www.forbes.com/sites/kevinandjackiefreiberg/2018/07/19/madiba-leadership-5-lessons-nelson-mandela-taught-the-world-about-change/#f9daa6141bac.

Stengel, Richard. 2008. "Mandela: His 8 Lessons of Leadership." *Time*, July 9, 2008. http://content.time.com/time/subscriber/article/0,33009,1821659-1,00.html.

destroy and instruments to squeeze things from the physical world to satisfy the wants of the body. In this way you are advanced. But you have neglected the most powerful resource you have—the power of the mind, the core of yourselves."

As a final consideration, we would like to look for a moment into an imaginary crystal ball of self-leadership possibilities for the future. Our belief is that the major breakthroughs in the next few decades will be in an arena that has generally been thought of as a bit strange and almost mystical. We are referring to the capabilities and powers we hold deep within ourselves that so far remain largely unexplored and uncharted: the powers of the mind.[2]

An interesting and insightful book on the subject is Barbara Brown's *Supermind*.[3] Brown argues that the brain and the mind are two distinct realities. Considerable effort has been devoted to exploring the physical functioning of the brain: electrochemical impulses, left and right hemisphere functioning, and so forth. Our understanding of the almost mystical powers of the mind, however, seems to have been reserved for usually questionable and unscientific witnessing from persons who have encountered strange experiences that defy scientific explanation: people lifting cars off endangered loved ones, miraculous physical healings through effort of mind, premonitions, and extrasensory perception (ESP).

Yet the evidence is vast enough and often credible enough to warrant a belief that mind power is a strong, untapped resource, perhaps the most powerful resource available to us. Take, for example, the mounting evidence regarding biofeedback—a process that involves the use of sophisticated monitors to provide participants with feedback regarding their own bodily functions, allowing them to exert control over certain physical processes long thought to be beyond intentional control. Experience with biofeedback has shown that we can control a number of our bodily functions, including heartbeat, blood pressure, skin surface temperature, and brain wave activity. The point is that through a learning process, we can control functions of our own bodies (even brain activity) that for years were believed to be beyond our control.

In this book, we have attempted to balance the emphasis placed on physical behavior with an equal emphasis on thought. Both play an important role in the total self-leadership picture. In the future, however, self-leadership advances will need to travel beyond the level of our current conscious awareness into the largely unconscious processes and powers of the mind. The purpose is not so much to use the mind as a window to our "true personalities," as Freud and other psychologists have done in the past, but instead to use it as a resource for gaining advanced self-leadership capabilities and personal effectiveness. Preliminary journeys into this exciting new frontier have begun. The ultimate in personal effectiveness in the future will likely be an advanced state of integration and harmony of our world, our behavior, our conscious thought processes, and the deeper recesses of the mind.

Before we end the book, we'd like you to consider the story of the koi, an interesting fish, also known as the Japanese carp. The amazing thing about the koi is that if you keep it in a small container, it will grow to only two to three inches in length. If you put it in a larger bowl or a small pond, it will grow to six to ten inches. When placed in a huge body of water, however, where it can grow without confinement, the koi has the potential to reach thirty-six to forty-eight inches in length.

Clearly, the growth of this fish is strongly related to the size of its world. We feel that, similarly, the size of a person's "pond"—the mental world in which she or he lives—can truly affect whether that individual fully develops in all aspects of life. We hope the ideas we have presented regarding self-leadership will help you to expand your world, remove the limits that you may have placed on what you believe you can accomplish, and grow to realize the enormous potential that exists inside you.

REAL-WORLD SELF-LEADERSHIP CASE

"Leaning In" with Sheryl Sandberg

A truly equal world would be one where women ran half our countries and companies and men ran half our homes.

—Sheryl Sandberg

Sheryl Sandberg, the chief operating officer at Facebook, has learned throughout her life and career to be an effective self-leader. Ranked sixteenth on the 2015 *Forbes* list of "America's Self-Made Women" and eighth on the 2015 *Forbes* list of "Power Women," Sandberg says she wasn't always confident in her ability to succeed: "I remember my first day at Facebook, driving to this new job, this hard job, and not being sure I could do it. I think about all the moments when I just didn't believe in myself: every test I was just about to fail, every job I wasn't sure I could do." Sandberg says that after seeing many women, including herself, quietly "lean back" and miss opportunities, she started to see a pattern and wanted to start talking about it.

In 2013, Sandberg published her first book, *Lean In: Women, Work, and the Will to Lead*, in which she addresses this pattern. Women, Sandberg notes, are getting more college degrees and more graduate degrees and are entering the workforce in record numbers, yet in industry after industry, women hold only 15 to 20 percent of the top jobs. "Women are held back by many things," she explains. "We're held back by bias, by lack of flexibility, by lack of

opportunity, but we also hold ourselves back: we don't sit at the table, we don't raise our hand, we don't let our voices be loud enough." Sandberg says she wrote the book for women of all ages, ranging from young women thinking about their futures to women who are out of the workforce and thinking about reentering to women who are volunteers and thinking about taking on greater leadership responsibilities. "I wrote this book to encourage women to believe in themselves and their dreams and to help men do their part to form a more equal world by making sure that all of us have opportunities based on our passions and interests, not just based on our gender," she states.

Sandberg wrote *Lean In* to help start conversations in workplaces and in schools, to encourage people to think differently about gender. Belinda Luscombe, writing in *Time* magazine, has observed that Sandberg is off to a good start: "It's probably not an overstatement to say Sandberg is embarking on the most ambitious mission to reboot feminism and reframe discussions of gender since the launch of *Ms.* magazine in 1971." Changing the outcomes for women in the workplace will likely entail changing how all people think and behave, and more effective self-leadership among women may be an important tool in this process.

Questions for Class Discussion

1. In what ways is Sheryl Sandberg a self-leader? Specifically, how may self-leadership

strategies have helped her to "lean in" during her career?

2. How could self-leadership strategies help more women to "believe in themselves and their dreams"?

Sources/Additional Readings

LeanIn.org, accessed August 8, 2015.

Luscombe, Belinda. 2013. "Confidence Woman." *Time*, March 7, 2013. http://ideas.time.com/2013/03/07/confidence-woman.

Sandberg, Sheryl, with Nell Scovell. 2013. *Lean In: Women, Work, and the Will to Lead.* New York: Alfred A. Knopf.

"Sheryl Sandberg." *Forbes*, accessed August 8, 2015. http://www.forbes.com/profile/sheryl-sandberg.

Chapter 1

1. Ralph M. Stogdill, *Handbook of Leadership: A Survey of Theory and Research* (New York: Free Press, 1974); Bernard M. Bass, *The Bass Handbook of Leadership: Theory, Research, and Managerial Applications*, 4th ed. (New York: Free Press, 2008).

2. For more on definitions of leadership, see Afsaneh Nahavandi, *The Art and Science of Leadership*, 7th ed. (Upper Saddle River, NJ: Prentice Hall, 2015); Peter G. Northouse, *Leadership: Theory and Practice*, 8th ed. (Thousand Oaks, CA: Sage, 2019).

3. See, for example, Mary Brophy Marcus, "Some Jobs Seem Riskier When It Comes to Heart Health," CBS News, March 1, 2006. https://www.cbsnews.com/news/some-jobs-seem-riskier-when-it-comes-to-heart-health/; Tarani Chandola, Annie Britton, Eric Brunner, Harry Hemingway, Marek Malik, Meena Kumari, Ellena Badrick, Mika Kivimaki, and Michael Marmot, "Work Stress and Coronary Heart Disease: What Are the Mechanisms?," *European Heart Journal* 29, no. 5 (2008): 640–48; H. Kuper and M. Marmot, "Job Strain, Job Demands, Decision Latitude, and Risk of Coronary Heart Disease Within the Whitehall II Study," *Journal of Epidemiology and Community Health* 57, no. 2 (2003): 147–53.

4. Quoted in David Love, "Serena Williams Road to 22: A Fierce Display of Mental Strength, Despite Media's Focus on Her Physical Appearance," Atlanta Blackstar, September 2, 2015, http://atlantablackstar.com/2015/09/02/serena-williams-road-to-22-a-fierce-display-of-mental-strength-despite-medias-focus-on-her-physical-appearance.

5. Patrick A. Wilson, "Serena Williams Is the Best Because of Her Brains—Not Just Her Body," *The Guardian*, August 31, 2015, http://www.theguardian.com/commentisfree/2015/aug/31/serena-williams-best-because-brains-not-body; Love, "Serena Williams Road to 22."

6. Joshi, Mayur. "Elite Athletes and Mental Strength: The Inseparable Connection," The Sportsman, September 19, 2017, https://www.thesportsman.com/articles/elite-athletes-and-mental-strength-the-inseparable-connection.

7. For more detailed academic discussions of the definition of self-leadership, see Charles C. Manz, "Self-Leadership: Toward an Expanded Theory of Self-Influence Processes in Organizations," *Academy of Management Review* 11, no. 3 (July 1986): 585–600; Greg L. Stewart, Stephen H. Courtright, and Charles C. Manz, "Self-Leadership: A Paradoxical Core of Organizational Behavior," *Annual Review of Organizational Psychology and Organizational Behavior*, vol. 6 (2019); Greg L. Stewart, Stephen H. Courtright, and Charles C. Manz, "Self-Leadership: A Multilevel Review," *Journal of Management* 37, no. 1 (January 2011): 185–222; Christopher P. Neck and Jeffery D. Houghton, "Two Decades of Self-Leadership Theory and Research," *Journal of Managerial Psychology* 21, no. 4 (June 2006): 270–95.

8. Stewart et al., "Self-Leadership: A Multilevel Review"; Charles C. Manz, "Leading Employees to Be Self-Managing and Beyond: Toward the Establishment of Self-Leadership in Organizations," *Journal of Management Systems* 3 (1991): 15–24.

9. See Albert Bandura, "Social Cognitive Theory," in *The Handbook of Theories of Social Psychology*, vol. 1, ed. Paul A. M. Van Lange, Arie W. Kruglanski, and E. Tory Higgins (London: Sage, 2012), 349–73.

10. See, for example, Edward L. Deci and Richard M. Ryan, "Self-Determination Theory," in Van Lange et al., *Handbook of Theories of Social Psychology*, 416–36.

11. Christopher P. Neck, *Medicine for the Mind: Healing Words to Help You Soar*, 4th ed. (New York: John Wiley, 2012).

Chapter 2

1. Quoted in Drake Baer, "What It's Like Inside Elon Musk's 'Reality Distortion Field,'" Business Insider, December 31, 2014, http://www.businessinsider.com/elon-musk-reality-distortion-field-2014-12.

2. Sir John Hargrave, "How Steve Jobs Created the Reality Distortion Field (and You Can, Too)," *Medium*, January 25, 2016, https://medium.com/@jhargrave/how-steve-jobs-created-the-reality-distortion-field-and-you-can-too-4ba87781adba

3. Rolfe Winkler, "Elon Musk Electrifies Techies," *Wall Street Journal*, MoneyBeat blog, June 3, 2013, http://blogs.wsj.com/moneybeat/2013/06/03/elon-musk-electrifies-techies.

4. Quoted in Baer, "What It's Like."

5. Winkler, "Elon Musk Electrifies Techies."

6. For overviews of self-regulation theory, see Charles S. Carver and Michael F. Scheier, "Self-Regulation of Action and Affect," in *Handbook of Self-Regulation: Research, Theory, and Applications*, 2nd ed., ed. Kathleen D. Vohs and Roy F. Baumeister (New York: Guilford Press, 2011), 3–21; Charles S. Carver and Michael F. Scheier, *On the Self-Regulation of Behavior* (New York: Cambridge University Press, 1998).

7. See, for example, Albert Bandura, "Social Cognitive Theory," in *The Handbook of Theories of Social Psychology*, vol. 1, ed. Paul A. M. Van Lange, Arie W. Kruglanski, and E. Tory Higgins (London: Sage, 2012), 349–73; Robert Wood and Albert Bandura, "Social Cognitive Theory of Organizational Management," *Academy of Management Review* 14, no. 3 (July 1989): 361–84.

8. Gary P. Latham and Edwin A. Locke, "Self-Regulation Through Goal Setting," *Organizational Behavior and Human Decision Processes* 50, no. 2 (December 1991): 212–47.

9. Roy F. Baumeister and Todd F. Heatherton, "Self-Regulation Failure: An Overview," *Psychological Inquiry* 7, no. 1 (January 1996): 1; Roy F. Baumeister, Todd F. Heatherton, and Dianne M. Tice, *Losing Control: How and Why People Fail at Self-Regulation* (San Diego, CA: Academic Press, 1994).

10. Charles C. Manz and Henry P. Sims Jr., "Self-Management as a Substitute for Leadership: A Social Learning Theory Perspective," *Academy of Management Review* 5, no. 3 (July 1980): 361–68; Mary Uhl-Bien and George B. Graen, "Individual Self-Management: Analysis of Professionals' Self-Managing Activities in Functional and Cross-Functional Work Teams," *Academy of Management Journal* 41, no. 3 (June 1998): 340–50; Katharina Ebner, Eva-Maria Schulte, Roman Soucek, and Simone Kauffeld, "Coaching as Stress-Management Intervention: The Mediating Role of Self-Efficacy in a Framework of Self-Management and Coping," *International Journal of Stress Management* 25, no. 3 (January 23, 2017).

11. For a more detailed overview of the expanded influence process of self-leadership as compared with related theories of self-influence, see Greg L. Stewart, Stephen H. Courtright, and Charles C. Manz, "Self-Leadership: A Multilevel Review," *Journal of Management* 37, no. 1 (January 2011): 185–222.

12. Edward L. Deci and Richard M. Ryan, "Self-Determination Theory," in Van Lange et al., *Handbook of Theories of Social Psychology*, 416–36; James M. Diefendorff, Nathalie Houlfort, Robert J. Vallerand, and Daniel Krantz, "Emphasizing the Self in Organizational Research on Self-Determination Theory," in *The Self at Work: Fundamental Theory and Research* (New York: Routledge/Taylor & Francis Group, 2018), 145–71.

13. Martin E. P. Seligman and Mihaly Csikszentmihalyi, "Positive Psychology: An Introduction," *American Psychologist* 55, no. 1 (January 2000): 5–14.

14. Rosemarie Kobau, Martin E. P. Seligman, Christopher Peterson, Ed Diener, Matthew M. Zack, Daniel Chapman, and William Thompson, "Mental Health Promotion in Public Health: Perspectives and Strategies from Positive Psychology," *American Journal of Public Health* 101, no. 8 (August 2011): e1–e9; Meg A. Warren, Stewart I. Donaldson, and Fred Luthans, "Taking Positive Psychology to the Workplace: Positive Organizational Psychology, Positive Organizational Behavior, and Positive Organizational Scholarship," in *Scientific Advances in Positive Psychology* (Santa Barbara, CA: Praeger/ABC-CLIO, 2017), 195–227.

15. Sonja Lyubomirsky, Kennon M. Sheldon, and David Schkade, "Pursuing Happiness: The Architecture of Sustainable Change," *Review of General Psychology* 9, no. 2 (June 2005): 111–31.

16. See, for example, Jeffrey Kerr and John W. Slocum Jr., "Managing Corporate Culture

Through Reward Systems," *Academy of Management Executive* 19, no. 4 (November 2005): 130–38; Terry L. Besser, "Rewards and Organization Goal Achievement: A Case Study of Toyota Motor Manufacturing in Kentucky," *Journal of Management Studies* 32, no. 3 (May 1995): 383–99.

17. Steven Kerr, "On the Folly of Rewarding A, While Hoping for B," *Academy of Management Journal* 18 (1975): 769–83.

18. For a recent review of this research, see Michael Domjan, "Theories of Reinforcement," in *The Essentials of Conditioning and Learning* (Washington, DC: American Psychological Association, 2018), 129–42.

19. Arnold P. Goldstein and Melvin Sorcher, *Changing Supervisor Behavior* (New York: Pergamon Press, 1977).

Chapter 3

1. See, for example, Carl E. Thoresen and Michael J. Mahoney, Behavioral Self-Control (New York: Holt, Rinehart & Winston, 1974); Charles C. Manz and Henry P. Sims Jr., "Self-Management as a Substitute for Leadership: A Social Learning Theory Perspective," *Academy of Management Review* 5, no. 3 (July 1980): 361–68; Katharina Ebner, Eva-Maria Schulte, Roman Soucek, and Simone Kauffeld, "Coaching as Stress-Management Intervention: The Mediating Role of Self-Efficacy in a Framework of Self-Management and Coping," *International Journal of Stress Management* (January 23, 2017).

2. Mary Uhl-Bien and George B. Graen, "Individual Self-Management: Analysis of Professionals' Self-Managing Activities in Functional and Cross-Functional Work Teams," *Academy of Management Journal* 41, no. 3 (June 1998): 340–50; Michael J. Mahoney and Diane B. Arnkoff, "Self Management: Theory, Research, and Application," in *Behavioral Medicine: Theory and Practice*, ed. Ovide F. Pomerleau and John Paul Brady (Baltimore: Williams & Wilkins, 1979); Manz and Sims, "Self-Management as a Substitute for Leadership"; Ebner, Schulte, Soucek, and Kauffeld, "Coaching as Stress-Management Intervention."

3. Jeff Chu, Stephanie Vozza, Jason Feifer, J. J. McCorvey, and Jillian Goodman, "Secrets of the Most Productive People," *Fast Company*, no. 191 (December 2014): 97–112.

4. Jill Duffy, "The Best To-Do List Apps of 2018," *PC Magazine*, January 11, 2018, https://www.pcmag.com/roundup/355449/the-best-to-do-list-apps; Steven Winkelman, "The Best To-Do List Apps for Android and iOS," *Digital Trends*, August 2, 2018, https://www.digitaltrends.com/mobile/best-to-do-list-apps/.

5. Anne Clarrissimeaux, "Never Give Up," *Success*, May 2, 2011, http://www.success.com/article/never-give-up.

6. James Clear, "How to Stick With Good Habits Every Day by Using the 'Paper Clip Strategy,'" *Huffington Post*, April 19, 2016, https://www.huffingtonpost.com/james-clear/how-to-stick-with-good-ha_b_9681338.html.

7. David Kirkaldy, "7 Leadership Lessons from Peyton Manning," Musings on the Mundane, February 24, 2015, http://www.davidkirkaldy.com/7-leadership-lessons-from-peyton-manning.

8. Quoted in "What Key Qualities Does Elon Musk Have That One Could Most Easily Emulate and Benefit from Emulating?," Quora, accessed January 2, 2016, https://www.quora.com/What-key-qualities-does-Elon-Musk-have-that-one-could-most-easily-emulate-and-benefit-from-emulating.

9. *Merriam-Webster OnLine*, s.v. "goal," accessed February 9, 2016, http://www.merriam-webster.com/dictionary/goal, emphasis added.

10. For more information about goal hierarchies, see Gary P. Latham and Gerard H. Seijts, "The Effects of Proximal and Distal Goals on Performance on a Moderately Complex Task," *Journal of Organizational Behavior* 20, no. 4 (July 1999): 421–29; Gary P. Latham and Edwin A. Locke, "New Developments in and Directions for Goal-Setting Research," *European Psychologist* 12, no. 4 (2007): 290–300.

11. Kim Benson, "Bricks, Goals and Will Smith . . . Say WHAT?" *Huffington Post*, June 23, 2010, https://www.huffingtonpost.com/kim-bensen/bricks-goals-and-will-smi_b_550365.html.

12. A plethora of studies on goal-setting have reached this conclusion. For a recent review of goal-setting theory and research, see Edwin A. Locke and Gary

P. Latham, "Goal Setting Theory: The Current State," in *New Developments in Goal Setting and Task Performance*, ed. Edwin A. Locke and Gary P. Latham (New York: Routledge, 2013), 623–30.

13. For a detailed overview of classic goal-setting research, see Edwin A. Locke and Gary P. Latham, *A Theory of Goal Setting and Task Performance* (Englewood Cliffs, NJ: Prentice Hall, 1990).

14. Luke Winn, "Kyle Dake," *Sports Illustrated Vault*, May 27, 2013, https://www.si.com/vault/2013/05/27/106326511/kyle-dake.

15. Quoted in "The Secrets to Taylor Swift's Success," *Seventeen*, July 9, 2009, http://www.seventeen.com/celebrity/a4935/taylor-swift-advice.

16. Richard J. Leider, *The Power of Purpose: Creating Meaning in Your Life and Work* (San Francisco: Berrett-Koehler, 1997), 1.

17. Ibid., 2.

18. Abraham H. Maslow, *Motivation and Personality*, 2nd ed. (New York: Harper & Row, 1970), 46.

19. Blake Mycoskie, "The Founder of TOMS on Reimagining the Company's Mission," *Harvard Business Review*, January–February 2016, https://hbr.org/2016/01/the-founder-of-toms-on-reimagining-the-companys-mission.

20. Ibid.

21. Simon Sinek, *Start With Why: How Great Leaders Inspire Everyone to Take Action* (New York: Portfolio, 2009).

22. Mycoskie, "Founder of TOMS."

23. Ibid.

24. Leider, *Power of Purpose*, 1.

25. Viktor E. Frankl, *Man's Search for Meaning*, rev. ed. (New York: Washington Square Press, 1984), 165.

26. British Library, Online Gallery, "The Quest for the Holy Grail," accessed August 6, 2018, http://www.bl.uk/onlinegallery/features/mythical/grail.html.

27. John Matthews, *The Grail Tradition* (Rockport, MA: Element, 1990), 6.

28. Quoted in Avery Comarow, "America's Best Leaders: Benjamin Carson, Surgeon and Children's Advocate," *U.S. News & World Report*, November 19, 2008, http://www.usnews.com/news/best-leaders/articles/2008/11/19/americas-best-leaders-benjamin-carson-surgeon-and-childrens-advocate.

29. Dorothea Brande, *Wake Up and Live!* (New York: Simon & Schuster, 1936), 44.

30. See for example, Alexander K. Koch, Julia Nafziger, Anton Suvorov, and Jeroen van de Ven, "Self-Rewards and Personal Motivation," *European Economic Review* 68 (May 2014): 151–67; Emma M. Brown, Debbie M. Smith, Tracy Epton, and Christopher J. Armitage, "Do Self-Incentives and Self-Rewards Change Behavior? A Systematic Review and Meta-Analysis," *Behavior Therapy* 49, no. 1 (January 2018): 113–23.

31. See, for example, Ryan J. Jacoby, Rachel C. Leonard, Bradley C. Riemann, and Jonathan S. Abramowitz, "Self-Punishment as a Maladaptive Thought Control Strategy Mediates the Relationship between Beliefs about Thoughts and Repugnant Obsessions," *Cognitive Therapy and Research* 40, no. 2 (April 2016): 179–87; Alan M. Saks and Blake E. Ashforth, "Proactive Socialization and Behavioral Self-Management," *Journal of Vocational Behavior* 48, no. 3 (June 1996): 301–23.

32. "Muhammad Ali—In His Own Words," BBC.com, January 17, 2012, http://www.bbc.com/sport/boxing/16146367.

Chapter 4

1. See Edward L. Deci, *Intrinsic Motivation* (New York: Plenum Press, 1975); Edward L. Deci, Richard Koestner, and Richard M. Ryan, "A Meta-Analytic Review of Experiments Examining the Effects of Extrinsic Rewards on Intrinsic Motivation," *Psychological Bulletin* 125, no. 6 (November 1999): 627–68; Maarten Vansteenkiste, Willy Lens, and Edward L. Deci, "Intrinsic versus Extrinsic Goal Contents in Self-Determination Theory: Another Look at the Quality of Academic Motivation," *Educational Psychologist* 41, no. 1 (2006): 19–31; Richard M. Ryan and Edward L. Deci, "Intrinsic and Extrinsic Motivations: Classic Definitions and New Directions," *Contemporary Educational Psychology* 25, no. 1 (January 2000): 54–67.

2. See, for example, Edward L. Deci and Richard M. Ryan, "The Empirical Exploration of Intrinsic Motivational Processes," in *Advances in Experimental Social Psychology*, vol. 13, ed. Leonard

Berkowitz (New York: Academic Press, 1980); Edward L. Deci and Arlen C. Moller, "The Concept of Competence: A Starting Place for Understanding Intrinsic Motivation and Self-Determined Extrinsic Motivation," in *Handbook of Competence and Motivation*, ed. Andrew J. Elliot and Carol S. Dweck (New York: Guilford Press, 2005), 579–97; Zachary W. Goldman, Alan K. Goodboy, and Keith Weber, "College Students' Psychological Needs and Intrinsic Motivation to Learn: An Examination of Self-Determination Theory," *Communication Quarterly* 65, no. 2 (April 2017): 167–91.

3. Myriam Chiniara and Kathleen Bentein, "Linking Servant Leadership to Individual Performance: Differentiating the Mediating Role of Autonomy, Competence and Relatedness Need Satisfaction," *Leadership Quarterly* 27, no. 1 (February 2016): 124–41.

4. See, for instance, Patrick E. McKnight and Todd B. Kashdan, "Purpose in Life as a System That Creates and Sustains Health and Well-Being: An Integrative, Testable Theory," *Review of General Psychology* 13, no. 3 (September 2009): 242–51; Jongho Shin, Myung-Seop Kim, Hyeyoung Hwang, and Byung-Yoon Lee, "Effects of Intrinsic Motivation and Informative Feedback in Service-Learning on the Development of College Students' Life Purpose." *Journal of Moral Education* 47, no. 2 (June 2018): 159–74.

5. See, for example, Maarten Vansteenkiste, Nathalie Aelterman, Gert-Jan De Muynck, Leen Haerens, Erika Patall, and Johnmarshall Reeve. "Fostering Personal Meaning and Self-Relevance: A Self-Determination Theory Perspective on Internalization. "*Journal of Experimental Education* 86, no. 1 (January 2018): 30–49.

6. Helen Claire Smith, "Finding Purpose Through Altruism: The Potential of 'Doing for Others' During Asylum." *Journal of Occupational Science* 25, no. 1 (April 2018): 87–99.

7. Felix Warneken, "Atlas Hugged: The Foundations of Human Altruism." In *Atlas of Moral Psychology* (New York: Guilford Press, 2018), 413–19.

8. Hans Selye, *Stress Without Distress* (New York: Signet Books, 1974).

9. Ning Li, Bradley L. Kirkman, and Christopher O. L. H. Porter, "Toward a Model of Work Team Altruism," *Academy of Management Review* 39, no. 4 (October 2014): 541–65.

10. Martin L. Hoffman, "Is Altruism Part of Human Nature?," *Journal of Personality and Social Psychology* 40 (1981): 121–37.

11. Erich Fehr and Urs Fischbacher, "The Nature of Human Altruism," *Nature* 425, no. 6960 (October 2003): 785–91; Tania M. Veludo-de-Oliveira, John G. Pallister, and Gordon R. Foxall, "Unselfish? Understanding the Role of Altruism, Empathy, and Beliefs in Volunteering Commitment," *Journal of Nonprofit & Public Sector Marketing* 27, no. 4 (October 2015): 373–96.

12. Quoted in James B. Stewart, "Looking for a Lesson in Google's Perks," *New York Times*, March 15, 2013, http://www.nytimes.com/2013/03/16/business/at-google-a-place-to-work-and-play.html.

13. Ibid.

14. Quoted in Jodi Kantor and David Streitfeld, "Inside Amazon: Wrestling Big Ideas in a Bruising Workplace," *New York Times*, August 15, 2015, http://www.nytimes.com/2015/08/16/technology/inside-amazon-wrestling-big-ideas-in-a-bruising-workplace.html.

15. Quoted in ibid.

16. https://news.stanford.edu/2005/06/14/jobs-061505/.

17. Cited in Deepak Chopra, *Magical Mind, Magical Body* (Niles, IL: Nightingale Conant, 1991).

18. See, for example, Deci, *Intrinsic Motivation*; Edward L. Deci, John Nezlek, and Louise Sheinman, "Characteristics of the Rewarder and Intrinsic Motivation of the Rewardee," *Journal of Personality and Social Psychology* 40, no. 1 (1981): 1–10; Deci, Koestner, and Ryan, "A Meta-Analytic Review of Experiments"; Qingguo Ma, Jia Jin, Liang Meng, and Qiang Shen, "The Dark Side of Monetary Incentive: How Does Extrinsic Reward Crowd Out Intrinsic Motivation," *NeuroReport* 25, no. 3 (February 2014): 194–98.

19. Kerrie L. Unsworth and Claire M. Mason. "Self–Concordance Strategies as a Necessary Condition for Self–Management," *Journal of Occupational and Organizational Psychology* 89, no. 4 (December 2016): 711–33.

20. Norman Vincent Peale, *A Guide to Confident Living* (Greenwich, CT: Fawcett Crest Books, 1948), 59.

Chapter 5

1. This concept is based on Social Cognitive Theory's Triadic Reciprocal Model as described in Chapter 2 and is based on the following citations: Albert Bandura, "Social Cognitive Theory," in *The Handbook of Theories of Social Psychology*, vol. 1, ed. Paul A. M. Van Lange, Arie W. Kruglanski, and E. Tory Higgins (London: Sage, 2012), 349–73; Robert Wood and Albert Bandura, "Social Cognitive Theory of Organizational Management," *Academy of Management Review* 14, no. 3 (July 1989): 361–84.

2. Christopher P. Neck, *Medicine for the Mind: Healing Words to Help You Soar*, 2nd ed. (New York: McGraw-Hill, 2007).

3. See, for example, Windy Dryden, *Rational Emotive Behaviour Therapy: Distinctive Features*, 2nd ed. (London: Routledge, 2015); Albert Ellis, *Better, Deeper, and More Enduring Brief Therapy: The Rational Emotive Behavior Therapy Approach* (New York: Brunner/Mazel, 1995); Albert Ellis and John M. Whiteley, eds., *Theoretical and Empirical Foundations of Rational Emotive Therapy* (Monterey, CA: Brooks/Cole, 1979); Michael Hickey and Kristene A. Doyle, "Rational Emotive Behavior Therapy," in *Cognitive Behavior Therapies: A Guidebook for Practitioners* (Alexandria, VA: American Counseling Association, 2018), 109–42.

4. Norman Vincent Peale, *The Power of Positive Thinking* (New York: Spire Books, 1956).

5. Norman Vincent Peale, *The Amazing Results of Positive Thinking* (New York: Fawcett Crest Books, 1959).

6. See, for example, Güler Boyraz and Owen Richard Lightsey Jr., "Can Positive Thinking Help? Positive Automatic Thoughts as Moderators of the Stress–Meaning Relationship," *American Journal of Orthopsychiatry* 82, no. 2 (April 2012): 267–77; Martin E. P. Seligman, *Learned Optimism: How to Change Your Mind and Your Life* (New York: Free Press, 1998); Abir K. Bekhet and Jaclene A. Zauszniewski, "Measuring Use of Positive Thinking Skills: Psychometric Testing of a New Scale," *Western Journal of Nursing Research* 35, no. 8 (September 2013): 1074–93; Meg A. Warren, Stewart I. Donaldson, and Fred Luthans, "Taking Positive Psychology to the Workplace: Positive Organizational Psychology, Positive Organizational Behavior, and Positive Organizational Scholarship," in *Scientific Advances in Positive Psychology* (Santa Barbara, CA: Praeger/ABC-CLIO, 2017), 195–227.

7. Watty Piper, *The Little Engine That Could* (New York: Platt & Munk, 1930).

8. See, for example, Steve Andreas, *More Transforming Negative Self-Talk: Practical, Effective Exercises* (New York: W. W. Norton, 2014); Thomas M. Brinthaupt and Christian T. Dove, "Differences in Self-Talk Frequency as a Function of Age, Only-Child, and Imaginary Childhood Companion Status," *Journal of Research in Personality* 46, no. 3 (June 2012): 326–33; Antonis Hatzigeorgiadis, Khelifa Bartura, Christos Argiropoulos, Nikos Comoutos, Evangelos Galanis, and Andreas D. Flouris, "Beat the Heat: Effects of a Motivational Self-Talk Intervention on Endurance Performance," *Journal of Applied Sport Psychology* 30, no. 4 (October 2018): 388–401; Małgorzata M. Puchalska-Wasyl, "Self-Talk: Conversation with Oneself? On the Types of Internal Interlocutors," *Journal of Psychology: Interdisciplinary and Applied* 149, no. 5 (July 2015): 443–60.

9. Christopher P. Neck, Heidi M. Neck, and Charles C. Manz, "Thought Self-Leadership: Mind Management for Entrepreneurs," *Journal of Developmental Entrepreneurship* 2, no. 1 (1997): 25–36.

10. Pamela E. Butler, *Talking to Yourself: Learning the Language of Self-Support* (San Francisco: Harper & Row, 1981).

11. Quoted in Carolyn White, "Sharpening Mental Skills," *USA Today*, August 8, 1996, C3.

12. Quoted in Ian Murtagh, "Serena Williams Reveals the Secret behind Her Wimbledon Success," *Daily Star*, July 13, 2015, http://www.dailystar.co.uk/wimbledon-2015/453369/Serena-Williams-reveals-secret-behind-Wimbledon-success.

13. Quoted in Steve Tobak, "Steve Jobs's Inspirational Words," CBS News, October 6, 2011, http://www.cbsnews.com/news/steve-jobss-inspirational-words.

14. See, for example, Ioana A. Cristea, Marcus J. H. Huibers, Daniel David, Steven D. Hollon, Gerhard Andersson, and Pim Cuijpers, "The Effects of Cognitive Behavior Therapy for Adult Depression on Dysfunctional Thinking: A Meta-Analysis," *Clinical Psychology Review* 42 (December 2015): 62–71; Marie-Anne Vanderhasselt and Rudi De Raedt, "How Ruminative Thinking Styles Lead to Dysfunctional Cognitions: Evidence from a Mediation Model," *Journal of Behavior Therapy and Experimental Psychiatry* 43, no. 3 (September 2012): 910–14; L. Esther de Graaf, Marcus J. H. Huibers, Pim Cuijpers, and Arnoud Arntz, "Minor and Major Depression in the General Population: Does Dysfunctional Thinking Play a Role?" *Comprehensive Psychiatry* 51, no. 3 (May 2010): 266–74.

15. David Burns, *Feeling Good: The New Mood Therapy* (New York: Morrow, 1980).

16. For a more extensive discussion of mental self-leadership and entrepreneurship, see Neck et al., "Thought Self-Leadership"; Christopher P. Neck, Jeffery D. Houghton, Shruti R. Sardeshmukh, Michael Goldsby, and Jeffrey L. Godwin, "Self-Leadership: A Cognitive Resource for Entrepreneurs," *Journal of Small Business & Entrepreneurship* 26, no. 5 (November 2013): 463–80.

17. See, for example, Deborah L. Feltz and Daniel M. Landers, "The Effects of Mental Practice on Motor Skill Learning and Performance: A Meta-Analysis," in *Essential Readings in Sport and Exercise Psychology*, ed. Daniel Smith and Michael Bar-Eli (Champaign, IL: Human Kinetics, 2007), 219–30; Peter Miksza, Kevin Watson, and Iantheia Calhoun, "The Effect of Mental Practice on Melodic Jazz Improvisation Achievement," *Psychomusicology: Music, Mind, and Brain* 28, no. 1 (March 2018): 40–49; Shane M. Murphy and Douglas P. Jowdy, "Imagery and Mental Practice," in *Advances in Sport Psychology*, ed. Thelma S. Horn (Champaign, IL: Human Kinetics, 1992), 221–50; Nick Sevdalis, Aidan Moran, and Sonal Arora, "Mental Imagery and Mental Practice Applications in Surgery: State of the Art and Future Directions," in *Multisensory Imagery*, ed. Simon Lacey and Rebecca Lawson (New York: Springer Science+Business Media, 2013), 343–63.

18. Quoted in "Mogul Fashions: A Success Story," *USA Today*, November 8, 1996, E2.

19. Ibid.

20. Helen Thayer, *Polar Dream: The Heroic Saga of the First Solo Journey by a Woman and Her Dog to the Pole* (New York: Dell, 1994), 231.

21. Quoted in Zac Clark, "The Secret to Tim Tebow's Success," *Stack*, February 1, 2012, http://www.stack.com/a/the-secret-to-tim-tebows-success.

22. Ibid.

23. Ed Magnuson, "Reagan's Big Win," *Time*, May 18, 1981, 14–16.

24. Jack Canfield and Mark Victor Hansen, *A Third Serving of Chicken Soup for the Soul* (Deerfield Beach, FL: Health Communications, 1996), 235–36.

25. Stefano Carnazzi, "Kintsugi: The Art of Precious Scars," *Lifegate*, https://www.lifegate.com/people/lifestyle/kintsugi.

26. Ibid.

27. Charles C. Manz, *The Power of Failure: 27 Ways to Turn Life's Setbacks Into Success* (San Francisco: Berrett-Koehler, 2002).

28. Jacques Wiesel, *Bloom Where You Are Planted* (Bloomington, IN: Xlibris, 2011).

29. J. Y. Cousteau with Frédéric Dumas, *The Silent World* (New York: Harper & Brothers, 1953), 6.

Chapter 6

1. Many of the ideas in this chapter have been adapted from material in Charles C. Manz, Christopher P. Neck, James Mancuso, and Karen P. Manz, *For Team Members Only: Making Your Workplace Team Productive and Hassle-Free* (New York: AMACOM, 1997).

2. Andre Martin and Vidula Bal, *The State of Teams* (Greensboro, NC: Center for Creative Leadership, 2015); Josh Berson, "New Research Shows Why Focus on Teams, Not Just Leaders, Is Key to Business Performance," *Forbes,*

March 3, 2016, https://www.forbes.com/sites/joshbersin/2016/03/03/why-a-focus-on-teams-not-just-leaders-is-the-secret-to-business-performance/#7835cf5024d5.

3. For a detailed overview of synergy in teams, see Amit Gal, "Synergy Work and Synergistic Membership: Towards a Theory of Beneficial Social Interactions in Teams," *Academy of Management Annual Meeting Proceedings* 2015, no. 1 (January 2015): 1; James R. Larson Jr., *In Search of Synergy in Small Group Performance* (New York: Psychology Press, 2010).

4. Cheryl Clark and Beach Clark, "Identifying Synergy in Small Group Competitions: An Applied Setting Approach," *Journal of Organizational Culture, Communications and Conflict* 19, no. 2 (June 2015): 121–33.

5. Our discussion of the behavioral and mental aspects of team self-leadership is adapted from Christopher P. Neck, Greg L. Stewart, and Charles C. Manz, "Self-Leaders within Self-Leading Teams: Toward an Optimal Equilibrium," in *Advances in Interdisciplinary Studies of Work Teams*, vol. 3, *Team Leadership*, ed. Michael M. Beyerlein, Douglas A. Johnson, and Susan T. Beyerlein (Greenwich, CT: JAI Press, 1996), 43–65.

6. For extended discussion of the group mind concept, see Erin Cooley, B. Keith Payne, William Cipolli III, C. Daryl Cameron, Alyssa Berger, and Kurt Gray, "The Paradox of Group Mind: 'People in a Group' Have More Mind Than 'a Group of People.'" *Journal of Experimental Psychology: General* 146, no. 5 (May 2017): 691–99; Thomas Szanto, "How to Share a Mind: Reconsidering the Group Mind Thesis," *Phenomenology and the Cognitive Sciences* 13, no. 1 (March 2014): 99–120; Jay J. Van Bavel, Leor M. Hackel, and Y. Jenny Xiao, "The Group Mind: The Pervasive Influence of Social Identity on Cognition," in *New Frontiers in Social Neuroscience*, ed. Jean Decety and Yves Christen (Cham, Switzerland: Springer International, 2014), 41–56.

7. See W. R. Bion, *Experience in Groups* (New York: Basic Books, 1961).

8. Quoted in David LaGesse, "America's Best Leaders: Jeff Bezos, Amazon.com CEO," *U.S. News & World Report*, November 19, 2008, http://www.usnews.com/news/best-leaders/articles/2008/11/19/americas-best-leaders-jeff-bezos-amazoncom-ceo.

9. Adapted from Glenn Van Ekeren, *The Speaker's Sourcebook* (Englewood Cliffs, NJ: Prentice Hall, 1988).

10. Brian Cavanaugh, *More Sower's Seeds: Second Planting* (New York: Paulist Press, 1992).

11. Bruce H. Jackson, "When Being Your Best Means Bringing Out the Best in Others," Korn Ferry International, January 21, 2016.

12. Special thanks to Craig Pearce, who contributed to this section on shared leadership. For additional reading on shared leadership, see Craig L. Pearce and Charles C. Manz, "The New Silver Bullets of Leadership: The Importance of Self- and Shared Leadership in Knowledge Work," *Organizational Dynamics* 34, no. 2 (2005): 130–40; Craig L. Pearce, Charles C. Manz, and Henry P. Sims Jr., *Share, Don't Take the Lead* (Charlotte, NC: Information Age, 2014); Craig L. Pearce and Charles C. Manz, "The Leadership Disease . . . and Its Potential Cures," *Business Horizons* 57, no. 2 (March 2014): 215–24.

13. If you are interested in learning more about shared leadership, we recommend that you read Craig L. Pearce and Jay A. Conger, eds., *Shared Leadership: Reframing the Hows and Whys of Leadership* (Thousand Oaks, CA: Sage, 2003). This collection includes an excellent chapter on the link between self- and shared leadership by Jeffery D. Houghton, Christopher P. Neck, and Charles C. Manz, as well as several other provocative chapters on shared leadership.

14. For a detailed discussion of groupthink, see Irving L. Janis, *Groupthink*, 2nd ed. (Boston: Houghton Mifflin, 1983); Irving L. Janis, "Groupthink," in *Leadership: Understanding the Dynamics of Power and Influence in Organizations*, 2nd ed., ed. Robert P. Vecchio (Notre Dame, IN: University of Notre Dame Press, 2007), 157–69.

15. For an extended discussion of the teamthink and groupthink concepts, see Neck and Manz, "From Groupthink to Teamthink"; Charles C. Manz and Christopher P. Neck, "Teamthink: Beyond the Groupthink Syndrome

in Self-Managing Work Teams," *Journal of Managerial Psychology* 10 (1995): 7–15.

16. For more details on virtual teams and recent research in this area, see Lucy L. Gilson, M. Travis Maynard, Nicole C. Jones Young, Matti Vartiainen, and Marko Hakonen, "Virtual Teams Research: 10 Years, 10 Themes, and 10 Opportunities," *Journal of Management* 41, no. 5 (July 2015): 1313–37; Bradley L. Kirkman, Benson Rosen, Paul E. Tesluk, and Cristina B. Gibson, "The Impact of Team Empowerment on Virtual Team Performance: The Moderating Role of Face-to-Face Interaction," *Academy of Management Journal* 47, no. 2 (April 2004): 175–92; Arvind Malhotra, Ann Majchrzak, and Benson Rosen, "Leading Virtual Teams," *Academy of Management Perspectives* 21, no. 1 (February 2007): 60–70; Mitzi M. Montoya-Weiss, Anne P. Massey, and Michael Song, "Getting It Together: Temporal Coordination and Conflict Management in Global Virtual Teams," *Academy of Management Journal* 44, no. 6 (December 2001): 1251–62.

17. For one of the few studies available, see Judith G. Oakley, "Leadership Processes in Virtual Teams and Organizations," *Journal of Leadership Studies* 5, no. 3 (1999): 3–17.

Chapter 7

1. From Brainy Quote, accessed July 30, 2015, http://www.brainyquote.com/quotes/quotes/a/arlenspect462442.html?src=t_health.

2. Portions of the material in this section are adapted from and inspired by Christopher P. Neck and Kenneth H. Cooper, "The Fit Executive: Exercise and Diet Guidelines for Enhancing Performance," *Academy of Management Executive* 14, no. 2 (2000): 72–83; and Christopher P. Neck, T. L. Mitchell, Charles C. Manz, Kenneth H. Cooper, and Emmet C. Thompson, "Fit to Lead: Is Fitness the Key to Effective Executive Leadership?" *Journal of Managerial Psychology* 15, no. 8 (2000): 833–40. We must note that before you embark on any exercise and/or nutritional program, you should obtain medical clearance from a qualified physician.

3. Rob Donat, interview by Christopher P. Neck, July 20, 2015.

4. Eric R. Goldberg, interview by Christopher P. Neck, July 21, 2015.

5. Tom Hatten, interview by Christopher P. Neck, July 22, 2015.

6. Matt Benedick, interview by Christopher P. Neck, July 27, 2015.

7. For more information about these studies and others that have examined the relationship between fitness and performance, see Matthew R. Rhea, Brent A. Alvar, and Rayne Gray, "Physical Fitness and Job Performance of Firefighters," *Journal of Strength and Conditioning Research* 18, no. 2 (May 2004): 348–52; Liam Boyd, Todd Rogers, David Docherty, and Stewart Petersen, "Variability in Performance on a Work Simulation Test of Physical Fitness for Firefighters," *Applied Physiology, Nutrition, and Metabolism* 40, no. 4 (April 2015): 364–70; Mark B. Stephens, Ting Dong, and Steven J. Durning, "Physical Fitness and Academic Performance: A Pilot Investigation in USU Medical Students," *Military Medicine* 180, no. 4 suppl. (April 2015): 77–78; C. C. A. Santana, L. B. Azevedo, M. T. Cattuzzo, J. O. Hill, L. P. Andrade, and W. L. Prado, "Physical Fitness and Academic Performance in Youth: A Systematic Review," *Scandinavian Journal of Medicine & Science in Sports* 27, no. 6 (June 2017): 579–603; David R. Frew and Nealia S. Bruning, "Improved Productivity and Job Satisfaction Through Employee Exercise Programs," *Hospital Materiel Management Quarterly* 9, no. 4 (1988): 62–69; Sandra E. Edwards and Larry R. Gettman, "The Effect of Employee Physical Fitness on Job Performance," *Personnel Administrator* 25, no. 11 (November 1980): 41–44, 61.

8. Norwood S. Lupinacci, Roberta Rikli, Jessie Jones, and Diane Ross, "Age and Physical Activity Effects on Reaction Time and Digit Symbol Substitution Performance in Cognitively Active Adults," *Research Quarterly for Exercise and Sport* 64, no. 2 (1993): 144–50.

9. David J. Bunce, Ann Barrowclough, and Ira Morris, "The Moderating Influence of Physical Fitness on Age Gradients in Vigilance and Serial Choice Responding Tasks," *Psychology and Aging* 11, no. 4 (December 1996): 671–82.

10. Scott M. Hayes, Daniel E. Forman, and Mieke Verfaellie, "Cardiorespiratory fitness Is Associated with Cognitive Performance in Older But Not Younger Adults," *The Journals of Gerontology: Series B: Psychological Sciences and Social Sciences* 71, no. 3 (May 2016): 474–82.

11. For more discussion of the benefits of being fit, see Kenneth H. Cooper and Tyler C. Cooper, *Start Strong, Finish Strong: Prescriptions for a Lifetime of Great Health* (New York: Penguin, 2008); Kenneth H. Cooper, *Faith-Based Fitness* (Nashville: Thomas Nelson, 1997).

12. For in-depth discussion of research on physical activity and psychological outcomes, see Eric Brymer, Keith Davids, and Liz Mallabon, "Understanding the Psychological Health and Well-Being Benefits of Physical Activity in Nature: An Ecological Dynamics Analysis," *Ecopsychology* 6, no. 3 (September 2014): 189–97; "Physical Activity and Psychological Benefits: Internal Society of Sport Psychology Position Statement," *Physician and Sportsmedicine* 20, no. 10 (1992): 179–84; Jeffrey E. Brandon and J. Mark Loftin, "Relationship of Fitness to Depression, State and Trait Anxiety, Internal Health Locus of Control, and Self-Control," *Perceptual and Motor Skills* 73, no. 2 (1991): 563–68.

13. Quoted in James M. Rippe, "CEO Fitness: The Performance Plus," *Psychology Today* 23, no. 5 (1989): 50–54.

14. See A. M. Paolone, R. R. Lewis, W. T. Lanigan, and M. J. Goldstein, "Results of Two Years of Exercise Training in Middle-Aged Men," *Physician and Sportsmedicine* 4 (December 1976): 72–77; D. Ornish, S. E. Brown, J. H. Billings, L. W. Scherwitz, et al., "Can Lifestyle Changes Reverse Coronary Heart Disease?," *Lancet* 336, no. 8708 (July 1990): 129–33; Lori A. Smolin and Mary B. Grosvenor, *Nutrition: Science and Applications*, 2nd ed. (Ft. Worth: Saunders College, 1997), 354.

15. "Cancer," HealthyPeople.gov, accessed July 31, 2015, http://www.healthypeople.gov/2020/topics-objectives/topic/cancer.

16. See, for example, Glenn A. Gaesser, Wesley J. Tucker, Catherine L. Jarrett, and Siddhartha S. Angadi, "Fitness versus Fatness: Which Influences Health and Mortality Risk the Most?" *Current Sports Medicine Reports* 14, no. 4 (July 2015): 327–32; D. Schmid and M. F. Leitzmann, "Cardiorespiratory Fitness as Predictor of Cancer Mortality: A Systematic Review and Meta-Analysis," *Annals of Oncology* 26, no. 2 (February 2015): 272–78; Cecilia Bergh, Ruzan Udumyan, Katja Fall, Henrik Almroth, and Scott Montgomery, "Stress Resilience and Physical Fitness in Adolescence and Risk of Coronary Heart Disease in Middle Age," *Heart (British Cardiac Society)* 101, no. 8 (April 2015): 623–29; Eugenia E. Calle, Michael J. Thun, Jennifer M. Petrelli, Carmen Rodriguez, and Clark W. Heath Jr., "Body-Mass Index and Mortality in a Prospective Cohort of U.S. Adults," *New England Journal of Medicine* 341 (1999): 1097–1105; Steven N. Blair, Harold W. Kohl III, Ralph S. Paffenbarger Jr., Debra G. Clark, Kenneth H. Cooper, and Larry W. Gibbons, "Physical Fitness and All-Cause Mortality: A Prospective Study of Healthy Men and Women," *Journal of the American Medical Association* 262, no. 17 (1989): 2395–401; Steven N. Blair, Harold W. Kohl III, Carolyn E. Barlow, Ralph S. Paffenbarger Jr., Larry W. Gibbons, and Caroline A. Macera, "Changes in Physical Fitness and All-Cause Mortality: A Prospective Study of Healthy and Unhealthy Men," *Journal of the American Medical Association* 273, no. 14 (1995): 1093–98.

17. Quoted in Catherine Romano, "In Sickness and in Health," *Management Review* 83, no. 5 (1994): 40.

18. "Heart Disease and Stroke Statistics—2015 Update: A Report from the American Heart Association," *Circulation 131* (January 27, 2015), e310, http://circ.ahajournals.org/content/131/4/e29.full.pdf.

19. Ibid.

20. Ryan Holmes, "How to Get Your Employees into Fitness," *Fortune*, September 18, 2014, http://fortune.com/2014/09/18/how-to-get-your-employees-into-fitness.

21. "Execs Say Physical Fitness Is Critical to Career Success; Obesity Considered a 'Serious Impediment,'" TheLadders.com, press release, November 28, 2005, http://www.theladders.com/press-releases/abouttheladderspressdetail_112805.

22. See, for example, Lucy Kelleway, "The CEO Fad for Extreme Exercise Has Gone Too Far,"

Financial Times, October 26, 2014, http://
www.ft.com/cms/s/0/262d8c6c-593d-
11e4-9546-00144feab7de.html#axzz3h
W7jjLD5; Danielle Braff, "Eating Up Fad Diets
Puts Your Health at Risk," *Chicago Tribune*,
July 11, 2014, http://articles.chicagotribune.
com/2014-07-11/health/sc-health-0709-
fads-20140711_1_twinkie-diet-low-calorie-diet-
rania-batayneh.

23. Neck and Cooper, "The Fit Executive."

24. Quoted in Neck et al., "Fit to Lead," 839.

25. Peter Salovey and John D. Mayer, "Emotional
Intelligence," *Imagination, Cognition, and
Personality* 9 (1990): 186.

26. See James J. Gross, "The Emerging Field
of Emotion Regulation: An Integrative Review,"
Review of General Psychology 2, no. 3 (1998):
271–99; James J. Gross, "Emotion Regulation:
Affective, Cognitive, and Social Consequences,"
Psychophysiology 39 (2002): 281–91;
Jane M. Richards and James J. Gross,
"Emotion Regulation and Memory: The
Cognitive Costs of Keeping One's Cool," *Journal
of Personality and Social Psychology* 79, no. 3 (2000):
410–24.

27. Gross, "Emotion Regulation," 282.

28. See, for example, Charles C. Manz, "Taking the
Self-Leadership High Road: Smooth Surface
or Potholes Ahead?" *Academy of Management
Perspectives* 29, no. 1 (February 2015): 132–51;
Mel Fugate, Charles C. Manz, Jeffery D.
Houghton, and Christopher P. Neck, "Emotional
Self-Leadership (ESL): A Process for Enhancing
Emotion Self-Influence, Emotion Authenticity,
and Personal Effectiveness" (paper presented at
the annual meeting of the Southern Management
Association, Savannah, GA, 2014).

29. Manz, "Taking the Self-Leadership
High Road"; Fugate et al., "Emotional
Self-Leadership"; Richards and Gross, "Emotion
Regulation and Memory"; Daren C. Jackson,
Jessica R. Malmstadt, Christine L. Larson,
and Richard J. Davidson, "Suppression and
Enhancement of Emotional Responses to
Unpleasant Pictures," *Psychophysiology* 37, no. 4
(2000): 515–22; Charles C. Manz, *Emotional
Discipline: The Power to Choose How You Feel* (San
Francisco: Berrett-Koehler, 2003).

30. See, for example, Barbara L. Fredrickson,
"Positive Emotions and Upward Spirals in
Organizations," in *Positive Organizational
Scholarship: Foundations of a New Discipline*, ed.
Kim S. Cameron, Jane E. Dutton, and
Robert E. Quinn (San Francisco:
Berrett-Koehler, 2003), 163–75.

31. See, for example, Khoa D. Le Nguyen
and Barbara L. Fredrickson, "Positive Emotions
and Well-Being," in *Positive Psychology: Established
and Emerging Issues* (New York: Routledge/Taylor
& Francis Group, 2018), 29–45;
Michelle N. Shiota, Claire I. Yee, Makenzie J.
O'Neil, and Alexander F. Danvers, "Positive
Emotions," in *Scientific Advances in Positive
Psychology* (Santa Barbara, CA: Praeger
/ABC-CLIO, 2017), 37–71.

32. See, for example, Andrew Steptoe, "Depression
and Negative Emotions," in *The Routledge
International Handbook of Psychosocial Epidemiology*
(New York: Routledge/Taylor & Francis Group,
2018), 136–55; Peter R. Breggin, *Guilt, Shame,
and Anxiety: Understanding and Overcoming
Negative Emotions* (Amherst, NY: Prometheus
Books, 2014).

33. For more on the potential for emotions to be
contagious, see Sigal G. Barsade, "The Ripple
Effect: Emotional Contagion and Its Influence
on Group Behavior," *Administrative Science
Quarterly* 47, no. 4 (December 2002): 644–75;
Elaine Hatfield, Megan Carpenter, and Richard
L. Rapson, "Emotional Contagion as a Precursor
to Collective Emotions," in *Collective Emotions:
Perspectives from Psychology, Philosophy, and Sociology*
(New York: Oxford University Press, 2014),
108–22; Eliska Prochazkova and Mariska E.
Kret, "Connecting Minds and Sharing Emotions
through Mimicry: A Neurocognitive Model
of Emotional Contagion," *Neuroscience and
Biobehavioral Reviews* 80 (September 2017): 99–114.

34. See, for example, Fugate et al., "Emotional Self-
Leadership"; Richards and Gross, "Emotion
Regulation and Memory"; Manz, *Emotional
Discipline*.

35. See, for example, Michael Hemphill, "A Note on
Adults' Color–Emotion Associations," *Journal
of Genetic Psychology* 157, no. 3 (1996): 275–80;
Hendrik N. J. Schifferstein and Inge Tanudjaja,

"Visualising Fragrances through Colours: The Mediating Role of Emotions," *Perception* 33, no. 10 (2004): 1249–66.

36. See, for example, Don Campbell, *The Mozart Effect: Tapping the Power of Music to Heal the Body, Strengthen the Mind, and Unlock the Creative Spirit* (New York: Quill, 2001); Elizabeth Miles, *Tune Your Brain: Using Music to Manage Your Mind, Body, and Mood* (New York: Berkley Books, 1997).

37. For example, see Stephen Warrenburg, "Effects of Fragrance on Emotions: Moods and Physiology," *Chemical Senses* 30 (2005): 248–49.

38. Dana L. Joseph, Jing Jin, Daniel A. Newman, and Ernest H. O'Boyle, "Why Does Self-Reported Emotional Intelligence Predict Job Performance? A Meta-Analytic Investigation of Mixed EI," *Journal of Applied Psychology* 100, no. 2 (March 2015): 298–342; Dana L. Joseph and Daniel A. Newman, "Emotional Intelligence: An Integrative Meta-Analysis and Cascading Model," *Journal of Applied Psychology* 95, no. 1 (January 2010): 54–78; Kenneth S. Law, Chi-Sum Wong, and Lynda J. Song, "The Construct and Criterion Validity of Emotional Intelligence and Its Potential Utility for Management Studies," *Journal of Applied Psychology* 89, no. 3 (June 2004): 483–96.

39. John D. Mayer, Peter Salovey, and David Caruso, "Models of Emotional Intelligence," in *Handbook of Intelligence*, ed. Robert J. Sternberg (Cambridge, UK: Cambridge University Press, 2000), 396–420.

40. Ibid.

41. John D. Mayer, Richard D. Roberts, and Sigal G. Barsade, "Human Abilities: Emotional Intelligence," *Annual Review of Psychology* 59 (2008): 511.

42. Quy Nguyen Huy, "Emotional Capability, Emotional Intelligence, and Radical Change," *Academy of Management Review* 24, no. 2 (1999): 325.

43. See, for example, Joseph et al., "Why Does Self-Reported Emotional Intelligence Predict Job Performance?"

44. Manz, "Taking the Self-Leadership High Road"; Fugate et al., "Emotional Self-Leadership"; Richards and Gross, "Emotion Regulation and Memory"; Jackson et al., "Suppression and Enhancement of Emotional Responses"; Manz, *Emotional Discipline*.

45. Larry W. Hunter and Sherry M. B. Thatcher, "Feeling the Heat: Effects of Stress, Commitment, and Job Experience on Job Performance," *Academy of Management Journal* 50, no. 4 (August 2007): 953–68; Ruby R. Brougham, Christy M. Zail, Celeste M. Mendoza, and Janine R. Miller, "Stress, Sex Differences, and Coping Strategies among College Students," *Current Psychology* 28, no. 2 (June 2009): 85–97. Portions of the material in this section are adapted from and inspired by Jeffery D. Houghton, Jinpei Wu, Jeffrey L. Godwin, Christopher P. Neck, and Charles C. Manz, "Effective Stress Management: A Model of Emotional Intelligence, Self-Leadership, and Student Stress Coping," *Journal of Management Education* 36, no. 2 (April 2012): 220–38.

46. Amy Cynkar, "Whole Workplace Health," *Monitor on Psychology* 38, no. 3 (March 2007): 28–31.

47. Susan Folkman and Richard S. Lazarus, "If It Changes It Must Be a Process: Study of Emotion and Coping during Three Stages of a College Examination," *Journal of Personality and Social Psychology* 48, no. 1 (January 1985): 152.

48. Ibid.

49. See, for example, Richard S. Lazarus, *Stress and Emotion: A New Synthesis* (New York: Springer, 2000).

50. Melissa J. Green and Gin S. Malhi, "Neural Mechanisms of the Cognitive Control of Emotion," *Acta Neuropsychiatrica* 18, nos. 3–4 (June 2006): 149.

51. Christopher P. Neck and Jeffery D. Houghton, "Two Decades of Self-Leadership Theory and Research: Past Developments, Present Trends, and Future Possibilities," *Journal of Managerial Psychology* 21, no. 4 (2006): 270–95; Christopher P. Neck and Charles C. Manz, "Thought Self-Leadership: The Impact of Mental Strategies Training on Employee Cognition, Behavior, and Affect," *Journal of Organizational Behavior* 17, no. 5 (September 1996): 445–67; Jeffery D. Houghton and Darryl L. Jinkerson, "Constructive Thought Strategies and Job Satisfaction: A Preliminary Examination," *Journal of Business and Psychology* 22, no. 1 (September 2007): 45–53.

52. Neck and Houghton, "Two Decades of Self-Leadership Theory"; Neck and Manz, "Thought Self-Leadership."

53. Neck and Manz, "Thought Self-Leadership"; Gregory E. Prussia, Joe S. Anderson, and Charles C. Manz, "Self-Leadership and Performance Outcomes: The Mediating Influence of Self-Efficacy," *Journal of Organizational Behavior* 19, no. 5 (September 1998): 523–38.

54. Susan Folkman and Judith Tedlie Moskowitz, "Positive Affect and the Other Side of Coping," *American Psychologist* 55, no. 6 (June 2000): 647–54; Susan Folkman and Judith Tedlie Moskowitz, "Positive Affect and Meaning-Focused Coping During Significant Psychological Stress," in *The Scope of Social Psychology: Theory and Applications*, ed. Miles Hewstone, Henk A. W. Schut, John B. F. de Wit, Kees van den Bos, and Margaret S. Stroebe (New York: Psychology Press, 2007), 193–208.

55. Susan Folkman, Judith Tedlie Moskowitz, Elizabeth M. Ozer, and Crystal L. Park, "Positive Meaningful Events and Coping in the Context of HIV/AIDS," in *Coping with Chronic Stress*, ed. Benjamin H. Gottlieb (New York: Plenum Press, 1997), 293–314; Judith Tedlie Moskowitz, Susan Folkman, Linda Collette, and Eric Vittinghoff, "Coping and Mood during AIDS-Related Caregiving and Bereavement," *Annals of Behavioral Medicine* 18, no. 1 (1996): 49–57.

56. Yan E. Shen, "Relationships Between Self-Efficacy, Social Support and Stress Coping Strategies in Chinese Primary and Secondary School Teachers," *Stress and Health* 25, no. 2 (April 2009): 129–38.

57. Adam R. Nicholls, Remco C. J. Polman, Andrew R. Levy, and Erika Borkoles, "The Mediating Role of Coping: A Cross-Sectional Analysis of the Relationship Between Coping Self-Efficacy and Coping Effectiveness among Athletes," *International Journal of Stress Management* 17, no. 3 (August 2010): 181–92; Marisa Salanova, Rosa María Grau, and Isabel M. Martínez, "Job Demands and Coping Behaviour: The Moderating Role of Professional Self-Efficacy," *Psychology in Spain* 10 (2006): 1–7.

58. Viktor E. Frankl, *Man's Search for Meaning*, rev. ed. (New York: Washington Square Press, 1984).

59. Ibid., 84.

60. Many of the ideas about optimism presented here and the research studies referenced are discussed in detail in Martin E. P. Seligman, *Learned Optimism: How to Change Your Mind and Your Life* (New York: Free Press, 1998).

61. See, for example, Albert V. Carron, Kim M. Shapcott, and Luc J. Martin, "The Relationship between Team Explanatory Style and Team Success," *International Journal of Sport and Exercise Psychology* 12, no. 1 (January 2014): 1–9; Viliyana Maleva, Kathryn Westcott, Mark McKellop, Ronald McLaughlin, and David Widman, "Optimism and College Grades: Predicting GPA from Explanatory Style," *Psi Chi Journal of Psychological Research* 19, no. 3 (Fall 2014): 129–35; Christopher Peterson, Martin E. P. Seligman, and George E. Vaillant, "Pessimistic Explanatory Style Is a Risk Factor for Physical Illness: A Thirty-Five-Year Longitudinal Study," in *Psychosocial Processes and Health: A Reader*, ed. Andrew Steptoe and Jane Wardle (New York: Cambridge University Press, 1994), 235–46; Peter Schulman, "Explanatory Style and Achievement in School and Work," in *Explanatory Style*, ed. Gregory McClellan Buchanan and Martin E. P. Seligman (Hillsdale, NJ: Lawrence Erlbaum, 1995), 159–71.

62. Martin E. P. Seligman and Peter Schulman, "Explanatory Style as a Predictor of Productivity and Quitting among Life Insurance Sales Agents," *Journal of Personality and Social Psychology* 50, no. 4 (April 1986): 832–38.

63. Carron et al., "The Relationship between Team Explanatory Style and Team Success"; David Rettew and Karen Reivich, "Sports and Explanatory Style," in Buchanan and Seligman, *Explanatory Style*, 173–85.

64. Harold M. Zullow, Gabriele Oettingen, Christopher Peterson, and Martin E. P. Seligman, "Pessimistic Explanatory Style in the Historical Record: CAVing LBJ, Presidential Candidates, and East versus West Berlin," *American Psychologist* 43, no. 9 (September 1988): 673–82.

65. For a detailed overview of these concepts, see Martin E. P. Seligman, *Authentic Happiness: Using the New Positive Psychology to Realize Your Potential* (New York: Free Press, 2004).

66. Many of the ideas about flow presented in this section are adapted from Mihaly Csikszentmihalyi, *Flow: The Psychology of Optimal Experience* (New York: Harper & Row, 1990).

67. Ibid., 2.

68. Ibid., 19.

69. Quoted in ibid., 53.

70. Quoted in ibid.

71. Quoted in ibid., 53–54.

72. Quoted in ibid., 58.

73. Ibid., 4.

74. https://www.brainyquote.com/quotes/leo_rosten_100873.

Chapter 8

1. Robert D'Intino contributed to the development and writing of this chapter.

2. See, for example, Jessie Ho and Paul L. Nesbit, "Personality and Work Outcomes: A Moderated Mediation Model of Self-Leadership and Gender," *International Journal of Management Excellence* 10, no. 2 (February 2018): 1292–1304; Sarah F. Bailey, Larissa K. Barber, and Logan M. Justice, "Is Self-Leadership Just Self-Regulation? Exploring Construct Validity with HEXACO and Self-Regulatory Traits," *Current Psychology* 37, no. 1 (March 2018): 149–61; Jeffery D. Houghton, T. W. Bonham, Christopher P. Neck, and Kusum Singh, "The Relationship Between Self-Leadership and Personality: A Comparison of Hierarchical Factor Structures," *Journal of Managerial Psychology* 19, no. 4 (2004): 427–41; Scott Williams, "Personality and Self-Leadership," *Human Resource Management Review* 7, no. 2 (1997): 139–55; Marco R. Furtner and John F. Rauthmann, "Relations Between Self-Leadership and Scores on the Big Five," *Psychological Reports* 107, no. 2 (October 2010): 339–53.

3. For a detailed overview of the MBTI and its development, see Isabel Briggs Myers and Mary H. McCaulley, *Manual: A Guide to the Development and Use of the Myers-Briggs Type Indicator* (Palo Alto, CA: Consulting Psychologists Press, 1985). See also Walter Renner, Jutta Menschik-Bendele, Rainer Alexandrovicz, and Paul Deakin, "Does the Myers-Briggs Type Indicator Measure Anything beyond the NEO Five Factor Inventory?" *Journal of Psychological Type* 74, no. 1 (December 2014): 1–10.

4. Robert L. Williams, John S. Verble, Donald E. Price, and Benjamin H. Layne, "Relationship of Self-Management to Personality Types and Indices," *Journal of Personality Assessment* 64, no. 3 (1995): 494–506.

5. For overviews of the Big Five model, see John M. Digman, "The Curious History of the Five-Factor Model," in *The Five-Factor Model of Personality: Theoretical Perspectives*, ed. Jerry S. Wiggins (New York: Guilford Press, 1996), 1–20; Robert R. McCrae and Oliver P. John, "An Introduction to the Five-Factor Model and Its Applications," *Journal of Personality* 60 (1992): 175–215; Michael K. Mount and Murray R. Barrick, "The Big Five Personality Dimensions: Implications for Research and Practice in Human Resource Management," *Research in Personnel and Human Resource Management* 13 (1995): 153–200; Michael B. Harari, Cort W. Rudolph, and Andrew J. Laginess, "Does Rater Personality Matter? A Meta-Analysis of Rater Big Five–Performance Rating Relationships," *Journal of Occupational and Organizational Psychology* 88, no. 2 (June 2015): 387–414.

6. Bailey et al., "Is Self-Leadership Just Self-Regulation?"; Ho and Nesbit, "Personality and Work Outcomes"; Houghton et al., "The Relationship Between Self-Leadership and Personality"; Furtner and Rauthmann, "Relations Between Self-Leadership and Scores on the Big Five."

7. Ho and Nesbit, "Personality and Work Outcomes"; A. L. Kazan and G. W. Earnest, "Exploring the Concept of Self-Leadership," *Leadership Link* (Winter 2000); Williams, "Personality and Self-Leadership."

8. Williams, "Personality and Self-Leadership."

9. Seokhwa Yun, Jonathan Cox, and Henry P. Sims Jr., "The Forgotten Follower: A Contingency Model of Leadership and Follower Self-Leadership," *Journal of Managerial Psychology* 21, no. 4 (2006): 374–88.

10. Heather E. Roberts and Roseanne J. Foti, "Evaluating the Interaction Between Self-Leadership and Work Structure in Predicting Job Satisfaction," *Journal of Business and Psychology* 12, no. 3 (1998): 257–67.

11. Greg L. Stewart, Kenneth P. Carson, and Robert L. Cardy, "The Joint Effects of Conscientiousness

and Self-Leadership Training on Employee Self-Directed Behavior in a Service Setting," *Personnel Psychology* 49, no. 1 (1996): 143–64.

12. Kazan and Earnest, "Exploring the Concept of Self-Leadership"; A. L. Kazan and G. W. Earnest, "Self-Leadership: Is It Only for the Young?" (paper presented at the annual meeting of the International Leadership Association, Toronto, 2000).

13. Kazan and Earnest, "Exploring the Concept of Self-Leadership"; Kazan and Earnest, "Self-Leadership."

14. Ho and Nesbit, "Personality and Work Outcomes"; Kazan and Earnest, "Exploring the Concept of Self-Leadership"; Kazan and Earnest, "Self-Leadership."

15. Susan Nolen-Hoeksema and Colleen Corte, "Gender and Self-Regulation," in *Handbook of Self-Regulation: Research, Theory, and Applications,* ed. Roy F. Baumeister and Kathleen D. Vohs (New York: Guilford Press, 2004).

16. Jenny Kurman, "Self-Regulation Strategies in Achievement Settings: Culture and Gender Differences," *Journal of Cross-Cultural Psychology* 32, no. 4 (2001): 491–503.

17. See, for example, Geert Hofstede, *Culture's Consequences: Comparing Values, Behaviors, Institutions, and Organizations Across Nations,* 2nd ed. (Thousand Oaks, CA: Sage, 2001).

18. For a detailed discussion of the relationship between cultural dimensions and self-leadership, see José C. Alves, Kathi J. Lovelace, Charles C. Manz, Dmytro Matsypura, Fuminori Toyasaki, and Ke (Grace) Ke, "A Cross-Cultural Perspective of Self-Leadership," *Journal of Managerial Psychology* 21, no. 4 (2006): 338–59.

19. See, for example, Russell E. Johnson, Mark Muraven, Tina L. Donaldson, and Szu-Han (Joanna) Lin, "Self-Control in Work Organizations," in *The Self at Work: Fundamental Theory and Research* (New York: Routledge/Taylor & Francis Group, 2018), 119–44; Denise de Ridder, Marieke Adriaanse, and Kentaro Fujita, *The Routledge International Handbook of Self-Control in Health and Well-Being.* New York: Routledge/Taylor & Francis Group, 2018.

20. Alan E. Kazdin, "Effects of Covert Modeling and Model Reinforcement on Assertive Behavior,"

Journal of Abnormal Psychology 83 (1974): 240–52; Alan E. Kazdin, "Effects of Covert Modeling, Multiple Models, and Model Reinforcement on Assertive Behavior," *Behavior Therapy* 7 (1976): 211–22.

21. For a comprehensive discussion of the plethora of research that examines the application of self-leadership techniques to sports settings, see Christopher P. Neck and Charles C. Manz, "Thought Self-Leadership: The Influence of Self-Talk and Mental Imagery on Performance," *Journal of Organizational Behavior* 13 (1992): 681–99.

22. See, for example, Andrew M. Lane, *Sport and Exercise Psychology,* 2nd ed. (New York: Routledge/Taylor & Francis Group, 2016); Robert J. Schinke, Kerry R. McGannon, and Brett Smith, *Routledge International Handbook of Sport Psychology* (New York: Routledge/Taylor & Francis Group, 2016).

23. See Andreas Ivarsson, Urban Johnson, Magnus Lindwall, Henrik Gustafsson, and Mats Altemyr, "Psychosocial Stress as a Predictor of Injury in Elite Junior Soccer: A Latent Growth Curve Analysis," *Journal of Science and Medicine in Sport* 17, no. 4 (July 2014): 366–70; Tara K. Scanlan and Michael W. Passer, "Sources of Competitive Stress in Young Female Athletes," *Journal of Sport Psychology* 1, no. 2 (1979): 151–59; Tara K. Scanlan and Michael W. Passer, "Factors Related to Competitive Stress among Male Youth Sport Participants," *Medicine and Science in Sports* 10, no. 2 (1978): 276–81.

24. Deborah L. Feltz and Daniel M. Landers, "The Effects of Mental Practice on Motor Skill Learning and Performance: A Meta-Analysis," *Journal of Sport Psychology* 5 (1983): 25–57.

25. Maxwell Maltz, *Psycho-cybernetics* (Englewood Cliffs, NJ: Prentice Hall, 1960), 35–36.

26. Rick Maese, "For Olympians, Seeing (in Their Minds) Is Believing (It Can Happen)," *The Washington Post,* July 28, 2016, https://www.washingtonpost.com/sports/olympics/for-olympians-seeing-in-their-minds-is-believing-it-can-happen/2016/07/28/6966709c-532e-11e6-bbf5-957ad17b4385_story.html?utm_term=.de0330156cec; Michael J. Mahoney, "Cognitive Skills and Athletic

Performance," in *Cognitive-Behavioral Interventions: Theory, Research, and Procedures,* ed. Philip C. Kendall and Steven D. Hollon (New York: Academic Press, 1979), 423–43.

27. Burt Giges, "Removing Psychological Barriers: Clearing the Way," in *Doing Sport Psychology* (Champaign, IL: Human Kinetics, 2000), 17–31.

28. R. Gary Ness and Robert W. Patton, "The Effect of Beliefs on Maximum Weight-Lifting Performance," *Cognitive Therapy and Research* 3, no. 2 (1979): 205–11.

29. See, for example, Erika D. Van Dyke, Judy L. Van Raalte, Elizabeth M. Mullin, and Britton W. Brewer, "Self-Talk and Competitive Balance Beam Performance," *Sport Psychologist* 32, no. 1 (March 2018): 33–41; Izet Kahrović, Oliver Radenković, Fahrudin Mavrić, and Benin Murić, "Effects of the Self-Talk Strategy in the Mental Training of Athletes / Efekti Self-Talk Strategije U Mentalnom Treningu Sportista," *Facta Universitatis: Series Physical Education & Sport* 12, no. 1 (March 2014): 51–58.

30. See Christopher P. Neck, Heidi M. Neck, and Charles C. Manz, "Thought Self-Leadership: Mind Management for Entrepreneurs," *Journal of Developmental Entrepreneurship* 2, no. 1 (1997): 25–36; Christopher P. Neck, Jeffery D. Houghton, Shruti R. Sardeshmukh, Michael Goldsby, and Jeffrey L. Godwin, "Self-Leadership: A Cognitive Resource for Entrepreneurs," *Journal of Small Business & Entrepreneurship* 26, no. 5 (November 2013): 463–80; Jeffrey L. Godwin, Christopher P. Neck, and Robert S. D'Intino, "Self-Leadership, Spirituality, and Entrepreneur Performance: A Conceptual Model," *Journal of Management, Spirituality & Religion* 13, no. 1 (January 2016): 64–78; Christopher P. Neck, Heidi M. Neck, Charles C. Manz, and Jeffrey L. Godwin, "'I Think I Can, I Think I Can': A Self-Leadership Perspective toward Enhancing Entrepreneur Thought Patterns, Self-Efficacy, and Performance," *Journal of Managerial Psychology* 14, nos. 5–6 (1999): 477–501.

31. Charles C. Manz and Charles A. Snyder, "Systematic Self-Management: How Resourceful Entrepreneurs Meet Business Challenges . . . and Survive," *Management Review* 72, no. 10 (1983): 68–73.

32. Douglas T. Hall and Jonathan E. Moss, "The New Protean Career Contract: Helping Organizations

and Employees Adapt," *Organizational Dynamics* 26, no. 3 (1998): 22–37.

33. Douglas T. Hall, "Protean Careers of the 21st Century," *Academy of Management Executive* 10, no. 4 (1996): 8–16.

34. Marc Abessolo, Andreas Hirschi, and Jérôme Rossier, "Work Values Underlying Protean and Boundaryless Career Orientations," *The Career Development International* 22, no. 3 (2017): 241–59; Alessandro Lo Presti, Sara Pluviano, and Jon P. Briscoe, "Are Freelancers a Breed Apart? The Role of Protean and Boundaryless Career Attitudes in Employability and Career Success," *Human Resource Management Journal* (March 2, 2018); Michael B. Arthur and Denise M. Rousseau, eds., *The Boundaryless Career: A New Employment Principle for a New Organizational Era* (New York: Oxford University Press, 1996); Hall and Moss, "New Protean Career Contract"; Hall, "Protean Careers of the 21st Century."

35. Hall, "Protean Careers of the 21st Century."

36. Frieda Reitman and Joy A. Schneer, "The Promised Path: A Longitudinal Study of Managerial Careers," *Journal of Managerial Psychology* 18, no. 1 (2003): 60–75.

37. Hall, "Protean Careers of the 21st Century," 11.

38. Ibid.

39. See, for example, Charles C. Manz, Kim S. Cameron, Karen P. Manz, and Robert D. Marx, eds., *The Virtuous Organization: Insights from Some of the World's Leading Management Thinkers* (Singapore: World Scientific, 2008).

40. On corporate social responsibility, see Abagail McWilliams and Donald Siegel, "Corporate Social Responsibility: A Theory of the Firm Perspective," *Academy of Management Review* 26, no. 1 (2001): 117–27. For a discussion of social entrepreneurship, see Peter A. Dacin, M. Tina Dacin, and Margaret Matear, "Social Entrepreneurship: Why We Don't Need a New Theory and How We Move Forward from Here," *Academy of Management Perspectives* 24, no. 3 (2010): 37–57. Regarding sustainability, see Marc J. Epstein, *Making Sustainability Work: Best Practices in Managing and Measuring Corporate Social, Environmental, and Economic Impacts* (San Francisco: Berrett-Koehler, 2008).

41. Peter F. Drucker, *Managing for Results* (New York: Harper & Row, 1964).

42. The cases described in this and the following three paragraphs are presented in Fred Luthans and Tim R. V. Davis, "Behavioral Self-Management: The Missing Link in Managerial Effectiveness," *Organizational Dynamics* 8, no. 1 (1979): 42–60.

43. See, for example, Charles C. Manz and Henry P. Sims Jr., "Leading Workers to Lead Themselves: The External Leadership of Self-Managing Work Teams," *Administrative Science Quarterly* 32 (1987): 106–28.

44. For a good description of some of the unique aspects of this plant, see Henry P. Sims Jr. and Charles C. Manz, "Conversations within Self-Managed Work Groups," *National Productivity Review* 1, no. 3 (Summer 1982): 261–69.

45. Ibid.

46. See, for example, Henry P. Sims Jr. and Charles C. Manz, *Company of Heroes: Unleashing the Power of Self-Leadership* (New York: John Wiley, 1996); Charles C. Manz and Henry P. Sims Jr., *The New SuperLeadership: Leading Others to Lead Themselves* (San Francisco: Berrett-Koehler, 2001).

Chapter 9

1. Charles C. Manz and Craig L. Pearce, *Twisted Leadership* (Palmyra, VA: Maven House Press, 2018).

2. For an interesting discussion of the power of the mind, see Mark Hyman, *The UltraMind Solution: Automatically Boost Your Brain Power, Improve Your Mood and Optimize Your Memory* (New York: Scribner, 2009).

3. Barbara B. Brown, *Supermind: The Ultimate Energy* (New York: Harper & Row, 1980).

INDEX